THE CHRISTIAN BOOK OF WHY

John C. McCollister

 Jonathan David Publishers, Inc.
Middle Village, New York 11379

THE CHRISTIAN BOOK OF WHY

JONATHAN DAVID PUBLISHERS, INC.
68-22 Eliot Avenue
Middle Village, New York 11379

1991	1993	1994	1992	1990
3 5	7 9	11 10	8 6	4

Library of Congress Cataloging in Publication Data

McCollister, John.
    The Christian book of why.

    Bibliography: p.
    Includes index.
    1. Christianity—Miscellanea. I. Title.
BR96.M36 1983   202'.02   83-15111
Paperback   ISBN 0-8246-0317-6

Printed in the United States of America

For
MY MOTHER AND FATHER,
who never hesitated
to answer their son
when he asked the question
"Why?"

In Appreciation

The author is grateful for the advice and encouragement he received while compiling *The Christian Book of Why.* Particular thanks is due Rabbi Alfred J. Kolatch, cherished friend and learned scholar, whose popular volume—*The Jewish Book of Why*—was the inspiration for this work.

The author thanks others who have contributed greatly to this book: the Rt. Rev. Herbert Edmondson, Fr. Sean Heslin, Fr. George Papadeas, Dr. Daniel Sain, and Dr. John Wheeler for their observations; and Dr. Anthony Buono and Dr. Jonathan Kolatch for their editorial suggestions.

Finally, the author owes a debt to those aware men and women who constantly examine their faith and dare to ask *"Why?"* Without these people, this book would have never been possible.

Contents

General Introduction

Christianity is really a very young faith. Not yet 2,000 years old, it is an infant when compared to other religions of this world. At the same time, its founder—Jesus—and his followers have established a unique set of laws, customs, and ceremonies.

Many books have been written about the Christian faith; their subjects include theology, Church history, the Christian life, and social issues. However, few if any devote themselves to an explanation of *why* Christians worship and live as they do.

The Christian Book of Why does not attempt to advise Christians on how to conduct their lives. It does not take sides in issues on which Christians have differed over the centuries. Instead, it merely explains *why* certain Christians choose to believe or behave as they do.

If some Christians elect to worship through a formal liturgy, while others prefer a church service in which structure is kept to a minimum, this book does not concern itself with which custom is the "proper" method of worship. It simply explains *why* each approach to worship is practiced.

If a bride wears a veil at her wedding, or the groom selects a close friend to act as his best man, this book does not judge the value of the custom. It simply explains *why* these things are done.

Many more questions could have been raised in this book, but time and space prohibit the inclusion of them all. The questions selected were deemed to be those of genuine interest and concern to today's lay person.

The Christian Book of Why is offered as a help for pastors, Sunday school teachers, parochial school personnel, instructors of religion at colleges and universities, and anyone who at one time or another has asked the question *"Why?"* about some dimension of the Christian faith.

John C. McCollister

Chapter 1

Jesus

INTRODUCTION

His name was Jesus. Has any man had a greater influence on civilization than he? Has anyone been as controversial?

The faithful call him "Savior," Messiah," and "Son of God"; others consider him only a prophet akin to Mohammed; and there are more than a few who display outward hostility toward him and those who follow his teachings.

What we know about the one whose birth date marks the designation of our years is precious little. Four brief records—Matthew, Mark, Luke, and John—present mere thumbnail sketches about the life of the Jewish carpenter who roamed remote Palestinian hills. What is more, their accounts cover only a fraction of his 33 years on earth. They tell of his birth, then allow us to eavesdrop on one brief encounter with learned rabbis in a temple when he was 12 years old (Luke 2:41–51). Whatever else transpired in the years between his birth and his baptism at about age 30 is unknown.

The events covering the last three years of his life are better documented. He took 12 rather obscure helpers with him and preached to anyone who would listen about the love of God and the obligation of human beings to share that love. In the end, he was executed by the Roman government. But he conquered death and became the guiding light of a movement that continues to this day.

Theologians are continually attempting to interpret and reinterpret the life of the one whom Christians call the "King of kings and Lord of lords," because they believe that no one can truly understand Christianity without first understanding its founder.

The following questions have been raised over the centuries by those who have heard the story and wondered about the person named "Jesus."

Why is Christianity really the knowledge of a person?

Christians are called not so much to know and follow a set of laws or a creed, as to know and follow a person—Jesus Christ. This emphasis stems from Jesus' words: " . . . that the world may know that thou hast sent me and hast loved them even as thou hast loved me" (John 17:23).

This knowledge is not stagnant or unproductive, but a knowledge that permeates Christians and overflows into action. Christians are called, therefore, to know, love, and follow Jesus in his life and work.

Why are Christians convinced that Jesus really lived?

Christians are convinced that Jesus truly lived on this earth because of the multiple historical data from both Christian and non-Christian sources that exists about him. More is written about Jesus than about any other historical figure of his time.

The Bible is the Christian's first source. The New Testament contains 27 different books written in the first century (some parts—including the "passion narratives"—are dated within five years of Jesus' death) all testifying to the fact that Jesus of Nazareth was born, lived, died, and rose again. Perhaps the Gospel writer John put it the most pointedly: "That which was from the beginning, which we have heard, which we have seen with our eyes, which we have looked upon and touched with our hands . . . we proclaim to you" (I John 1:1-3).

Jesus is also mentioned by non-Christian writers such as the Jewish historian Flavius Josephus (about 37 A.D.) who states: "Now there was about this time, Jesus, a wise man . . . a doer of wonderful works. He drew over to him both many of the Jews and many of the Gentiles." Noted historians of the second century, including the Roman historian Cornelius Tacitus (about 110 A.D.) and his student Suetonius (about 125 A.D.), describe Jesus of Nazareth as a leader of his people. In addition, the Roman historian Pliny the Younger (about 115 A.D.) refers to Jesus in his work *Epistles.*

An obscure Syrian Stoic, Mara bar Serapion, also alludes to Jesus about the year 73 A.D. in a letter to his son studying at Edessa on the Black Sea. He reminds his son that the truly great and wise have often been persecuted and put to death by their contemporaries. As examples, he specifically mentions Socrates, Pythagoras, and the "wise King of the Jews" put to death by his people even though he had given them "new laws."

We might sum up the extrabiblical data about Jesus as follows:

1. The name of Christians is derived from the one called Jesus Christ (Josephus, Pliny the Younger, Tacitus, Suetonius).

2. Christ lived in Palestine (Josephus, Tacitus).

3. Christ was condemned to death under Tiberius (Tacitus) by Pontius Pilate (Josephus, Tacitus). Since Tiberius reigned from 14 to 37, and Pilate was procurator of Judea from 26 to 36, the years in which Jesus was put to death are narrowed to the decade between 26 and 36.

4. Christ was condemned to death (Tacitus) through crucifixion (Josephus).

For these reasons, coupled with the oral tradition—i.e., the word of mouth accounts passed on by eyewitnesses—Christians accept the fact that Jesus existed, and they base their faith on his life and teachings.

Why did Jesus come to the earth?

Christians teach that Jesus came to this earth to give eternal life to all people. As he said: "I came that they may have life, and have it abundantly" (John 10:10). This knowledge is imparted through a knowledge of the Father and the Son: "And this is eternal life, that they may know thee the only true God, and Jesus Christ whom thou hast sent" (John 17:3).

According to Jesus, this knowledge must be put into practice: "Not everyone who says to me, 'Lord, Lord,' shall enter the kingdom of heaven, but he who does the will of my Father who is in heaven" (Matthew 7:21).

Jesus also came to the earth to set human beings free from sin and death: "You will know the truth, and the truth will make you free" (John 8:32).

In short, Christians believe that Jesus came to earth to fulfill the promises made by God to the Jewish people about a Messiah.

Why is Jesus called the "Messiah"?

Christians call Jesus the "Messiah," because he fulfilled the messianic expectations of the chosen people (the Jews) contained in the Old Testament:

These are my words which I spoke to you . . .
that everything written about me in the law of

Moses and the prophets and the psalms must
be fulfilled. . . . Thus it is written that the Christ
[Greek for "Messiah"] should suffer and on the
third day rise from the dead (Luke 24:44–46).

A summary of these messianic pronouncements can be
given as follows:

1. After the fall, the promise of a Deliverer is given. He
will be born of a woman and crush the head of the serpent
(the devil) (Genesis 3:15).

2. The chosen people is formed for the purpose of
blessing all nations through the foretold Redeemer (Genesis
12:3).

3. The concept of the Messiah begins to be revealed: He
will come from the tribe of Judah and rule over the nations
(Genesis 49:10–11). He will be a prophet like Moses (Deuteronomy 18:15–19).

4. He will be a King from the family of David (II Samuel
7:16; Psalm 2; 89; 110). He will be called "Immanuel" (Isaiah
7:13–14) and a "wonderful child" (Isaiah 9:1, 2, 6, 7).

5. He will be born of a virgin (Isaiah 7:14), at Bethlehem
(Micah 5:2–5), spend part of his childhood in Egypt (Hosea
11:1), and be brought up in Nazareth (Isaiah 11:1. Note: there
is a similarity in sound and in meaning between the Aramaic
word for "Nazareth" used in the text of Matthew 2:33 and
the Hebrew word translated as "branch" in this Isaiah text).

6. The Messiah will have a forerunner like Elijah (Mal-
achi 3:1; 4:5), will conduct his ministry in Galilee (Isaiah 9:1),
and work miracles of healing (Isaiah 32:5, 6).

7. He will be rejected by his nation, be stricken, and
suffer—a man of sorrows (Isaiah 53). He will be betrayed by
a friend (Psalm 41:9), for 30 pieces of silver (Zechariah 11:12),
and led like a sheep to the slaughter (Isaiah 53:7).

8. He will die with the wicked, be scorned and reviled,
and be pierced in the hands and feet (Psalm 22).

9. He will be victorious over sin and death (Isaiah 25:6–9;
53), rising on the third day (as indicated by Jonah's time

inside the fish—1:17), and inaugurate a glorious age (Psalm 72).

10. He will bring a new covenant to all (Jeremiah 31:31), and will be known as the Desire (or Expectation) of nations (Haggai 2:6, 7) whom he will include in his kingdom (Hosea 1:10).

Why is Jesus called the "Expectation of the Nations"?

The Church has always regarded Jesus as the Messiah foretold by the prophets. At the same time, it has pointed him out as the "Expectation (or Desire) of the Nations."

Before Christ, there was a religious feeling in the air that God listens to the pleas of his people, dispenses justice and mercy, and holds out the hope of deliverance. Most of the nations subject to Rome harbored the hope of a divine messenger or other intervention that would set them free and bring happiness.

The Babylonians expected a kind of messianic age, and even some type of savior. The Egyptians awaited a king-redeemer and a new age of happiness. The Persians expected a powerful hero and sage-like Zoroaster who would establish God's kingdom.

The ancient Romans were convinced that out of Judea was to come a master and ruler of the world. The Chinese also believed that a great wise man would appear.

The Hindus believed that the supreme God would reveal himself to human beings, first in Krishna, then in Buddha, and then in a new world and era of happiness.

The ancient Germans looked forward to the renewal of the present world.

The Greeks expected a Saint of the West, and the Romans of Jesus' day expected a king whom they would recognize. The poet Virgil wrote about a king in conjunction with a virgin.

The outstanding example of this expectation of the nations is provided in the story of the Magi who came seeking the "King of the Jews" after Christ's birth (Matthew 2). Note: more about the Magi (Wise Men) appears later in this chapter.

Why is Jesus called "Christ" or *the* Christ"?

The term "Christ" is the English form of the Greek word *Christos,* meaning "the anointed one." Just as kings of the Old Testament were anointed upon taking office, so Christians consider Jesus as the anointed King of kings and Lord of lords (Revelation 19:16). In other words, the full meaning behind the Greek term is that of the "Messiah."

Christians, by the way, properly refer to Jesus as *the* Christ, because the term is a title, not what we would call a surname. Jesus' real name was "Jesus [or Joshua] ben Joseph." It was the custom of the Jews to use as a surname the father's first name preceded by the Hebrew word *ben* or the Aramaic word *bar,* meaning "the son of."

In time, however, the term "Christ" became affixed to the name Jesus, and Christians usually combined them to form the term "Jesus Christ."

Why was the Savior named "Jesus"?

"Jesus" is the Latin form of the Hebrew name Joshua, which means "God will save." In biblical times, the name of a person was an indicator of a person's function in life. The name selected for the son of Mary and Joseph was not an arbitrary selection. As announced by the angel in a vision to Joseph, the child was to be named "Jesus," for he would "save his people from their sins" (Matthew 1:21).

Why is Jesus called the "God Incarnate"?

The word "incarnate" comes from the Latin, meaning "in the flesh." The term "God Incarnate" therefore means "God in the flesh."

This belief is central in Christian theology. It implies that Jesus possessed two natures—one human and one divine. This was expressed by the Gospel writer John who said: "And the Word became flesh and dwelt among us, full of grace and truth" (1:14).

Although this teaching is now considered basic to the faith, it was the center of one of the earlier disputes in the history of the Church. Some Christians believed that Jesus was only divine, not human. They felt that God had come to earth in the appearance of a human being. This would explain why Jesus could live his entire life on earth without sinning. Other Christians claimed that Jesus was only human, not God. They pointed to the human characteristics of Jesus: he needed food and drink, he grew, he slept, he suffered, he died.

The first council of the Church (held in Nicaea in 325) dealt with this controversy. For the first time, the Church had to articulate the New Testament theology of Jesus as the God Incarnate, and it pronounced what is known even today as the "Nicene Creed." The Creed reads, in part:

> We believe in one Lord, Jesus Christ,
> the only Son of God, eternally begotten of
> the Father,
> God from God, Light from Light,
> true God from true God,
> begotten, not made,
> one in Being with the Father. . . .
> For us and for our salvation
> he came down from heaven. . . .
> He was born of the virgin Mary,
> and became man.

Why did Jesus refer to himself as the "Good Shepherd"?

"I am the good shepherd," said Jesus, ". . . [who] lays down his life for the sheep" (John 10:11).

Jesus compared himself to a dedicated shepherd who would sacrifice anything for the welfare of his flock, even to the point of death. In this comparison, Jesus thought of the people who followed him as sheep under his care.

For this same reason, the spiritual leader of a congregation is often called a "pastor"—the Latin word for "shepherd."

Why was Jesus called the "Lamb of God"?

When John the Baptist (the cousin of Jesus) was baptizing in the Jordan River, he saw Jesus coming toward him and said: "Behold, the Lamb of God, who takes away the sin of the world" (John 1:29). This rather strange title given Jesus by his cousin has been used by Christians throughout the centuries as a description of the one whom they believe to be the Son of God.

The designation of Jesus as the "Lamb of God" is linked with the lamb used by the Jews as a sacrifice for their sins during the days of the Patriarchs (Genesis 22:7–8). Christians believe that by his death on the cross, Jesus became the sacrifice for their sins. He became for them their "lamb."

This picture of Jesus is most vividly presented in the last book of the New Testament when God's Son is portrayed as ruling the kingdom of heaven alongside the Father, and appearing in the form of a lamb who was slain for sins (Revelation 5:6).

Why is Jesus sometimes called the "New Adam"?

Saint Paul described Jesus as "the image of the invisible God, the first-born of all creation . . . " (Colossians 1:15). To the church in Corinth (one of the first centers of Christian worship) he wrote: "For as in Adam all die, so also in Christ shall all be made alive" (I Corinthians 15:22).

Christians believe that the first Adam (in the book of Genesis) was created without sin and was therefore able to dialogue with Almighty God. After Adam sinned, he and the entire human race no longer enjoyed that luxury. Jesus, according to Christian teachings, was also without sin. Consequently, he was the second man who lived upon earth and possessed a perfect state of being—thus the designation "New Adam."

Why is it a mistake to think that Jesus was born in the year 1 A.D.?

Most people think that Jesus was born in the year 1 A.D., since the years of the calendar supposedly indicate the number of years that have passed since the first Christmas. However, this assumption is erroneous.

A Roman astronomer named Dionysius Exiguus ("Dionysius the Little") committed one of history's biggest numerical blunders in the sixth century when he reformed the calendar to pivot about the birth of the Christ child. He dated Jesus' birth 753 years after the founding of Rome. Scholars later would discover a four to seven year error in his calculations. In fact, the Bible itself indicates that the astronomer's designation was wrong.

The Gospels record that Magi visited the Christ child during the reign of King Herod (Matthew 2:1). Herod died in the spring of 4 B.C. Consequently, most authorities feel that Jesus was born around the year 5 B.C., perhaps as early as 7 B.C.

Any fleeting thought of changing the calendar to coincide with the birth of Jesus immediately gives way to the insurmountable confusion that would result.

Why was the mother of Jesus so young when he was born?

Throughout the centuries, artists have sometimes portrayed Mary, the mother of Jesus, as a rather mature—almost middle-aged—woman who was selected by God to raise his Son. However, in all probability, Mary was a very young girl when Jesus was born. During biblical times, a girl became engaged shortly after reaching puberty (12 to 15 years of age). A man became engaged normally when he completed his apprenticeship in a particular trade (which would make him about 25 years old).

The reason a man chose such a very young bride was because the life expectancy of a woman in those times was perhaps 40 years.

In reality, the marriages for both sons and daughters were arranged by the parents. The couple had some input into the matter, but the final word came from the endorsement of the parents. The marriage ceremony followed a period of engagement that usually lasted for about one year. It was during Mary's period of engagement that she was told by an angel that she was selected to bear God's Son.

Why did Jesus' earthly father want to divorce Mary?

When Joseph, a young carpenter who lived in the small village of Nazareth, learned that his fiance, Mary, was pregnant, he intended to divorce her (Matthew 1:19).

Engagement in ancient times was a legal betrothal, far more binding than our modern engagements. In fact, although a couple were only betrothed and not officially married, they could break an engagement only by divorce. On top of this, if either was proved to be unfaithful during the engagement period, this was considered adultery and, as such, punishable by death if the offended party demanded it.

The news of Mary's pregnancy was shocking to Joseph who knew that he could not be the father. According to Jewish custom, Joseph could decide among three courses of action:

1. marry the girl quickly, and hope that their friends and neighbors would not gossip about a "six-month baby" after the birth;

2. publicly divorce Mary as an adulteress, thus submitting her to a lifetime of shame;

3. have the marriage contract set aside quietly and allow Mary to leave town in order to have her baby.

Joseph (whom Matthew called a "just man" [1:19]) chose the third option.

In a dream, however, Joseph was told by an angel of God that the unborn child was of God, not of man (Matthew 1:20). As a result, he quickly married Mary and supported her during the final months of her pregnancy and through the delivery of her child.

Why did Mary place the infant Jesus in a manger?

After his birth, the infant Jesus was wrapped in swaddling cloths by his mother and laid in a manger (Luke 2:7). A manger was a feeding trough for the cattle and other animals. It provided, however, a comfortable area bedded by hay and grain as well as minimal protection from the elements—the best available under the circumstances.

Tiny Bethlehem was unable to accommodate the masses who arrived for the census ordered by the Roman government. It was a time for all the people to visit the city of their birth. The homecoming of the family of King David included Joseph, the new husband of Mary, and hundreds of others who filled the available guest rooms. Consequently, Mary was forced to have her baby in a stable—actually a cave, a place normally reserved for animals. In that cave, the manger was the safest place to set the baby.

Why is the star which appeared at Jesus' birth a mystery?

The Gospel of Matthew reports that the birth of Jesus in Bethlehem was marked by the appearance of a new star in the East (2:2–11). The star is mentioned only once in the New Testament with no explanation other than that it suddenly appeared. Consequently, the star of Bethlehem is cloaked in mystery, and scholars still debate the exact cause of this phenomenon.

Dr. John Roberts of Olivet College lists the three possible explanations most often cited by his fellow scientists:

1. It was a "nova," or an exploding star.
2. It was a comet, possibly Halley's.
3. It was really a conjunction of the planets Jupiter and Saturn.

Many Christians, including Dr. Roberts, add a fourth possibility which, they feel, more closely parallels the intent of Matthew's account. They consider the star as a special creation planted in the heavens by God as an announcement of the birth of his Son.

If the Bethlehem star was indeed a new creation, the implication would be that God preordained the events of that first Christmas centuries earlier, assuming the natural laws of the universe were maintained.

Modern science tells us that most of the stars decorating the skies are 500 to 600 light years away, meaning that this is the length of time it takes for the light from these stars to reach the earth. If the star of Bethlehem were a part of the normal galaxy of stars, this would mean that the precise moment of Jesus' birth was planned hundreds of years before it happened.

In spite of the mystery that surrounds the scientific explanation of the star, Christians include this as a part of the Christmas story as being the sign which led the Wise Men to the Christ child.

Why were three kings *not* at the manger in Bethlehem?

"We three kings of Orient are. . . . " Christians sing this familiar carol each year at Christmas. When they do, they make at least two, if not three errors. In the first place, we have no idea how many Wise Men made the trip to Bethlehem. Secondly, they were not really "kings" in the usual sense of the term. Finally, they were not from the Orient, but from the Near East—probably Persia.

The historical background of this era tells us that there were indeed magi—i.e., wise men (or astrologers)—who were extremely well educated for their day, especially in religion and astronomy. Therefore, when the new star in the heavens announced the birth of Jesus (Matthew 2:2), the Magi were alert to the phenomenon and went to find the one they called "King of the Jews."

The Bible never mentions any visit of the Wise Men to the manger of the Christ Child. Instead, it relates that they visited the house in which he was living at the time (Matthew 2:11). Historians, such as Dr. Paul Maier, conclude that the visit of the Magi did not occur until a year after Jesus' birth because of the time necessary to interpret the meaning of the star and to complete the long journey from Persia to Bethlehem.

Why have Christians always pictured *three* Wise Men as visiting the Christ child?

Normally, Christians think of three Wise Men visiting the baby Jesus because of the three gifts—gold, frankincense, and myrrh—that they presented to the parents. As to the actual number of Wise Men who visited Jesus, however, we are not certain. Most authorities feel that for the sake of safety while traveling, many more than three men probably would have made the journey.

Later Christian meditation on the Gospel story has assigned names to the three Magi: Caspar, Melchior, and Balthazar.

Why were shepherds chosen as the first people to worship the Christ child with Mary and Joseph?

If the Wise Men who followed the star represented the best in scholarship in ancient times, shepherds composed the other side of the spectrum. The job of a shepherd was assumed by those unable to do much else for an honest living. They were far from the intellects of the day.

Modern biblical scholars, including Dr. Fred Meuser, speculate that perhaps this was the very reason God chose shepherds to be the first people outside the immediate family to worship the Christ child. When the angelic heralds announced to them that night that the Savior was born, these rather simple men who guarded the sheep wasted no time debating the subject because it did not conform to logical thinking. Instead, they immediately left the flocks and hurried to the manger and worshiped the new born baby (Luke 2:8-20).

Why was Jesus nearly executed before he was two years old?

When the Wise Men were searching for the baby Jesus, their journey took them to Jerusalem. Here they asked several people: "Where is he who has been born king of the Jews? For we have seen his star in the East, and have come to worship him" (Matthew 2:2).

When Herod the Great heard about this, he became enraged, for he had been given the title "King of the Jews" by order of the Roman Senate in 40 B.C. In order to eliminate another claimer to his throne, Herod commanded that the baby—who was now about one-and-one-half years old—be found first by his own men and killed.

Mary and Joseph were warned by an angel that Herod was about to kill the baby and fled with their son. That night they set out from Bethlehem for Egypt where they remained until Herod's death shortly thereafter.

Why was Jesus circumcised?

In line with the tradition of the Jews, Jesus' parents took their child to the Temple for circumcision. Circumcision was a mark of the covenant between God and the Children of Israel (Genesis 17:11).

During circumcision, the Jewish child was officially named. The name "Jesus" was given to the son of Mary as ordered by the angel before the Savior's birth (Luke 2:21).

In the Early Church, one of the first disputes arose out of the fact that St. Peter insisted that those males who wanted to become Christians must first be circumcised as was Jesus and every other faithful Jew. St. Paul, on the other hand, preached that all the convert to Christianity needed was a "circumcision of the heart" (Romans 2:29). After a meeting of the leaders of the Church at Jerusalem (sometimes called the "Council of Jerusalem"), Paul's view prevailed.

Why did Jesus choose 12 disciples?

The Gospel of Mark tells us that Jesus went up to a mountain and called to himself those he desired (3:3). There he chose 12 disciples, since 12 corresponds to the 12 tribes of Israel.

The mission of the disciples and their involvement with the tribes of Israel are clearly spelled out in the New Testament:

> As my Father appointed a kingdom for me, so do I appoint for you that you may eat and drink at my table in my kingdom, and sit on thrones judging the 12 tribes of Israel (Luke 22:29-30).

Why did Jesus perform miracles?

Some 40 miracles of Jesus are recorded in the New Testament. They range from demonstrating Jesus' control over nature such as the time he attended a wedding feast and changed water into wine (John 2:1-11) to his control even over the powers of death as shown when he raised his friend Lazarus from the grave (John 11:17-44).

Jesus performed miracles for two reasons. First, he sought to relieve the suffering of people. Once when he had encountered a large crowd that gathered to hear him, Jesus felt compassion for those who were sick, and he healed them (Matthew 14:14). On another occasion, a massive crowd of about 5,000 was with him for three days without food. With only five loaves of bread and two small fish, he fed the entire assembled group (Mark 6:34-44).

Underlying all of his miracles, however, was a second and more important lesson. Each miracle was designed to reveal the fact that Jesus held the power of God to perform such works. Miracles, then, supported the belief that Jesus was the God Incarnate—"God in the flesh."

"Believe the works," said Jesus, "that you may know and understand that the Father is in me and I am in the Father" (John 10:38).

Why did Jesus instruct his disciples to "tell no one what you saw" after he performed a miracle?

When Jesus worked a miracle, he often told his disciples as well as the other people who viewed the phenomenon not to tell anyone what they had seen (Luke 8:56).

Why would Jesus say such a thing? Surely, one might suspect that publicity about his supernatural power would have drawn others to see and hear him. Yet this was the precise reason why Jesus urged the witnesses to remain silent about what they had seen for themselves.

During Jesus' time, as is the case today, there were those who claimed to have been given power from Almighty God. They demonstrated this alleged authority by performing "tricks." However, when the secret of their magic was revealed, these false prophets were driven out of town. Jesus feared that those who heard of his mighty works would link him with these charlatans.

Jesus knew, also, that any faith based upon seeing some sort of miracle performed was a rather shallow faith. Once such a faith began to wane, the person would demand to see another miracle. Yet always remaining in the back of the person's mind was the question: "Was this really a miracle, or was it another 'trick'?"

Throughout the Bible, the miracles of God and of the Christ were never meant to create a faith; they were meant, instead, to strengthen an already existing faith. The Roman Catholic philosopher, Maurice Blondel, explained this when he wrote:

Miracles are miraculous only to those who are

already prepared to recognize the operation of God in the commonest events and actions.

In the last analysis, Blondel concludes, it is faith that dictates the interpretation of the fact.

Why do some scholars refuse to believe that Jesus actually performed miracles?

While most Christians accept as fact that Jesus performed miracles during his ministry here on earth, some scholars openly challenge the belief that these miracles actually happened.

One noted scholar, Charles Guignebert, Professor of the History of Christianity in the Sorbonne, claimed: "It is the interpretation of the fact as a miracle which depends upon the credulity of the witness." Guignebert went on to say that most of the happenings attributed to Jesus can be rationally explained; hence the so-called miracles are only natural phenomena blown out of proportion by those who reported them.

Another professor, Rudolph Bultmann, explained the record of Jesus' miracles by saying, in effect, that they never happened at all. Instead, he concluded, the reporting of these were attempts by the writers of the four Gospels (Matthew, Mark, Luke, and John) to explain the character of Jesus as they interpreted it.

Orthodox Christian scholars disagree with Guignebert, Bultmann, or anyone else who views the miracles of Jesus from the perspective of the nonbeliver. They argue that belief in Jesus' miracles requires having faith that he possessed the power to perform these miracles; otherwise anyone could explain away the miracles as "tricks" or the reporting about them as "lies."

Most of the Christian authorities, in fact, look with suspicion upon any challenge to the miracles of Jesus as written in the New Testament. They feel that once people refuse to accept the miracles as presented, they may as well disregard the remaining accounts of Jesus' life, even the greatest miracle of all—his resurrection.

Why did Jesus teach in parables?

Jesus taught his disciples and other interested listeners through a familiar method of education in his day—parables. Parables were stories (whether true or fictitious) that revealed moral truths.

Teaching in parables was a part of Jesus' Jewish tradition. The Old Testament records several parables. For example, when the prophet Nathan confronted David with the word of the Lord's judgment for his murder of Uriah in order to steal Uriah's wife, he brought the king to repentance by telling the parable of the rich man's sheep and the poor man's beloved lamb (II Samuel 12:1-4).

Some of the most oft-quoted sections of the New Testament are the stories told by Jesus in which he used ordinary experiences to illustrate grander points. He compared, for instance, the Kingdom of Heaven to a mustard seed which, if planted correctly in good soil, would grow by leaps and bounds. Other stories centered upon the exemplary life such as the familiar story of the Good Samaritan (Luke 10:25-37) which demonstrated that the true neighbor is not necessarily the person who lives next door, or who is of the "right race and nationality," but the person whose heart is big enough to care for someone in need.

Why did Jesus found a Church?

Jesus came to rescue the human race, according to Christian belief, from the clutches of sin and death, and hold out the hope of eternal life. Someone or some organ would have to continue that struggle against evil after his ascent into heaven. This organ was the Church. For this reason, Jesus told St. Peter:

> You are Peter, and on this rock I will build my church, and the powers of death shall not prevail against it. I will give you the keys to the kingdom of heaven, and whatever you bind on earth shall be bound in heaven, and whatever you loose on earth shall be loosed in heaven (Matthew 16:18-20).

The Church and Christ are as closely connected as the body and head of a person. The Church, according to traditional Christian teaching, is to form its members into the full maturity of Christ the head (Ephesians 4:15-16).

Why did Jesus call the Pharisees "hypocrites"?

> Woe to you, scribes and Pharisees, hypocrites! for you are like whitewashed tombs, which outwardly appear beautiful, but within they are full of dead men's bones . . . (Matthew 23:27).

These stinging words of Jesus were levied against a popular Jewish sect of his day known as the "Pharisees," which was only 200 years old and numbered some 6,000 members. (In time, this group would be equated with Judaism.) Throughout his ministry, Jesus was extremely critical of the Pharisees of his day who were deeply concerned with the strict observance of the many laws set up in the Jewish community. To the Pharisees, adherence to the letter of the law was the essence of Judaism.

Jesus, on the other hand, felt that many Pharisees were interested only in the outward signs of righteousness while forgetting that genuine religion was that which comes from the heart. Jesus felt that such Pharisees were so intent on keeping the letter of the law that they missed the more important dimensions of life and faith.

Once, for example, when Jesus healed a man with a withered hand on the Sabbath, some Pharisees openly questioned whether or not it was proper to do so, since no work was to be performed on the seventh day (Matthew 23:23). Jesus responded to their challenge by asking:

> What man of you, if he has one sheep and it falls into a pit on the sabbath, will not lay hold of it and lift it out? Of how much more value is a man than a sheep! So it is lawful to do good on the sabbath (Matthew 12:11-12).

This is not to imply, of course, that Jesus was completely opposed to the mission of the Pharisees in this world. On the contrary, Jesus saw in the Pharisees the clearest example of traditional Judaism and regarded them as men who attempted to apply the writings of the law (the Torah) to the changing needs of the people. Hence, he counseled his hearers to "practice and observe whatever [the Pharisees] tell you" (Matthew 23:3).

At the same time, however, Jesus dissuaded the people from doing what many Pharisees did, for they preached but did not practice (Matthew 23:3). Jesus became increasingly frustrated at their emphasis on the exterior show of religion without manifesting evidence of love for their fellow human beings.

In light of this, it is ironic that one Pharisee, Saul of Tarsus, eventually joined the followers of Jesus, became an influential leader of the Early Church, and authored what many regard as the finest treatise on love in the New Testament (I Corinthians 13). He was known later as St. Paul.

Why did Jesus pose a threat to the Sadducees?

Jesus' popularity with the people in Jerusalem disturbed another religious sect of his day—the Sadducees. The Sadducees, rivals of the Pharisees, were aristocratic and wealthy. They had a vested interest in maintaining the status quo in both religion and the government. They did not want anyone "rocking the boat," so to speak. Therefore, when the people flocked to hear Jesus and responded so zealously to his preaching that some wanted to make him a king (John 6:15), he posed a threat to the current religious and political scenes. The concern of the Sadducees was heightened all the more when people referred to Jesus as the "King of the Jews."

The Sadducees were largely responsible for Jesus' death inasmuch as the chief priests and elders who were prominently involved in the Passion Narratives were, for the most part, Sadducees. They were also actively involved, later, in opposing the apostles' teaching of the resurrection of Jesus.

Why did the Pharisees and the Sadducees join forces against Jesus?

The Pharisees and the Sadducees were strongly opposed to one another during Jesus' time because of a marked difference in philosophy. The Pharisees preached strict observance of the Jewish laws and opposed the Roman government. The Sadducees rejected the literal interpretation of the Jewish laws and were sympathetic toward the Roman overlords.

Jesus threatened both groups when he challenged the Roman government (backed by the Sadducees) and the Jewish laws (stressed by the Pharisees).

A few days before Jesus' death, a group of Pharisees and Sadducees set aside their differences and conspired to entrap him by approaching him together and asked whether or not it was proper to pay taxes to Caesar. If Jesus had answered "Yes," he would have supported civil law and angered the Pharisees; had he answered "No," he would have supported civil disobedience and angered the Sadducees. Jesus saw through the attempt to trap him and settled the issue by demanding: "Render to Caesar the things that are Caesar's, and to God the things that are God's" (Matthew 22:21).

After the Romans destroyed Jerusalem and the Temple in 70 A.D., the Sadducees disappeared from Jewish life, for they no longer had any institutions to hold them together. The Pharisees, on the other hand, grew and held the Jewish community together, for they were the product of a true religion. The members of the Pharisees were no longer called "scribes," but "rabbis."

Why did Jesus ride into Jerusalem on Palm Sunday?

Jesus entered into Jerusalem on the Sunday prior to his death by riding on a donkey. Crowds stood along the roadside shouting "Hosanna" (meaning "Lord, help us"). Some threw palm branches in the path of the donkey; hence the name "Palm Sunday" is used to designate this event.

Many commentators feel that Jesus deliberately rode into Jerusalem in order to fulfill his Mission—to die so that he could rise from death.

Jesus predicted he was going to be killed, and he knew that Jerusalem would be the place of his death. Before the entrance into the city on Palm Sunday, Jesus took his 12 disciples aside and said:

> Behold, we are going up to Jerusalem; and the Son of man will be delivered to the chief priests and scribes, and they will condemn him to death, and deliver him to the Gentiles to be mocked and scourged and crucified, and he will be raised on the third day (Matthew 20:18-19).

Why did Jesus eat a Passover meal?

The Passover meal for Jesus was an annual event he celebrated throughout his life. Passover was and still is one of the holiest of all seasons for the Jews. It commemorates the exodus from Egypt and is the Jewish holiday of freedom. Passover is a week-long celebration inaugurated by a supper—a "Seder"—shared, even to this day, with family and very close friends.

For Jesus, the Passover meal was not only an opportunity to participate in a long-standing tradition, but also a chance to meet for the last time with all 12 of his disciples in order to announce to them what was about to take place.

At the same time, it was an ideal occasion for leaving his followers a memorial banquet that would unite him with his followers of all ages—the Lord's Supper.

Why did Jesus eat his last Passover meal one day early?

Jesus ate his last Passover meal with his 12 disciples on the evening prior to the start of the week-long observance. Had he followed the Hebrew tradition to the letter of the law, he would have celebrated the meal on the "Seder night," which, at this time, would have been on a Friday. Instead, Jesus met with his close companions on a Thursday evening.

But Jesus knew that he would be sent to his death on that Seder night. Earlier in the week he told his disciples: "You know that after two days the Passover is coming, and the Son of man will be delivered up to be crucified" (Matthew 26:2). At the close of the meal on Thursday evening, Jesus reminded his disciples that he would not drink again of the fruit of the vine until that day when they were together in heaven (Matthew 26:29).

Why did Jesus use unleavened bread at his last supper?

Certain foods, including unleavened bread (matza), is eaten at the traditional Passover observance. This is to commemorate the hurried departure of the Israelites from Egypt: "The people took their dough before it was leavened" (Exodus 12:34).

In Deuteronomy, the practice of eating is prescribed for the seven-day Passover celebration:

> Seven days you shall eat it with unleavened bread . . . for you came out of the land of Egypt in hurried flight—that all the days of your life you may remember the day when you came out of the land of Egypt (16:3).

On the evening before his crucifixion, Jesus took the bread (matza), blessed it, and, before distributing it to his disciples, said: "Take, eat; this is my body" (Matthew 26:26).

Since Jesus used unleavened bread at his last supper—which Christians believe is the foundation for their observance of Holy Communion—many denominations (such as the Roman Catholic, Lutheran, Episcopal, and Eastern Orthodox) insist that unleavened bread be served whenever the Communion is offered.

Why was wine used at Jesus' last supper?

Wine was always used at Sabbath meals and at other festivals, including the Seder night which marked the beginning of the Passover observance. Jesus' last supper with his disciples was the Seder. When he served the wine, however, he added a new dimension with the words: "This is the blood of the covenant, which is poured out for many for the forgiveness of sins" (Matthew 26:28).

According to Jewish practice, two cups of wine are normally served at festivals. A special prayer called a kid-

dush (which means "sanctification") is recited over one cup of wine, and the grace at the end of the meal is prayed over a second cup. At Passover, two extra cups of wine are added.

Because Jesus used wine at his last supper, many Christians (particularly the Roman Catholics, Lutherans, Anglicans and Eastern Orthodox) use wine during their services of Holy Communion which has its roots in the Seder.

Why did Jesus go to the Garden of Gethsemane to pray before his arrest and trial?

The garden known as Gethsemane is a small 140-by-150 foot retreat on the western slope of the Mount of Olives that was a favorite of Jesus who often met there with his disciples (John 18:2). It was a quiet spot where he conducted private devotions as he did on the night in which he was betrayed and arrested.

The spot today is preserved by an enclosed wall built by the Franciscans (a monastic group) in 1848. However, as with many of the sites associated with the life of Jesus, there is some dispute about the claim that this was the actual place where Jesus prayed.

Why was Jesus arrested by the Romans?

When Jesus was arrested in the Garden of Gethsemane following his vigil of prayer, his capture must have had the authorization of the Roman government—the agency empowered to enforce civil law.

Although Jesus had not violated the civil law, but only the Jewish law in the eyes of the religious leaders, the Sanhedrin—the superior judicial body in Jewish life at that time—had lost the power to pass capital sentences. Therefore, if Jesus was to be executed, it had to be by order of the official representative of the Roman government—Pontius Pilate.

The arrest of Jesus was made by a company armed with weapons, sent by the religious leaders and led by Judas who betrayed him (Mark 14:43). One Gospel writer, John, mentions that a cohort of Roman soldiers was present (John 18:12). Some New Testment authorities such as Vincent Taylor conclude that the presence of a detachment of soldiers strongly implies a collusion between the religious leaders and Pilate.

Why was Jesus' trial and execution carried out so quickly?

The arrest, trial, and execution of Jesus covered a span of less than 24 hours—a violation of both the Roman and the Jewish codes of justice.

Under Roman law, those accused of a crime would receive a trial, sentencing (if found guilty) and, after a week or ten days, appropriate punishment. The reason for this delay between sentencing and punishment was to allow time for appeals or restitution in the event a verdict was rendered without just cause.

Under Jewish law, a trial could be conducted only during the day and settled by night. For a criminal proceeding which carried with it a potentially severe punishment, however, sentencing would not be pronounced until one day after the trial when the minds of the judges had theoretically cooled.

The reason for Jesus' hastened form of "justice" was twofold. First, the mob of onlookers—both Jews and Romans—was angry and demanded instant punishment. Second, the trial was conducted just hours before the Seder night of Passover. According to Jewish law, no one could be put to death during the seven days of the Passover celebration. Therefore, in the minds of many in the mob, if the sentence was not carried out immediately, there might have been a chance for the condemned Jesus to escape punishment.

Although the Jews had no power to execute people, Pontius Pilate was willing to do whatever he could to maintain peace and harmony within the Jewish community. Most authorities agree that Pilate's order for a quick execution before sundown was a consensus in order to please the religious leaders.

Why did Jesus deny that he was an earthly king?

Jesus spent his entire public life trying to avoid being identified as a political Messiah. He took painstaking care to instruct his apostles and the crowds that followed him in the spiritual mission he pursued. He emphasized that he had come to tell the people about their heavenly Father and to bring them into a proper loving relationship with that Father and with each other.

After his arrest and conviction by the Sanhedrin, when he stood before Pontius Pilate, accused of claiming to be a king, the procurator asked him the inevitable question: "Are you the King of the Jews?" Jesus answered in a way consistent with his life: "My kingship is not of this world." He went on to add: "You say that I am a king. For this I was born and for this I have come into the world, to bear witness to the truth" (John 19:36–37).

Even in the face of death, Jesus maintained that his kingship was spiritual only.

Why was Jesus scourged and crowned with thorns?

It was customary for all who were to die by crucifixion to be scourged—possibly in an attempt to render them less sensitive to the pains of crucifixion. In a scourging, the victim was tied to a pillar and beaten by two or more men at a time. The instrument of the scourging was a leather whip studded with pieces of metal or bone. Some victims died under the beating itself.

In the case of Jesus, the soldiers decided to have some sport with him. He was wearing a gorgeous apparel which Herod had placed on him. This reminded the soldiers of royalty. So they made him a mock-king. They made a crown out of thorns and affixed it to his head. To complete the humiliation, a soldier's cloak was thrown about Jesus' shoulders, and a reed was placed in his right hand as a scepter. Then the soldiers mockingly bowed down before this "king."

Why did Pontius Pilate wash his hands at the trial of Jesus?

When Pontius Pilate saw the tragic state of Jesus after the scourging and the humiliation of the soldiers, he thought the people who had brought him for condemnation would agree that the man had suffered enough. Therefore, he brought Jesus before them, confident of their willingness to dismiss him.

Instead, Pilate was surprised to hear that they wanted the condemnation carried out. Indeed, the procurator would have a full-scale riot on his hands unless something was done; and the Romans would not take too kindly to anything less than death. Hence, Pilate washed his hands before the crowd in a kind of grandstand play, proclaiming his innocence in the death of Jesus. This action, however, was really the last word in Jesus' condemnation, and the sentence had to be carried out.

Why was Jesus forced to carry his crossbeam on his way to the crucifixion?

One of the added insults to the condemned prisoner in Jesus' time was to force him to carry the crossbeam (called the *patibulum*) that would be used for his own crucifixion. The vertical post of the cross (called *stipes crucis*) was normally planted solidly in the ground prior to his arrival at the place of execution.

Why was Simon of Cyrene compelled to carry Jesus' crossbeam?

Ordinarily, the condemned criminals carried the instrument of their death (the crossbeam) to the place of execution. However, Jesus was so exhausted by the events leading up to the cross—the sleepless night, the various trials, the scourging and crowning—that the soldiers feared he might die before arriving at Calvary. Hence, they made use of a practice that was made necessary from time to time.

They enlisted a passerby to carry the crossbeam. His name was Simon of Cyrene, the father of Alexander and Rufus (Mark 15:21). Nothing further is known about him. It is possible that his sons were Christian, for Paul in his letter to the Romans (16:13) sent greetings to a certain Rufus, who is believed to be the same one mentioned in the Gospel of Mark.

Why did Jesus tell the women of Jerusalem to weep?

On the way to Calvary, "a great multitude . . . of women" followed Jesus "who bewailed and lamented him" (Luke 23:27). Jesus turned to them and told them to weep not for him but for themselves and their children.

According to many scholars, Jesus was probably referring here to the destructive days that lay ahead, including the fall of Jerusalem in 70 A.D.

Why was Jesus killed by crucifixion?

Crucifixion was the standard mode of execution for non-Romans by the Roman government and practiced on a large scale in Judea during the Roman occupation.

Crucifixion was a slow, humiliating form of execution in which the condemned was literally nailed to a cross made of wood.

The victim was laid upon the ground with the crossbeam resting under his shoulders and outstretched arms. A soldier placed his knee on the inside of the elbow and held the forearm flat to the rough piece of wood. He then placed the point of a five-inch, square-cut iron nail over the little hollow spot in the wrist, raised a hammer over the nail head, and brought it down sharply. He repeated the procedure with the other wrist. (Note: the nails were not placed in the hands as often believed.)

When the wrists were secured, and the executioner was satisfied that the victim could not free himself from the crossbeam, he and another soldier raised the prisoner onto the vertical post already in the ground onto which the criminal's feet were nailed only a few inches above the ground. As a result, the crucified spent his last agonizing hours of life realizing that he was suspended less than a foot away from the earth.

Why was Jesus stabbed with a spear by a Roman soldier?

Jesus and the two criminals who were crucified with him were still hanging on crosses as sundown approached, marking the start of Passover. In order that the condemned would be put to death before the Seder night, the soldiers followed the standard procedure of breaking the bones of the victims until they died. When they got to Jesus, however, it appeared that he had already expired. In order to be certain, one of the soldiers "pierced his side with a spear" (John 19:34).

Christians believe that this action by the soldier fulfilled the prophecies about the Messiah: "He keeps all his bones; not one of them is broken" (Psalm 34:20) and "They [shall] look on him whom they have pierced" (Zechariah 12:10).

Why did blood and water flow from Jesus' side?

The dead do not bleed, normally, but when the soldier stabbed Jesus in the side with a spear, the biblical account reads: "At once there came out blood and water" (John 19:34).

According to one explanation, the soldier's spear might have pierced Jesus' heart. The human heart holds blood after death, and the other sac holds a serum called "hydropericardium." The puncture of this area by an object could then cause blood and water to flow over the body of Jesus.

Mystical writers have given various interpretations of this phenomenon. The most common alludes to the great love that the heart of Jesus has for all human beings.

Why was Jesus' body wrapped in a shroud?

Immediately after Jesus was removed from the cross, his body was quickly wrapped in a shroud before being set inside the tomb.

Shrouds have been part of the Jewish custom for burial since the time of the Exodus. Normally made of simple, inexpensive muslin or linen, the shroud not only preserved the body a bit longer, but also held a symbolic meaning.

Everyone was buried in a simple shroud, so that both rich and poor would be equal before Almighty God. In contrast to the belief of the ancient Egyptians that the dead could take earthly possessions with them, the Jews used shrouds without pockets, indicating that none of a persons's material belongings can be taken along after death.

Why is the "Shroud of Turin" a controversial part of Jesus' burial?

The Shroud of Turin is an ancient linen cloth measuring 14 feet by 4 feet which is said to have been the burial garment placed over the body of Jesus before he was placed in the tomb following his crucifixion. In 1978, Pope Paul VI declared that the Shroud was "the most important relic in the history of Christianity."

Of most fascination to those who view the Shroud is the purported image of Christ that marks the cloth. Its image is said to represent the facial and body features of Jesus. These were imprinted on the cloth, thereby presenting absolute proof that the man, Jesus, was dead and buried.

Skeptics throughout the centuries have dubbed this Shroud a "fake." The popular television series, "Sixty Minutes," aired a broadcast in 1981 which featured statements by representatives of both sides of the controversy.

The debate began when a man named Geoffrey de Charney purchased the Shroud and displayed it before the public in 1357 in Lirey, France. Charney died without disclosing to anyone exactly how he got the cloth.

The Shroud was placed in storage after Charney's death and, in 1449, was displayed once again by his granddaughter, Margaret. Three years later, she sold it to the Duke of Savoy. In 1532, it was damaged by a fire in the Sainte Chapelle of Chambery.

In 1898, photographs were taken of the Shroud which indicated that the image (of a man crowned with thorns, whipped, lanced, and crucified) could not have been painted during the Middle Ages. The negatives surprisingly yielded a *positive image*. Studies conducted on the Shroud have indicated that the cloth at some stage and in some way came in contact with radiation.

Throughout the years, the Shroud has been subjected to chemical tests, X-rays, gamma rays, even computer analysis. Modern scientists, armed with the evidence of investigators, are far from unanimous in their opinions as to the Shroud's authenticity. Some voice support for the claim that it is real; others use the same evidence to prove otherwise.

The issue is even more clouded by the absence of any reference to the cloth with the image of Jesus either in the New Testament or in the writings of the Early Church. On top of this, after the Crusades, as many as 40 "shrouds" were circulated within the Christian communities, all with the claim of authenticity.

Why did Joseph of Arimathea give his tomb for Jesus' burial?

An observer of the crucifixion of Jesus was a man named Joseph of Arimathea who asked permission of Pontius Pilate to have the body of Jesus in order that he might bury it in his private tomb near the spot of the execution. Pilate granted his wish.

The Bible paints a rather complex and sometimes contradictory picture of this character who appears in the New Testament only during this description of Jesus' burial. All four of the Gospel writers mention him. Matthew calls him "a rich man . . . who also was a disciple of Jesus" (27:57). Mark merely states that he was sympathetic to Jesus' teachings and a member of the council (perhaps a Sanhedrin of his city) "who was himself looking for the kingdom of God" (15:43). Luke calls him a "good and righteous man"

(23:50), and John says he was a "disciple of Jesus, but secretly" (19:38).

Nothing more is mentioned about Joseph of Arimathea in the Bible. Records kept by the Early Church fathers give no indication as to what happened to him. The apocryphal *Gospel of Nicodemus* states that Joseph played a prominent role in the foundation of the first Christian community at Lydda. In the twelfth century, the English historian, William of Malmesbury, shares the legend that Joseph reached England with the Holy Grail (the cup used by Jesus at the Last Supper) and erected the first church in England at Glastonbury.

Today, scholars are still baffled by the fact that the Bible remains silent about the fate of this man whose kindness must have brought needed comfort to the family and friends of the crucified Jesus.

Why did the friends of Jesus wait until Sunday to visit the body in the tomb?

All four Gospel accounts of Jesus' death and burial relate that Mary Magdalene, Mary the mother of James and Salome, and some friends did not visit the tomb to anoint the body of the crucified Jesus until Sunday—two days after the execution. This was in line with the Jewish law that forbids any mourning of a departed loved one on the Sabbath (Saturday). The Sabbath was a day of joy and was not to be marred by mourning. Isaiah himself wrote: " . . . and [you shall] call the sabbath a delight" (53:13). In keeping with this tradition, the relatives and companions of Jesus did not visit the tomb on Saturday.

Even today, according to Jewish practice, mourning is not observed on Sabbaths and holidays. It is the custom for mourners on the Sabbath to dress up, attend worship, and observe the Sabbath until nightfall, at which time they may resume mourning.

Why did Jesus' followers come to believe in his resurrection from the dead?

The followers of Jesus had been hoping that he would be the one to set Israel free. His unexpected death on Good Friday left them bewildered, despairing, and fearing for their lives. So they locked themselves in the Upper Room.

On the following Sunday, they learned from some of the women of their group that Jesus' tomb was empty and an angel had announced that he had risen. Then two disciples came rushing in from the country (Emmaus) with the word that the Savior had risen and appeared to them. Finally, that night, Jesus himself came to the disciples through the bolted doors and imparted to them his peace and the power to forgive sins.

Over the course of the next few weeks, Jesus appeared to the disciples more times under varying circumstances. In all, the New Testament lists 13 appearances of Jesus:

1. To Mary Magdalene on Easter morn in Jerusalem (Mark 16:9).

2. To other women on Easter morn in Jerusalem (Matthew 28:9).

3. To Peter at an unspecified time and place (I Corinthians 15:5).

4. To two disciples on Easter day at Emmaus (Luke 24:15–31).

5. To ten apostles on Easter evening at Jerusalem (John 20:19–24).

6. To the Eleven on the Sunday after Easter at Jerusalem (John 20:26–28).

7. To seven disciples fishing at an unspecified time at the Sea of Galilee (John 21:1–24).

8. To the Eleven at an unspecified time at a mountain in Galilee (Mt 28:16–17).

9. To 500 brethren at an unspecified time and place (I Corinthians 15:6).

10. To James at an unspecified time and place (I Corinthians 15:7).

11. To "all the apostles" at an unspecified time and place (I Corinthians 15:7).

12. To the Eleven on Ascension Day at Bethany (Acts 9:1-5).

13. To Saul at an unspecified time on the Road to Damascus (Acts 9:1-5; I Corinthians 15:8).

These recorded appearances (and probably others not recorded) were enough to convince the followers of Jesus that he had indeed risen from the dead as he had said. They recalled that on three separate occasions Jesus had predicted his death and resurrection on the third day (Matthew 16:21; Mark 8:31-33; Luke 18:31-34). And they believed.

Why are there differences about some of the details of Jesus' life?

The four Gospel accounts—Matthew, Mark, Luke, and John—record the story of the one called "Jesus." Unfortunately, perhaps, the four writers sometimes differ on particulars and, in certain instances, present information not confirmed by the other three witnesses. Matthew, for example, tells about Jesus feeding over five thousand people at one time (14:13-21); Mark says that there were four thousand people (8:1-10). At Jesus' crucifixion, John quotes Jesus as saying things from the cross never mentioned by any of the other three writers. Yet most authorities do not consider these inconsistencies strange in light of the circumstances of the times.

Not only were the ancient scribes not blessed with our modern sophisticated recording devices, but the actual writing down of the happenings didn't take place until probably 40 years after Jesus' death and resurrection. Until then, the stories about Jesus were passed from one generation to another by the so-called oral tradition—the relating of stories by word of mouth. It is easy to see, therefore, how some details could become distorted over the span of years.

Many scholars, in fact, take these very discrepancies in the Gospels as added proof of their historicity. Instead of making all the accounts identical, the early Christians respected them too much to tamper with the text. It came down to the Church as it had been handed down by the eyewitnesses who originally made oral reports on which the Gospels were based.

Anyone who has ever listened to eyewitness reports at a trial (under oath) can testify to the variance in the reports of the same incident on the part of these witnesses. The substance will be the same, but the nonessentials will vary. Far from being proof of the falsity of the Gospels, minor discrepancies are just another proof of their historicity.

Chapter 2

Practices and Beliefs That Unite and Divide

INTRODUCTION

We are one in the Spirit,
We are one in the Lord.
We are one in the Spirit,
We are one in the Lord.
And we pray that all unity may one
    day be restored.
And they'll know we are Christians
    by our love, by our love,
Yes, they'll know we are Christians
    by our love.*

These are the words of a popular folk-hymn sung in churches throughout the nation. They express an admirable wish, but one that is far from reality.

Christians have *never* been "one" in the fullest sense of the word. Their history is colored with different shades of beliefs and practices that unite them and divide them. Even their earliest leaders—Peter and Paul—openly disagreed on whether or not a person had to become a Jew before becoming a Christian. The controversy grew so intense that the small bands of followers chose sides, creating a diversity

---

*Copyright © 1966, 1967 by F.E.L. Church Publications Ltd.

within a group that so desperately needed a unified effort to withstand the persecutions levied against them on all sides.

In the centuries that followed, the practices and beliefs that divided Christians increased both in number and in intensity. Why the discord? Some of it stemmed from petty jealousies and rivalries which developed between Christian leaders; some resulted from geographic or nationalistic loyalties. But we come closest to the heart of the problem when we admit that most of the current differences between Christians reflect genuine concerns of people who seek honest answers to honest questions.

Unfortunately, what often started out as a minor difference that might have been settled through dialogue progressed to a major issue on which no one was willing to bend.

These beliefs and practices cannot always be confined to denominational affiliations. On the contrary, they have set Baptist against Baptist while, at the same time, mobilizing a Lutheran and a Roman Catholic to fight side-by-side in support of an issue.

Fortunately, in most instances, these heated debates generally center upon *secondary* issues which compose the fringe on the garment of dogma. For the most part, Christians are in general agreement about the *major* issues concerning the faith. Most of them understand that their striving for *unity* does not compel a *uniformity* of interpretation on each issue.

Christians will continue to work toward unification, and they'll sing their folk-songs that proclaim their "oneness." Indeed, some progress may be made in the coming years. Yet at the precise moment Christians think that complete unity is just around the corner, someone will raise a question, another will offer an answer, and a third will challenge either the wisdom of the response or the right of anyone to raise the question in the first place.

The following questions and answers attempt to show some of the issues that have united and divided Christians throughout the world in the past and continue to do so even in our day.

Why do Christians worship the Trinity even though the word is never mentioned in the Bible?

If Christians are united on any issue it is this: the God whom they worship is a "Trinity," with three persons—the Father, the Son, and the Holy Spirit. At the same time, the word "Trinity" never appears in the Bible.

This unique concept is not, as some outsiders have been led to believe, a collection of three different gods. Instead, Christians view the Father, the Son, and the Holy Spirit as three complete persons composing one God. While some may argue that this concept falls outside the arena of sound logic, Christians accept the realization that the ways of God often surpass human reason.

As to the fact that neither the word "Trinity" nor the phrase "Triune God" ever appears in the Old or the New Testament, Christians are quick to point out that the concept of the Trinity is both implicit and explicit throughout the Holy Scriptures. Several passages allude to it. The most convincing text centers on the formula for baptism given by Jesus to his apostles:

> Go, therefore, and make disciples of all nations baptizing them in the name of the Father and of the Son and of the Holy Spirit (Matthew 28:19).

This teaching about the Triune God was not without controversy. Christians in the Early Church engaged in spirited debates over the specific wording and implication of the dogma. As a result, the Council of Nicaea (325) defined the official Christian belief about the Trinity and published what we know today as the Nicene Creed. It states that:

> We believe in one God
> the Father, the Almighty,
> maker of heaven and earth,
> of all that is seen and unseen.
> We believe in one Lord, Jesus Christ,

the only Son of God,
eternally begotten of the Father,
God from God, Light from Light,
true God from true God,
begotten, not made,
of one Being with the Father. . . .
We believe in the Holy Spirit, the Lord,
    the giver of life,
    who proceeds from the Father [and the Son].
    With the Father and the Son he is worshipped
    and glorified. . . .*

The Nicene Creed is confessed by the majority of Christians, although some, such as the Baptists, the Disciples of Christ, and the United Church of Christ, refuse to endorse it or any other creed.

Why do the majority of Christians accept creeds?

A creed is a formal statement of belief. The majority of Christians—Anglicans, Roman Catholics, Lutherans, Methodists, Presbyterians, and others—do not feel that such statements conflict with the teachings of the Bible. They regard creeds as offering condensations of the basic teachings of the faith.

Christians in the Early Church often came from humble backgrounds and were not schooled in the academic disciplines of reading and writing. Consequently, they were unable to read any of the Holy Scriptures that contained the story of Jesus and his Church.

In an effort to crystallize their beliefs into a unified form, Christians committed certain statements to memory and confessed to others what they believed.

*Copyright ©1970, 1971, 1975 by International Consultation on English Texts.

The earliest recorded confession, introduced around the year 150, was a summary of the teachings of the apostles of Jesus. Hence, it is still known as the Apostles' Creed. It not only gave the early Christians a summary of the teachings of the Church but also reminded them of the hope of eternal life for all who accepted Christ as Savior—something that they welcomed at a time when some of their fellow believers were killed for what they believed.

The creed which they memorized is confessed to this day at public worship by most Christians. It states:

I believe in God, the Father almighty,
    creator of heaven and earth.

I believe in Jesus Christ, his only Son, our Lord.
    He was conceived by the power of the Holy Spirit
        and born of the Virgin Mary.
    He suffered under Pontius Pilate,
        was crucified, died, and was buried.
    He descended to the dead.
    On the third day he rose again.
    He ascended into heaven,
        and is seated at the right hand of the Father.
    He will come again to judge the living and the dead.

I believe in the Holy Spirit,
    the holy catholic Church,*
    the communion of saints,
    the forgiveness of sins,
    the resurrection of the body,
    and the life everlasting. Amen.**

Why do some Christians reject creeds?

Throughout the history of the Church, Christians have

---

*Many Protestants use the phrase "the holy *Christian* Church" instead of "the holy *catholic* Church."

**Copyright © 1970, 1971,1975 by International Consultation on English Texts.

used certain statements of belief called "creeds." The most widely accepted are the Apostles' Creed and the Nicene Creed as summaries of the basic teachings of the faith.

At the same time, some believers insist upon freedom of thought and expression in both the pulpit and the pew. They embrace the absolute autonomy of the individual. Groups such as the Baptists, the Disciples of Christ, and the United Church of Christ feel that no person or congregation should be bound to any man-made expression of faith, because the Bible reveals all we need to know.

These Christians would rather shift the responsibility for a faith from a Church council that penned a written statement to the individual who must ultimately decide what to believe.

Why do Roman Catholics and Protestants use different versions of the Apostles' Creed?

In the Roman Catholic version of the Apostles' Creed, the believer confesses: "I believe in the holy catholic Church," while most Protestants say: "I believe in the holy Christian Church."

Although the word "catholic" is merely another word for "universal," many of the leaders of the Protestant Reformation in the 16th century—including Ulrich Zwingli—feared that people might mistake the use of this term to mean the Roman Catholic Church. Therefore, Protestants of this era substituted the word "Christian" for "catholic," a tradition which still exists in many circles.

In 1978, interestingly enough, the Lutheran Church published its *Lutheran Book of Worship* in which the word "catholic" has been returned to its rightful place in the creed. The *Book of Common Prayer*—the basis for worship in the Anglican Church—has used the word "catholic" in its version of the creed since 1789.

Why does the traditional version of the Apostles' Creed refer to the "quick and the dead"?

The traditional version of the Apostles' Creed states: "And he [Christ] shall come again to judge both the quick and the dead." The word "quick" in this instance refers to the living, who will be yet on this earth during what Christians refer to as the "Second Coming of Christ."

According to the New Testament, at a time known to no human being, God will destroy the existing heavens and earth, and Jesus will judge both the living and the dead on the basis of their faith (I Peter 4:5).

Although this phrase is repeated in the Apostles' Creed by many Christians during Sunday morning worship, certain Christians—members of the Assemblies of God and the Adventists, for example—place a heavier emphasis upon the "Day of Judgment" than do others.

Why does the Apostles' Creed speak of the "communion of saints"?

The "communion of saints" is another term for the Church. The Apostles' Creed states, in part: "I believe in the holy catholic [or Christian] Church, the communion of saints. . . . " If, after the word "Church," we mentally insert the words "which is," we catch the spirit of the phrase even better.

Roman Catholic Bishop Fulton J. Sheen of New York, national director of the Society for the Propagation of the Faith, once gave an added dimension to this concept of the communion of saints. On one of his popular television broadcasts in the late 1950s, Bishop Sheen mentioned that this "communion" which Christians share with one another refers not just to the saints (another name for the "redeemed") who live on earth, but also to those who have died in the faith and dwell with God. He spoke of this communion as having both a horizontal (reaching out to all other humans) and a vertical (reaching upward to those in heaven) relationship.

Theologians from the Lutheran, Eastern Orthodox, Methodist, and Presbyterian churches have gone on record as endorsing Bishop Sheen's insight.

Why have some Christians been excommunicated from the communion of saints?

Excommunication is the name given to the official declaration of the Church (or of a congregation) by which a believer is excluded from the communion of the faithful and from receiving the sacraments, especially that of Holy Communion. It is placed upon a person who is living a life inconsistent with the teachings of the faith. Most often, the person is living in a way that at least externally constitutes "mortal sin" without showing any feeling of remorse.

The most widely publicized ban of excommunication in recent years was placed upon Jacqueline Kennedy, widow of America's 35th President, when she married Aristotle Onassis, a divorced shipping tycoon. Since Mrs. Kennedy's Roman Catholic Church considered a divorced person as still married, it looked upon her marriage to Onassis as perpetuating a state of adultery—a mortal sin. Hence, the excommunication.

Excommunication has been issued by the Roman Catholic, Lutheran, Anglican, and Eastern Orthodox churches. In some Protestant circles where independent congregations are autonomous, the vote of the congregation is all that is needed to excommunicate a fellow member.

Excommunication—sometimes called the "capital punishment of ecclesiastical discipline"—is not, necessarily, a "once, for all time" punishment. It is used, instead, as a last resort in an attempt to call attention to the open rebellion against a law of God. Once excommunicated persons have altered their life-style and seek forgiveness for their sin, the Church has the authority to lift the ban and to restore them to full membership.

Why are some sins called "mortal"?

Some sins are obviously worse than others. Christians of the Roman Catholic and Eastern Orthodox communions, as well as some in the Lutheran and Anglican fellowships, refer to the most serious sins as "mortal." According to their belief, these sins are "death-dealing" in that they kill God's life and love within us.

The traditional definition of mortal sin was given in the Roman Catholic *Baltimore Catechism* as "a grievous offense against the law of God which deprives the soul of sanctifying grace, makes the soul an enemy of God, takes away the merit of all its good actions, deprives it of the right of everlasting happiness in heaven, and makes it deserving of everlasting punishment in hell."

According to a modern Roman Catholic catechism, *Christ Among Us,* mortal sin is a "fundamental choice of ourself over God." Although individual Christians must follow their own consciences in judging whether an action on their part constitutes a mortal sin, most Christians who accept this designation of sin would include as mortal: adultery, stealing, lying, and blasphemy.

Although they are serious in nature, mortal sins can be forgiven. (More on this in Chapter 5.)

Why are some sins called "venial"?

Those who accept the designation of "mortal" sins deem the sins which pose no serious threat to the relationship of a person with God as "venial," meaning "easily forgiven."

Venial sins may weaken a person's relationship with

God and neighbor, just as a careless argument would disturb the harmonious relationship in a marriage. Nonetheless, the consequences cannot be compared to those of "mortal" sins.

Why is the rejection of the Holy Spirit considered the "unforgiveable sin"?

Jesus is quoted in the Gospel of Mark as saying: "Whoever blasphemes against the Holy Spirit never has forgiveness, but is guilty of an eternal sin" (3:29).

Why was Jesus so stern at this point? Christian theologians have traditionally taught that rejection of the Holy Spirit is the same as the rejection of Christ as Lord. Since human beings cannot, by reason alone, accept the belief that Jesus is God's Son, they can only hope to do so with the help of the Holy Spirit. Once they reject the influence of the Holy Spirit, then they close the door to all possibility of accepting Christ, the only mediator between God and the human race (I Timothy 2:5).

The Lutheran theologian, John T. Mueller, wrote:

> The sin against the Holy Spirit is unpardonable because it is directed not against the divine person of the Holy Spirit, but against his divine office or his gracious operation upon the human heart.

Why do some Christians believe that newborn infants are born in a state of sin?

The teaching that newborn infants are born in sin dates back to the time of St. Augustine (354–430) who was the Bishop of Hippo. Augustine preached that all who were born into this world were sinners from the moment they left the womb.

Some Christians—particularly those of the Anglican, Roman Catholic, Lutheran, Eastern Orthodox, Methodist, and Presbyterian churches—still believe that any child born to sinful parents must, by nature, also be in a state of sin. The child, according to their thinking, possesses "original sin."

The background of the story of original sin may be found in Genesis, chapter 2. Adam and Eve are pictured in a luxurious garden with complete freedom to do whatever they wished. Both the man and the woman were naked and not ashamed; they had complete openness and esteem one for the other. Then, tragedy struck. The two chose to reject a specific command of God. From that moment on, they were no longer guiltless, but sinners.

Since Adam and Eve were not perfect, any offspring they produced could not be perfect; two imperfects cannot create a perfect. Any succeeding generation would also be born into a state of sin based upon the same logic.

St. Paul referred to this when he wrote: "By one man's disobedience many were made sinners" (Romans 5:19). In the same spirit, the Psalmist wrote: "I was brought forth in iniquity, and in sin did my mother conceive me" (Psalm 51:5).

Just as physical heredity transmits certain defects from the parent to the child, the accumulation of mankind's defects and corruption is passed from one generation to another and inherited by all—even infants.

Why can't some Christians accept the concept of "original sin"?

With few exceptions, members of the Baptist, Assemblies of God, and the so-called Pentecostal churches cannot envision a merciful God who would consider a newborn infant as sinful. They do not believe that the state of sin ("original sin," as others call it) is inherited. Instead, they feel that individuals are held accountable for their own actions, not those of their parents or grandparents.

The debate over original sin is closely tied to a person's theology about baptism. Christians who believe that infants are born in the state of sin also believe that through baptism God "washes away" this sin. They, therefore, would want their children baptized as soon as possible. On the other hand, those who do not accept the concept of original sin see no imminent need for baptism. They choose to wait until their children reach the age of accountability (about the age of 14). For more about baptism, see Chapter 5.

Why do some Christians believe that the Virgin Mary had no original sin?

St. Augustine spoke about an early Christian belief concerning Mary, the mother of Jesus, when he said that all human beings are born sinners "except the Holy Virgin Mary, whom I desire, for the sake of the honor of the Lord, to leave entirely out of the question when the talk is of sin." Traditionally, Roman Catholics, Eastern Orthodox, most Anglicans, and some Lutherans accept this teaching that Mary was filled with the grace of God from the beginning of her life and was preserved from original sin from the moment of her conception.

Although nothing appears in the Bible to substantiate this teaching, certain Christians feel that since Mary was chosen for the unique responsibility of bearing God's only Son, she would be a woman untainted with sin.

On December 8, 1854, Pope Pius IX pronounced that this day would mark the worldwide observance of what is called the "Immaculate Conception." On this date every year, all Roman Catholics are obligated to participate at Mass.

Why is Mary often called the "Mother of God"?

The term "Mother of God" is associated with the Virgin Mary primarily by the Roman Catholics, Eastern Orthodox, and Anglicans. This unique title stems from the belief that Mary was to Jesus all that any mother is to her son. Since Jesus was the Son of God (a basic Christian teaching), it follows that Mary should be called the "Mother of God."

Most Protestants recoil at the use of this title. While few would hold that Jesus was not born of Mary, they are suspicious that certain elements in the Church (mentioned above) have exalted Mary to a position of authority that surpasses God's intention. This fear was expressed quite loudly during the early 1950s when Pope Pius XII announced that Mary ascended into heaven in bodily form—this is the Roman Catholic dogma known as the "Assumption."

Why do some Christians believe that Mary ascended into heaven in bodily form?

An official teaching of the Roman Catholic Church was announced on November 1, 1950, by Pope Pius XII that the Virgin Mary at the end of her earthly life was taken into heaven in bodily form to live with her son. The pronouncement resulted from questions raised as far back as the sixth century when Christians venerated (i.e., set apart for worship) the alleged tomb of the Blessed Virgin but were unable to find any relics of her body as they did when venerating the tombs of the apostles and other saints of the Church.

"Could it be that Mary, like Moses, Elijah, and Jesus, ascended into heaven in bodily form?" they asked. The 1950 announcement answered the question in the affirmative—a general feeling of the Church, according to a Roman Catholic Catechism, *Christ Among Us.*

Protestants, as a whole, do not accept this teaching,

because the Bible never mentions a bodily assumption of the Virgin Mary.

Why are so many Christians today anxious to be "reborn"?

A declaration made by a growing number of Christians in practically every denomination of the Church today is: "You must be born again." Their emphatic statement is based upon a story in the New Testament about a Pharisee named Nicodemus who attempted to discover the secret of Jesus' close association with Almighty God. When the Pharisee raised some pointed questions, Jesus responded: "Truly, truly, I say to you, unless one is born anew, he cannot see the kingdom of God" (John 3:3).

Some contemporary spokesmen for the faith, such as the Reverend Jerry Falwell, trumpet this popular theme on radio and television. Perhaps the most famous person in recent years to announce publicly that he was "born again" was our nation's 39th President, Jimmy Carter.

Persons who claim to be "born again" can usually recall the exact moment in their lives when they accepted Jesus as their Lord. At that moment, they say, they were given a "new life." Their conversion experience normally resulted in some marked changes in attitude and life-style. These changes might manifest themselves in such things as good works, increased participation at public worship, a greater willingness (even eagerness) to speak with others about the word of God, and, for some, the unusual phenomenon known as "speaking in tongues."

Why is "speaking in tongues" a part of the Christian tradition?

"Speaking in tongues" (or glossolalia) is the name of a

unique occurrence mentioned several times in the New Testament and growing in popularity during recent times.

The Bible tells the story of its introduction into the Church during the first Pentecost (50 days after Easter) when the Holy Spirit filled a large room in which thousands of people from various nations had gathered to hear St. Peter tell of his personal experiences with Jesus. Suddenly, the people reacted to the presence of the Holy Spirit by speaking in a strange, but common language (Acts, chapter 2).

Throughout the history of the Church, some people have repeated this reaction to the presence of the Holy Spirit through "speaking in tongues."

This phenomenon first appeared on the American scene during the period known as the "Great Awakening" (which began around the middle of the eighteenth century and lasted for approximately 40 years) when Sunday morning worshipers often witnessed people who went into a trance and spoke aloud by making strange, incoherent sounds akin to babbling. When they awoke from the trance, one or more of the assembled group "interpreted" what was said. This unusual form of expression is as popular now as ever before.

"Speaking in tongues" traditionally has been linked with Christians of the Pentecostal churches—e.g., Assemblies of God. In the past, the more liturgical communions—the Roman Catholic, Eastern Orthodox, Lutheran, and Anglican—discarded the practice as a mere emotional response. The present movement, however, is shared by members even among some of the more conservative, liturgical congregations.

In the middle 1970s, Lutherans, Roman Catholics, and Anglicans began organizing annual conventions on the Holy Spirit in major metropolitan areas throughout the nation. The conventions draw literally thousands of people each year and offer the opportunity for believers to praise the Lord through the "gifts of the Spirit"—including "speaking in tongues."

Why is "speaking in tongues" called a "gift of the Spirit"?

Christians who demonstrate the work of the Holy Spirit through "speaking in tongues" cannot claim this is a result of effort on their part. On the contrary, it is a gift from God. As St. Paul wrote: "To each is given the manifestation of the Spirit for the common good. To one is given . . . various kinds of tongues, to another the interpretation of tongues" (I Corinthians 12:7-10). Since it is a gift, those who speak in tongues cannot boast that they are, therefore, better than their brothers and sisters in the faith who do not share this experience.

Why does someone appear to be in a trance when "speaking in tongues"?

"When I speak in tongues," said a young man in Minneapolis while attending a Lutheran Convention on the Holy Spirit, "I don't really know what's happening to me. I just 'blank out.'"

The young man's experience is not unique. Those who share this expression of the faith appear to be in a trance-like condition while uttering the strange words. Immediately after the uttering ceases, they return to their normal state, still unaware of what happened to them over the past few minutes.

The Rev. Eugene "Gene" Ewing, popular traveling evangelist in the midwest, leads revival services at which participants regularly "speak in tongues." He explained the phenomenon at a Columbus, Ohio rally this way: "When a person speaks in tongues, he enters a trance and allows his entire body to be open to the working of the Holy Spirit. In this state he does nothing mentally, physically or spiritually to check its [the Holy Spirit's] activity."

Why are some Christians suspicious of those who "speak in tongues"?

Although "speaking in tongues" is a phenomenon growing in popularity within nearly every denomination of the Christian Church, not every believer endorses it. In fact, some Christians look with suspicion at those who condone this practice.

They point to the words of St. Paul:

> I speak in tongues more than you all; nevertheless, in church I would rather speak five words with my mind, in order to instruct others, than ten thousand words in a tongue (I Corinthians 14:19).

Some not only echo the feeling of St. Paul that questions the value of such expression, but go so far as to look upon it as fakery or the result of emotional instability.

Because of the sharp difference of opinion about this expression of the faith, some Christians fear that this movement will do more to divide the Church in the 1980s than any one controversy.

Why are Christians divided on the issue of drinking alcoholic beverages?

Christians are as divided on the subject of drinking alcoholic beverages as is the general population of the United States. Some see nothing wrong with drinking in moderation, while others pledge not to partake of any substance containing alcohol. Ironically, Christians on both sides of the fence point to Holy Scripture for support.

Those who abstain from using alcohol often cite St. Paul's warning: "Do not get drunk with wine, for that is debauchery" (Ephesians 5:18). The best way to avoid drunkenness, they feel, is to refrain from drinking alcohol altogether.

As for those who are able to handle alcohol without personal consequences, there is the fear that knowledge about their drinking might "lead astray" someone who cannot control the use of alcohol.

Those who choose to abstain from alcohol may keep this as a personal commitment without attempting to convert others to their way of thinking. On the other hand, some are much more zealous in their treatment of the subject. The famed evangelist, Billy Sunday, sparked America's enactment of its Prohibition Law in the 1920s when he spoke to huge rallies on the evils of "demon rum."

Today, some Baptist congregations, as well as others of the more conservative groups, require their members to vow abstinence from alcohol. Some among them employ what might be labeled a "double standard" by requiring a pledge only from their clergymen to refrain from using alcohol as an example for their members to follow.

Those who wish to consume alcoholic beverages in moderation quote St. Paul as do those who abstain from alcohol. They refer to Paul's claim: "For freedom Christ has set us free" (Galatians 5:1). In this spirit, these Christians consider themselves as free from prohibitions that bind others. That includes drinking alcohol.

These same people quote St. Paul's words to Timothy: "No longer drink only water, but use a little wine for the sake of your stomach and your frequent ailments" (I Timothy 5:23). And they are quick to point out that Jesus, himself, drank wine at the Last Supper. They conclude, consequently, that if the Master used wine, why can't they?

Why have so many Sunday prohibitions been imposed on Christians?

The Christian faith is an outgrowth of the religion of the Jews. From this tradition comes the observance of the Sabbath as a day of rest for servants as well as masters. It is a day that commemorates Israel's redemption from Egyptian bondage and the creation of the world.

Christians of the Early Church replaced the Jewish Sabbath (which was Saturday, the seventh day of the week) with Sunday, the first day of the week, in memory of Jesus' resurrection which occurred on that day. Accordingly, some of the early Christian leaders added their own dimensions to Sunday observances in line with the spirit inherited from the Jews.

In the third century, Tertullian wrote that all anxiety should be set aside on Sunday. In 321, Emperor Constantine established Sunday as a day of rest for everyone except farmers. In 469, Emperor Leo the Great even included farmers in the prohibition against Sunday labor.

Puritans of sixteenth-century England referred to Sunday as the official "Sabbath," borrowing the term from the Jews. They published strict codes surrounding the Sabbath which came to be known in the New Haven Colony of America as "blue laws."

Why were "blue laws" a part of the Christian scene in early America?

Stern laws governing Sunday activities were called "blue laws" because they were published in volumes bound with blue paper. Some people were convinced that the term stems from the color of bruises inflicted on those who failed to observe them.

These "blue laws" included specific "dos" and "don'ts" for the "exemplary servant of the Lord." They prohibited, for example, any labor whatsoever on Sunday. Children who played with toys on Sunday were chastised unless the toys were of a religious nature, such as a replica of Noah's Ark. Bible reading, both before and after long hours spent at public worship, was the thing you did.

Remnants of the "blue laws" persist today in communities, particularly those in the New England states. In Ocean Grove, New Jersey, for instance, the streets are roped off at midnight on Saturday and remain closed through Sunday as a way of prohibiting traffic from moving during "the Lord's Day." As late as the 1950s, the state of Pennsylvania prohibited major-league baseball games from being played after 7:00 P.M. so that people would have enough time to attend Vespers which traditionally began at 7:30. And in New York, still no professional sporting event can begin before 1:00 P.M. so that it will not interfere with religious services. Of course, many states prohibit the sale of alcoholic beverages on Sunday.

Why do some Christians feel that Sunday should not be a day on which all work must cease?

Not all Christians refrain from working on Sunday. The New Testament records the time Jesus was condemned by the religious leaders of the Jews for performing certain acts of mercy on the Jewish Sabbath, and he responded: "The sabbath was made for man, not man for the sabbath" (Mark 2:27).

In this light, some Christians feel that Jesus freed them from the many rules and regulations that had confined the activities of the Jews on the Lord's Day.

Why do some Christians call each other "brother" or "sister"?

Parishioners in Baptist and Methodist congregations in the southeastern states of America commonly address one another as "Brother John," "Brother Ben" or "Sister Abigail," yet they are unrelated—in the biological sense, that is. The rather unusual titles are carry-overs from the Jews who are often referred to as the "Children of Israel" in the Bible. Through the use of the titles "brother" and "sister," these Christians remind themselves that they are "Children of God" with the Lord as their "Heavenly Father."

Jesus amplified this theme when he taught his disciples what is known today as the "Lord's Prayer" with the invocation: "Our Father, who art in heaven. . . . " If God is the "Father," it follows that his disciples must be his "children"—brothers and sisters in the faith.

Although the terms are used sparingly today, they were quite common among Christians in the Early Church when a strong bond united them during the persecutions at the hands of the Roman Government.

Why are Christians divided on the issue of sexual relationships?

One of the most sensitive and sometimes confusing issues confronting modern Christians is the proper approach toward sexual behavior. Because the sexual mores of the nation and attitudes toward sex have changed considerably within the last few years, Christians find themselves taking a variety of stands on some of the more controversial dimensions of sexuality. Add to this the recent innovations in birth control methods, and previously unchallenged answers become no longer acceptable in some circles.

The teaching of the Church, traditionally, has been extremely conservative—perhaps "puritanical" is a better word—in its pronouncements about sexual behavior among Christians, husbands and wives included. Peter Lombard, the influential theologian of the twelfth century, warned Christians that the Holy Spirit left the room when a married couple engaged in sexual intercourse—even if it were for the purpose of conceiving a child.

Other Church leaders insisted that God required sexual abstinence during all holy days. Some went so far as to advise couples not to have sex relations on Thursdays, in honor of Jesus' arrest; on Fridays, in memory of his crucifixion; on Saturdays, in honor of the Virgin Mary; on Sundays in remembrance of Christ's resurrection; and on Mondays, out of respect for the departed souls. That left only Tuesday and Wednesday.

Modern Christians choose a more positive approach to sexual relationships in marriage. Roman Catholic theologian Anthony Wilhelm wrote in 1975:

> A couple's sexual expression of their love is a wonderful privilege given them by God. The married man and woman celebrate each other's beauty and goodness, with truly creative interaction, sharing intimate knowledge of each other. "With my body I thee worship," runs the mutual pledge. . . .

In Europe, some contemporary pastors actually bless the marriage bed of the newly married couple as a sacred place in which they will find the love of God in each other.

Traditionally, too, the Church has spoken with one voice against any sexual relationship between unmarried people. Sexual intercourse has been held as the symbol and expression of a permanent union and a life-long commitment of a husband and a wife. Nevertheless, a marked change in attitude is openly admitted among the Christian community.

A 1965 survey conducted at Penn State University of 150 men and women, mostly ministers or professors and their wives, revealed that while 33 percent were opposed to premarital sex, 40 percent favored it selectively. The remainder had no comment.

Why do some Christians oppose birth control?

St. Augustine (354–430) was the first Christian leader to

speak out against birth control. In his writing entitled *Marriage and Concupiscence,* he condemned those who engaged in what he called "the poisons of sterility." He went so far as to conclude that husbands and wives who do any "evil thing" to prevent conception are "married in name only."

In a 1931 encyclical letter on Christian Marriage, Pope Pius XI reiterated Augustine's approach:

> Any use whatsoever of marriage exercised in such a way that the act [of sexual intercourse] is deliberately frustrated in its natural power to generate life is an offense against the law of God and of nature, and those who indulge in such are branded with the guilt of grave sin.

Some Christians, particularly Roman Catholics, have traditionally considered birth control as one of the principal enemies of marriage and the home. In their opinion, it is contrary to the prescribed purpose of sexual relations, namely, the procreation of the races. Recently, however, this long-held view is challenged by even some of the more conservative representatives of the Catholic Church.

One of the most newsworthy items that resulted from the Second Vatican Council was the action of some leading cardinals and bishops who publicly questioned the Church's traditional teaching and asked for a new look at the problem. In June 1964, Pope Paul VI responded by appointing a commission of bishops, theologians, physicians, and lay people to study the problem and offer recommendations. The commission voted four to one that the Catholic Church liberalize its teaching about contraception. However, the Pope issued the encyclical *Humanae Vitae* (On the Regulation of Birth) four years later in which he stated that the Church will continue to teach "that each and every marriage act must remain open to the transmission of life." In short, birth control was still forbidden.

Reaction to the encyclical was swift. Both priests and lay people disagreed with the Pope's statement, including 172

American teaching theologians who asserted that Catholics may follow their consciences, even though the Pope had spoken. It should be noted at this time, however, that when he issued the encyclical, the Pope was not speaking infallibly.

Why do some Christians openly advocate birth control?

While many Roman Catholics as well as some Christians of other denominations strongly oppose the use of birth control methods based upon their conviction that such artificial methods deliberately frustrate the natural power given by God to generate human life, other Christians not only favor using birth control in their personal sexual activities, but actually encourage its use by other men and women whose lives would be adversely affected by additional births. They feel that a woman whose life would be threatened if she should become pregnant or a ghetto family unable to support another child can best serve themselves and those for whom they are responsible by using methods of birth control.

Christians who support birth control do not look upon contraception as contrary to the will of God. Rather, they regard it as an outgrowth of a person's concern for the welfare of the world. They feel, also, that when the birthrate endangers the quality of life of those dwelling in a particular nation or environment, producing a generation able to sustain itself is more in keeping with the will of God than creating a society which must gear all its efforts into just keeping alive.

The conflicting theologies about birth control among Christians clash especially in the foreign mission fields. In India, for instance, where the population has already outgrown the food supply, Roman Catholic missionaries forbid the use of contraceptives, while Lutheran, Presbyterian,

Methodist, and Baptist missionaries sponsor free clinics at which methods of effective birth control are taught to young women.

Why are Christians divided on the matter of abortion?

The July 23, 1973, editorial of *The New York Times* read, in part:

> Nothing in the [Supreme] Court's approach [to abortion] ought to give affront to persons who oppose all abortion for reasons of religion or individual conviction. They can stand as firmly as ever for those principles, provided they do not seek to impede the freedom of those with an opposite view.

Dr. Roger Shinn of Union Theological Seminary in New York City took strong issue with this approach when he wrote:

> If a person or group honestly believes that abortion is the killing of persons, there is no moral comfort in being told, "Nobody requires you to kill. We are only giving permission to others to do what you consider killing."

Many Christians in every denomination believe that abortion is a murderous attack on the life of an unborn child. They contend that abortion is much worse than birth control in that while birth control prevents life, abortion destroys existing life. Joseph Stimpfle, Roman Catholic Bishop of Augsburg, said in 1980: "He who performs an abortion, except to save the life of the mother, sins gravely and burdens his conscience with the killing of human life."

Pope Paul VI referred to an unborn child as *personne en devenir*—a person in the process of becoming.

The Roman Catholic Church has pronounced that all

who perform, or even assist in any way, in an abortion are guilty of a crime to which the Church attaches the penalty of excommunication. The Lutheran Church in 1982 published in the *Evangelical Catechism:* "The practice of using abortion for personally convenient or selfish reasons must be rejected." Most other denominations have gone on record with similar statements.

At the same time, fellow believers in these same denominations argue that the issue is not so sharply defined. They question whether or not a fetus is a human being. Some go so far as to say that a woman has the right to decide what is best for her. They feel that the will of the Lord would not be served were the woman compelled by law or by her church to endure nine months of carrying a child only to give birth to an unwanted offspring.

Rachel Wahlberg wrote in the September 8, 1971, issue of *The Christian Century:* "To be free and not slaves, women must have power of decision over their reproductive systems."

The issue of abortion has been, and will remain, a source of heated debate within the Christian Church. John L. McKenzie brought this into focus when he wrote in the *National Catholic Reporter:* " . . . those who make decisions of common concern must expect the decisions to be examined by those who are concerned."

Why are Christians divided on the issue of homosexuality?

The Christian Church has historically taught that human sexual relations were meant, from the first days of creation, to be shared by a male and a female. Any other relationship is forbidden.

The first official pronouncement against homosexual activity was issued in the fourth century when St. Asterius, the Bishop of Amasia, in what is now Italy, spoke against the men in his diocese who celebrated New Year's Eve by dressing in women's clothing, referring to this as an "abomination to the Lord."

Today, the vast majority of Christians in every denomination regard homosexuality as a sin against God and society. They point to the classic illustration in the Bible which tells of the destruction of Sodom and Gomorrah, two cities in which homosexuality was openly practiced (Genesis 19:1-19).

While the Bible and the Church have clear pronouncements against homosexuality, there are some Christians in nearly every denomination who, although not homosexuals themselves, feel that this sort of relationship is something which cannot be helped, since certain people are born with this attraction for another of the same sex. They conclude that it is not the homosexual's choice to be as he or she is. Therefore, they encourage others in the Church to accept these people with love and understanding.

A Christian counseling center opened in 1982 in downtown Miami, Florida, with the sole purpose of assisting homosexuals in their struggles to cope with a society and a Church that "locks them out."

In San Francisco, meanwhile, some Christian clergymen have even performed homosexual "marriages." When asked about their actions in light of the obvious biblical condemnation of homosexuality, one of the pastors remarked: "The Bible was written for one time; these are new times."

Why are so many Christian traditions linked to Judaism?

Christians owe a tremendous debt to the Jewish people. Consequently, many of the so-called "Christian" traditions are really extensions of Jewish observances conducted long before Jesus was born.

One of the reasons for this inheritance of tradition stems from the fact that Jesus was a Jew, born to a family that faithfully observed Jewish law. He was circumcised on the eighth day as were all Jewish boys, schooled in Jewish teachings, celebrated the festivals such as Passover, and, according to Christian belief, was the fulfillment of the Jewish prophecies regarding the coming of God's Messiah into the world.

On top of this, the first disciples of Jesus were Jews as were the earliest converts to Christianity. It should come as no surprise, then, that many of the teachings and traditions of the Church have their foundations in the religion of Israel. For example, two Christian traditions—baptism and Holy Communion—which are observed in just about every denomination, have their roots in Jewish practices. (More on this will be found in Chapter 3.)

This spiritual bond between Christians and Jews was the subject of a 1982 call by Roman Catholic bishops for Church theologians to clarify the common heritage with the Children of Israel.

Why do so many Christians remain anti-Semitic?

One of the greatest tragedies in the Bible is expressed by the writer of the fourth Gospel: "He [Jesus] came to his own home, and his own people [the Jews] received him not" (John 1:11). After waiting for the Messiah for centuries, most of the Jews of Jesus' generation failed to acknowledge him as the fulfillment of their own prophecies. For this reason, according to the Gospels, they cooperated with the Roman government in asking for Jesus' death on Calvary.

Today, many Christians still blame the Jews for the death of their Savior. Nothing, of course, could be further from the truth, since the Jewish leaders did not possess authority to order the death of any citizen. The evidence notwithstanding, some Christians refuse to listen to reason and prefer to label the Jews as "murderers of Jesus." Although this twisted reaction against the Jews has often been a source of embarrassment for the majority of Christians, it has been successful over the years in fueling the fires of hatred. The Holocaust is just the latest in a long line of mistreatments meted out to the descendants of Abraham, Isaac, and Jacob.

The Second Vatican Council (which opened on October 11, 1962) issued a statement concerning Jewish responsibility for the death of Jesus in which it clearly indicated that if there was any responsibility, it was shared only by a small group at the time of Christ. In no way did the entire nation or subsequent Jews share any part of such responsibility.

The Council, in fact, stressed that Christians and Jews should explore the things they share in common through biblical and theological studies and fraternal dialogues. In the words of Pope Pius XI, Christians are "spiritual Semites."

Today, dialogue between Christians and Jews is as meaningful as ever as exemplified by the formation of the National Conference of Christians and Jews with headquarters in New York City. Most observers agree that a more productive spirit prevails among Christians causing them to concentrate on things which bind them and the Jews rather than on specific past actions that have divided them.

Why was Martin Luther so anti-Semitic?

Martin Luther (1483–1546), the person most historians acknowledge as the leading force of the Protestant Reformation, was an outspoken critic of the Jews. He openly accused the Jews as "Christ killers."

Luther's anti-Semitic remarks were used by Adolph Hitler in his attempts to justify the atrocities levied against the Jews in Germany during World War II. In 1981, Israel's Prime Minister Begin traced modern anti-Semitic feelings to Martin Luther.

Psychologists who study Luther's personality have generally agreed that the Reformer's greatest strength—a willingness to speak out against what he felt were wrongs—was also his greatest weakness when he spoke and acted before having all the facts at his disposal.

But Luther was a product of his time. He did not always rise above local prejudice. For instance, he attacked the theory of Copernicus who said that the sun, not the earth, was the center of the universe. By today's standards, he was wrong in his scientific outlook, of course. Likewise, most modern Christians concur that Luther was wrong in echoing the popular prejudices against the Jews shared by the majority of his contemporaries.

Luther's strong statements against the Jews, in fact, were officially censured in 1983 by the Lutheran World Federation at its meeting in Stockholm, Sweden. The Federation repudiated "the sins of Luther's anti-Jewish remarks . . . and his violent verbal attacks against the Jews." In addition, the Federation pledged that "Lutheran writings will never again serve in their churches as a source for the teaching of hatred for Judaism and the denigration of the Jewish people."

Rabbi Marc H. Tanenbaum, interreligious affairs director of the American Jewish Committee, hailed the Federation's declaration as "one of the most significant achievements of the year-long observance of Martin Luther's 500th birthday."

Why do Christians often have a misconception of angels?

Although the Bible is not precise in describing them, angels are most often pictured by artists as wearing white robes, with halos over their heads, and blessed with the power to fly with huge wings attached to their shoulders. This picture, as majestic as it may appear to be, does not conform to the image presented in the Holy Scriptures.

Angels are spirits that appear in a variety of forms. One appeared to Adam and Eve in the Garden of Eden; another to Abraham; one appeared at the empty tomb of the risen Christ; a band of angels announced Jesus' birth to shepherds on a hillside in Bethlehem.

Angels are mentioned at least 300 times in the Bible. From Genesis to Revelation, their chief function is to serve as messengers from God.

Some denominations have a highly developed theology of angels, and others do not. Some theologians even question whether angels as such exist. Regardless of their approach to this question, all believe that angels remind us that God communicates with his people. He is present to our beings by his message, his blessings, and his judgment. Angels, in short, manifest God's concern for his people.

Why does the Church use the rite of exorcism?

The specially designated service of exorcism most often associated with the Roman Catholic Church, although used by clergymen of the Lutheran and Episcopal denominations on rare occasion, is a direct result of the belief that demons—the fallen angels who rebelled against God—have power to act upon the faithful for their own evil purposes.

Although dramatically portrayed in books and movies, exorcism is little more than a prayer to God (public or private) to restrict the work of these forces upon a particular individual. The Church recognizes, even today, the possibility of demon possession, and has prescribed a service of exorcism which includes the following command:

> Hear, accursed Satan, I adjure you by the name of the eternal God and of our Savior Jesus Christ, depart with your envy, conquered, trembling, and groaning. May you have no part in these servants of God [*names inserted*] who already have thoughts of heaven and who are about to renounce you and your world and achieve a blessed immortality.

Exorcism has its roots in the Bible when Jesus charged his disciples not only to preach the gospel of salvation, but to heal the sick and cast out demons in his name (Matthew 10:1 and Luke 11:14ff). St. Paul used this authority when he drove out the evil spirit of a slave girl (Acts 16:16-18).

Church Fathers such as Justin Martyr (100-165), Tertullian (160-230), and Origen (185-284) were among those who exorcised evil spirits from the bodies of possessed Christians.

Throughout the history of the Church, certain clergymen (sometimes lay people as well) were appointed to fulfill the role as "exorcist" as the need arose. The office, however, is rarely used today and, in 1972, was suppressed by the Roman Catholic Church as a regular charge. However, any priest can carry out an exorcism as part of his priestly office—provided he has the permission of his bishop.

Why do Christians regard the Bible as the most important book in the world?

Christians regard the Bible so highly because they believe it is the record of God's self-revelation to human beings. Although the Bible is called one book, it is really composed of many books—hence its name which comes from *biblia,* which in Greek means "books"—some by unknown authors and all written between the tenth century B.C. and the first century A.D.

The Bible (1) sets forth God's unique revelation; (2) is inspired by God; (3) delineates God's saving plan for time and eternity; and (4) focuses on God incarnate, Jesus Christ, savior of the world.

The Bible has been termed "the most perfect of all books and the most certain of all knowledge—the most august, the most effective, the most wise, the most useful, the most solid, the most necessary, the most basic, and the most elevated" (Cornelius a Lapide).

The Bible teaches the best way of living, the noblest way of enduring suffering, and the most consoling way of dying.

Why is the Bible said to give the "History of Salvation"?

The Bible sets forth God's intervention in human history and his communication to human beings of his saving plan—which is contained in a message as well as a series of events. We call this combination the "History of Salvation."

The main purpose of the Bible is not to provide scientific information, sociological and political data, or any other kind of secular knowledge for its own sake. The Bible speaks of faith—of the Israelite community and of the Christian community. It contains the memoirs of a faith community testifying that God is the Lord of history and that Christ's death-resurrection is the central event of all history.

Why is the Bible called the "inspired word of God"?

The belief that the Bible is God's inspired word stems from the Bible, itself. St. Paul's Second Letter to Timothy (3:16) reads: "All Scripture is inspired by God and profitable for teaching, for reproof, for correction, and for training in righteousness."

The Greek word for "inspired" used in this passage is *theopneustos*, which literally means "God-breathed." The traditional dogma of inspiration held by most Christian denominations expresses the idea that because the Bible had its origin in the Holy Spirit, it is the word of God. Another way of putting it is that the Bible is divine truth to be trusted in all its aspects, and is the norm for judging all doctrines and teachings.

Why are so many Christians today at odds with the dogma of divine inspiration?

While the Christian Church is generally in agreement that the Bible is the inspired word of God, most Christians are divided on the issue as to what degree it is inspired.

A substantial number of Christians (primarily those of the more fundamental groups—Baptists, Assemblies of God, and others) believe that the men who penned the books of the Bible were mysteriously told by Almighty God the exact words to write.

Other Christians feel that it is impossible to accept a literal inspiration of the Bible. They point to the fact that the Holy Scriptures are filled with some errors in grammar, spelling, and scientific pronouncements. Instead, these people feel that the essence of the message is what is really important, not the individual words.

Why has it been so necessary to compose different translations of the Bible?

The many translations of the Bible that are available to modern Christians are a direct result of the fact that scholars have debated for centuries the meaning of specific words and passages in the Bible. The reasons for this prolonged debate are three: language, connotation, and human error.

The Bible was written in languages foreign to the English-speaking world. Hebrew was the language of the Old Testament; Greek the language of the New Testament. Whenever a translation is attempted from one language to another, some of the meaning is either lost or cannot be conveyed exactly as the author intended. How can any translator, for instance, capture the subtle differences between the three Greek words meaning "love" when English has only one word to express all three?

Connotation is another problem. Words which may have communicated a thought hundreds of years ago will not necessarily carry that same meaning in a contemporary content. Jesus, as did the prophets of the Old Testament, taught by using customs and figures of speech common to the people of the times. To understand, for example, the message behind the parable of the Good Samaritan, one must be aware of the existing feelings at that time between the Jews and the foreign nations. Otherwise, the story loses much of its impact.

Human error plays a major part whenever a text is translated and transmitted over centuries. Any writer knows how difficult, if not impossible, it is to edit and transcribe his own work without error. This problem increases when translators, secretaries and scribes become involved.

If some Christians argue that the Holy Spirit would not allow such things to happen, they are forced to deal with the facts that modern scholarship has revealed plenty of errors—innocent, perhaps, but errors nonetheless—caused because of an oversight on the part of some translator or transmitter.

As older manuscripts are discovered, and we have a clearer picture of what the original text might have contained, we gain some fresh insights into the Scriptures. These insights call for new translations.

Some of the more popular translations through the ages have been:

• The *Vulgate* translated into Latin in 405 by St. Jerome
• Luther's *German Bible,* the 1534 translation made popular because of the new invention of the printing press
• *Douay Bible* published in Douay, France, in 1609, used by Roman Catholics
• *King James Version* published in 1611 and brought to America by the first settlers
• *Revised Standard Version* used by most Protestants today, published in 1952
• The *Jerusalem Bible* translated by Roman Catholic scholars in 1968
• The *New English Bible* completed in 1970 for the people of Great Britain
• The *New American Bible* completed in 1970 by American scholars under the aegis of the Roman Catholic Bishops of the United States
• *Good News for Modern Man,* a rather free translation, completed in 1977 by order of the American Bible Society.

Why is the Bible organized as it is?

For all but Roman Catholic Christians, the Bible consists of 66 books—39 in the Old Testament and 27 in the New Testament. These 66 books are often referred to as the "canonical books." The word "canon" means "rod" or "rule." Today, these books generally are accepted by the Church as the basis for its dogma and as a guide to daily living.

By the year 130, the four Gospels and the 13 letters of St. Paul were considered the basis for all New Testament teachings. Later, as other writings were considered, scholars debated as to whether or not they should become part of the Bible. As a response, the Council in Rome met in 382 and established the books now contained in both the Old and the New Testaments as being the basis for all teaching and preaching for the Christian Church.

Why do Roman Catholics have more books in their Bibles than do Protestants?

As already noted, the Protestant version of the Holy Bible numbers 66 books. Roman Catholics, however, accept additional books adopted by the Council of Trent (1545–1563) as being inspired by God and containing the basis for faith and morals.

The Catholic Bible includes: Tobias (Tobit), Judith, Wisdom, Ecclesiasticus (Sirach), Baruch, and the two books of Maccabees, along with additions to the books of Esther and Daniel. Protestants call these books the "Apocrypha," meaning "hidden writings," and may use them as literature for private devotional studies.

Although the official Protestant Bibles do not contain them, the sixteenth-century reformer Martin Luther put the books of the Apocrypha in a separate section of his German Bible translation between the two testaments. Luther felt that while the books were not on a par with the canonical writings of Holy Scripture—i.e., they should not serve as the basis for Church teachings—they could be beneficial literature for use in private meditation.

Why do Christians refer to the last 27 books of the Bible as the "New Testament"?

The word "testament" means "covenant." Christians believe that God made two covenants with his people. The first involved the testament with Israel when God said: "I will be your God; you shall be my people" (Exodus 6:6ff). This was the "old testament." The "new testament" is the covenant made between God and those who accept Jesus as the Lord.

Why are the Gospels known as the "heart" of the New Testament?

The Gospels have a special preeminence in the New Testament for they are the principal witness of the life and teaching of Jesus, the Incarnate Word, our Savior. The word *gospel* means "good news," and it is applied to the good news of human salvation proclaimed by Jesus. It has logically also been applied to the four separate accounts in which the good news of Jesus has been handed down throughout the centuries—those of Matthew, Mark, Luke, and John.

The four Gospels faithfully hand on what Jesus, while living among human beings, did and taught for their eternal salvation until the day he was taken up to heaven (Acts 1:1-2). The highlight of each Gospel is the Passion Narrative—the account of Jesus' sufferings, death, and resurrection. They also include incidents from his public ministry and some have accounts of his infancy.

Perhaps St. Augustine best expressed the reason why Christians prize the Gospels above the other books of the Bible when he said: "Everything that Christ, ascended to heaven, willed to have us read about his actions and words he caused to be written by the evangelists as if by his own hands.... Thus the readers of the Gospel will receive what is told them by the disciples of Christ as if they saw the Lord himself writing it with his own hand."

Why are the Beatitudes regarded as the heart of the Gospel?

The Beatitudes (Matthew 5:3-10) are "eight words" pronounced by Jesus midway up a mountain around June of the year 28. They give in a nutshell the type of life Jesus wants for all human beings and they have been called the most important words in history. They are addressed to all people, believers and nonbelievers alike, and twenty centuries later they still constitute the sole beacon that shines in the darkness of a selfish world.

The Beatitudes form the core of the Sermon on the Mount which is itself a summary of the teachings of Jesus. We might say the Sermon with the Beatitudes is to the New Testament what the Ten Commandments are to the Old.

The individual Beatitudes are all positive in tone; it is only later to illustrate the infractions that we do not cease to commit that Jesus will detail all sorts of prohibitions or rather warnings.

"Blessed are the poor in spirit, for theirs is the kingdom of heaven.

"Blessed are those who mourn, for they shall be comforted.

"Blessed are the meek, for they shall inherit the earth.

"Blessed are those who hunger and thirst for righteousness, for they shall be satisfied.

"Blessed are the merciful, for they shall obtain mercy.

"Blessed are the pure in heart, for they shall see God.

"Blessed are the peacemakers, for they shall be called the sons of God.

"Blessed are those who are persecuted for righteousness' sake for theirs is the kingdom of heaven" (Matthew 5:3-10).

Why is the Bible divided into chapters and verses?

In 1226, Professor Stephen Langton of the University of Paris (who later became Archbishop of Canterbury) divided the text of the Bible into chapters—in order to make it easier to read. Then in 1551, the printer Robert Stephen inserted verse numbers in the text in accord with the arrangement Santos Pagnini had worked out in 1528—for easy reference.

As a result, Christians and all who read the Bible have a

ready-made and universal method of citing from the Scriptures with ease and with total understanding. A staggering amount of biblical information can be imparted through a judicious use of this reference-method.

Why are the findings of biblical archeology regarded by Christians as indispensable for understanding the Bible?

In the words of G. Frederick Owen, "God kept two copies of the historic records of his special dealings with and revelation to human beings. One was the *Bible* which had been written on parchment and by great effort placed into the hands of human beings. The other was written in the *ruined remains* and in the *strange languages of* those lands whence the Bible came."

Archeology enables us to have access to this second copy of God's record and to compare it with the first. Archeology is the study of the past based on material finds—piles of ruins ("tells"), constructions, tombs, and the like. *Biblical archeology* is concerned with excavations and finds (arms, ceramics, ornaments) from biblical localities and seeks to catalogue everything that pertains to the Bible. It seeks not so much to demonstrate the truth of the Bible account as to set forth the historical truth—which can then be compared with the biblical account.

The story of biblical archeology is a fascinating one but it cannot be given here. What must be noted is that archeology has made a great contribution to biblical studies. Many of its findings (1) confirm the Bible accounts (e.g., the conquest of Samaria, II Kings 13); (2) aid its understanding (e.g., related texts found at Nuzi and Mari); (3) complement the dates of the Bible (e.g., reign of Omri; tribute of Jehu); (4) insert the Bible within the wider context of the history and culture of the ancient East (migration of Amorites and Arameans as the background for the prehistory of Israel);

and (5) force us to rethink the meaning of some biblical episodes (e.g., the conquest of Jericho).

Why are the Dead Sea Scrolls important for Bible study?

In 1947 a Bedouin shepherd boy playfully hurled a stone into a cave at Khirbet Qumran, on the northeast coast of the Dead Sea. Hearing a jar break, he entered the cave and found several jars containing ancient manuscripts. Thus began one of the most sensational biblical discoveries of the twentieth century—a discovery that has aided the study of the Bible immeasurably.

From 1947 to 1956, scholars found 11 caves with ancient manuscripts—all but one of them in Hebrew. All told, the remains of more than 500 different manuscripts, or large portions of manuscripts, and thousands of fragments were found—both biblical and nonbiblical. Every book of the Old Testament was represented except Esther (and no book of the Apocrypha but Tobit). Most of the manuscripts had been written about 100 B.C. and were in the possession of a group of Essenes (people who had split from the Jewish community in Palestine).

Scholars are still working with this huge treasure of texts, but the most important to date are: (1) a complete text of Isaiah dating from the second century B.C. and (2) a commentary on Habakkuk. Until this discovery the oldest Hebrew manuscripts were from the tenth century A.D.

The scrolls are already regarded as important sources of information about Hebrew literature, Jewish history between the Testaments, and the history of the Old Testament texts. They established the fact that the Hebrew text of the Old Testament was fixed before the beginning of the Christian era and they have already made significant contributions to critical studies and to translations of the Old Testament.

Why is the Bible read at religious services?

The Bible is read aloud at religious services because it is the word of God. Christians use that word both to listen to God speaking to them and to respond to him. The author of the *Imitation of Christ* made this point very well: "You have given us . . . two tables set on either side of the treasury of the holy Church. One is the table of the holy altar, having on it the holy bread—the precious body of Christ; the other is the table of the divine law, containing holy doctrine, instructing us in the true faith and leading us securely even beyond the inner veil wherein is the Holy of Holies" (Bk IV, ch. 11).

Some Christian churches—especially the liturgical churches—also believe that Christ becomes present in any official proclamation of his word. The Gospel proclaimed aloud is thus not a static word, but a living word, one that actualizes a saving mystery of Christ. Through that word, Jesus speaks to his assembled people just as he spoke to the crowds of Palestine—and we can respond to him just as they did.

Why do Christians read the Bible in private?

The Bible, besides being the book of the praying Church, is also the book that Christians read in private. It tells us about the greatest person who ever walked the earth and the greatest life ever lived. It puts us in touch with him. Every Christian takes up the Bible to read God's word and be transformed by it. Reading the Bible is a dialogue. It is God's word to us today.

We read the Bible to learn how to live, to conform ourselves to God's thoughts, so that we may be conformed to his image. The Bible is a principal means of Christian growth.

We also read the Bible as an act of prayer and devotion. It helps us to adore our Creator and stay in touch with him.

All exemplars of the Christian faith over the centuries have been readers of the Bible.

Why do Christians make use of special helps in reading the Bible?

The Bible was written in times, places, languages, and cultures with which Christians are unfamiliar. In order to understand it properly, they need helps that will explain the text for modern people. These helps bring out what the sacred writers intended to say as they used the literary forms of their day and culture. Hence, Christians may use one or more of the following helps:

1. Bible dictionary—which contains short descriptive articles about people, places, things, and customs mentioned in the Bible.
2. Bible encyclopedia—which includes many more entries and expanded treatments of subjects found in dictionaries.
3. Bible commentary—which provides a detailed exposition of the Bible verse by verse and gives an all-around knowledge of the Bible.
4. Bible concordance—which is an alphabetical index of principal words of the Bible in partial texts, indicating the places where the words occur in their full contexts.
5. Gospel harmony—which gives a combination of the four Gospels into one continuous narrative or an arrangement of the Gospels into four parallel columns so that similarities and differences in them can be easily compared.

Why can the Bible yield three different senses?

As the word of God to human beings, the Bible is well nigh inexhaustible in its meanings and interpretations. One passage can provide light for a multiplicity of themes and be subject to many uses. Christians have traditionally seen at least the following three senses in the Bible.

1. A literal sense—the direct and immediate meaning of the text according to the ordinary rules of language. This is the most usual way of reading the Bible—with the aid of the Bible helps mentioned in the last question.

2. A spiritual sense—a meaning that goes beyond the literal sense but is based on it. For example, the text concerning the bronze serpent in the Old Testament (Numbers 21:9) also referred to Christ on the Cross, and the text about Jonah in the belly of the fish (Jonah 2:1) also referred to Christ in the tomb (and his resurrection).

3. An accommodated sense—an accommodation of the text to a subject not intended by the sacred writer. This is not a true sense of Scripture. It is made use of principally by the Church in the Liturgy for the edification of the faithful.

Why do Christians have Bible Societies?

Bible Societies (nonprofit organizations) exist for the dissemination of the Sacred Scriptures—involving translation, publication, and distribution. The first formal Bible Society was formed in Germany in 1710: the Van Canstein Bible Institute of Saxony. Gradually, Bible Societies arose in England, Wales, Ireland, the Scandinavian countries, and France—most of them supported by the British and Foreign Bible Society.

In the United States, local Bible Societies started in 1808-1809 in New York, Boston, Hartford, Princeton, and Philadelphia. In 1916 many of the local societies banded together into the American Bible Society. In 1946 the United Bible Societies was established incorporating many of the larger national societies.

As a result of the work of these Bible Societies (and many other persons and organizations), the Bible is available today in more than one thousand of the most used languages and dialects in the world. And with every passing day it is being made available in other languages and to other peoples.

Why do some theologians refer to certain stories in the Bible as "myths"?

Not everyone in the Christian Church accepts every word in the Bible as divinely inspired. Some theologians believe that certain stories (such as Adam and Eve in the Garden of Eden, or Jonah and the whale) are "myths"—i.e., invented stories, which may or may not be true, that communicate a lesson. Those who accept this theory regard these familiar biblical tales as fables, not historic events.

In the opinion of these theologians, these "myths" were never meant to be taken literally. This approach, of course, is in direct contrast to the literalists who claim that every word in the Bible is the result of God's direct revelation. Literalists, therefore, would never endorse the concept of "myths."

Why do many Christians dread the number "666"?

This strange number—666—mentioned in the Book of Revelation (13:18) refers to a creature called the "Antichrist."

The "Antichrist" is the arch-antagonist of the Lord who, according to Christian teaching, will appear during the last days of the earth's existence to bring torment and temptation to faithful Christians who remain on the earth in one last attack against the Church. Although he will be destroyed by Christ before the Day of Judgment, Christians fear that the Antichrist will confront them without warning and attempt to lead them away from the faith.

The Book of Revelation is filled with symbols; numbers are but one kind. In this instance, the number "six" represents evil, and the Antichrist is recorded as a triple alliance of evil. Hence the number 666.

Why is it necessary to believe that our bodies end up in heaven?

Each Sunday morning most Christians at worship confess in the Apostles' Creed: "I believe in the resurrection of the body."

Nothing in the Bible indicates that we shall assume a different physical form after the Day of Judgment than before. The emphasis of the Christian teaching is on the resurrection to eternal life when the souls of the faithful will dwell with God and each other forever. The apostle John stressed the fact that the tombs of the dead will be opened at the Judgment, and the bodies of the dead will come forth (John 5:28–29).

However, the body that ascends to heaven will be a "spiritual" body—one not bound by space and time as it was while living on earth. St. Paul wrote that at death we sow a "physical" body and reap a "spiritual" body (I Corinthians 15:44).

Exactly what this "spiritual" body will look like, no one knows for certain. We are only told that as the Lord will create a new heaven and a new earth (Revelation 21:1), so he will give us new bodies fit for a world free from sin.

Why is cremation prohibited by some Christians?

When Christianity became a recognized religion in the year 325, it began to have an impact upon the customs and observances of civilizations throughout the world. One of the earliest recorded evidences of that influence was the successful campaign of the Christians against the accepted practice of the Romans who cremated their dead on funeral pyres. It seems as though Christians in the Early Church stressed the teaching of the resurrection of the physical body on the Day of Judgment—a day that many of them felt would occur within their lifetimes. Cremation, then, would destroy this body, thereby preventing its resurrection to eternal life.

By the fifth century, Christians were able to have this practice banned in Rome altogether. However, by the nineteenth century, some of the more liberal-minded Christians throughout the world revived cremation without any strong opposition from ecclesiastical leaders.

Today, some Christians still abhor the thought of cremating the dead. They point to God's comment to Adam: "You are dust, and to dust you shall return" (Genesis 3:19). If a body is cremated, and the ashes kept in an urn or scattered over the ocean, it cannot be returned to the earth from which it came.

In addition, they call attention to the words of St. Paul who wrote about the Day of Judgment: "Our commonwealth is in heaven, and from it we await a Savior, the Lord Jesus Christ, who will change our lowly body to be like his glorious body...."(Philippians 3:20–21). The resurrection of the dead, then, included the resurrection of the body from the grave. Cremation eliminates the existence of any body.

Although most denominations today have no official restriction against cremation, some of the more conservative Christians strongly urge that ashes of the deceased be interred or, better, be deposited in consecrated soil.

Why do many Christians insist on being buried in consecrated ground?

Many Christians leave specific instructions with their

nearest kin that at the time of death they must be laid to rest in ground that has been set aside by the Church [consecrated] for burial of the faithful.

In 1348, the English bishop, Edyndon, explained that "the Church believes in the resurrection of the body of the dead. Sanctified by the reception of the sacraments, it [the body] is consequently not buried in pagan places, but in specially consecrated cemeteries, or in churches, where with due reverence they are kept like the relics of the saints, till the day of resurrection."

The demand for burial in consecrated ground is not a recent requirement by any stretch of the imagination. In ancient times, burials always took place outside the walls of cities and towns. Because of the fear of both disease and ghosts, it was not lawful to bury the dead within city limits. In 752, an English monk, St. Cuthbert, obtained official permission from the Pope to have the churchyards of his city parishes recognized as suitable places for the burial of the dead. The bishop explained to the Pope that even in death, the Christian would be separated from the nonbeliever. The Pope was persuaded and ordered that the grounds around the city churches be consecrated by bishops in order to provide fit places of rest for the faithful.

Why are most consecrated cemeteries surrounded by protective walls and gates?

In 1267, Bishop Quevil of England ordered that all cemeteries in his diocese be enclosed, and that no animal be permitted to graze on the grass which grew there. Even the local priests were admonished for allowing their cattle to roam these holy places. The Bishop ordered, then, that "all cemeteries must be guarded from defilement, both because they are holy [in themselves], and because they are made holy by the relics [the remains] of the saints."

Why were suicide victims sometimes not buried in consecrated ground?

Until quite recently, Roman Catholics and some in the Lutheran, Eastern Orthodox, and Episcopal churches would not permit victims of suicide to be buried in consecrated cemeteries. The reason behind this practice was that they believed that the taking of one's life was a violation of the commandment: "You shall not kill" (Exodus 20:13). By taking their own lives, the victims had invaded the providence of Almighty God who, alone, holds power over life and death.

The added tragedy, of course, is that persons who take their lives cannot hope to repair their sins through confession and absolution. They have committed a mortal sin (one that can result in eternal damnation) without benefit of forgiveness. For this reason, they could not be buried in consecrated land reserved for those who have sinned, but have been granted absolution.

Today, most Christians hold a much more charitable attitude toward the victim of suicide. Father Sean Heslin, pastor of St. Paul's Roman Catholic Church in Daytona Beach, Florida, explained: "Who are we to judge whether or not in the seconds before death the victim did not ask for forgiveness? Who are we to judge whether or not the victim was mentally able to determine right from wrong? This violent act upon the body would indicate that the victim was not rational at the time." For this reason, with very few exceptions, the remains of suicide victims today are buried in consecrated ground without any reservation.

Why do Irish Christians conduct joyous wakes before funerals?

During the several days between the death of a loved one and the funeral, it is a common practice for friends and relatives to keep the body of the deceased under close observation. This watching or "wake" of the dead has been a standard practice of Christians from nearly every nation, although the custom is associated most often with the Irish because of the legendary party spirit of the ritual, punctuated by occasional overindulgence of alcoholic beverages.

This stark contrast to the normal atmosphere of somber mourning, according to those who participate in wakes, is in harmony with the celebration of the gift of eternal life granted to all those who die in the Lord. Since the soul of the deceased is about to spend eternity with Christ and his angels, the joyous wake is only an appropriate expression.

Why are some Christians buried facing the East?

In the Early Church especially, Christians who died were buried facing the East, an outcome of the belief that the final summons to judgment will come from the East as does the rising of the sun.

The custom remains quite popular today in some of the northern European nations. Hence, in Wales, the east wind is still known as the "wind of the dead man's feet."

Why do some Christians believe in a place called "purgatory"?

"Purgatory" is the designation by the Roman Catholic Church and some Anglicans given to the place in which souls are detained before entering heaven. For them, purgatory is a place of cleansing in which the soul is prepared to spend eternity with the other saints of God.

The Council of Florence (1438–1445) explained the purpose or function of purgatory when it issued a statement saying: "The souls [of the deceased] are cleansed by purgatorial pains after death, and in order that they may be rescued from these pains." The pronouncement seemed to say that it would be totally unfitting for any soul still defiled by the slightest sin to appear before Almighty God in heaven.

References in Holy Scripture to a place of purgation are sketchy, at best, but some of the early Christian writers—Tertullian, St. Basil, and St. Augustine, to name a few—stated that purgatory was a reality.

For those who believe in purgatory it is a common practice to pray for the welfare of those souls being made ready for eternal life.

Purgatory, of course, will cease to exist after the Day of Judgment, since all souls at that time will be made ready for entrance either into heaven or into hell.

Why are most Christian denominations opposed to the concept of purgatory?

Outside of the Roman Catholics and some Anglicans, the vast majority of Christian denominations do not accept the teaching about purgatory. Perhaps the evangelist Billy Graham stated their feeling best when he said during a Los Angeles youth rally: "When your grandmother died, that instant she became aware of more things than you'll ever learn in the collective universities you are attending." His message rang clear. There is no waiting period between death and entrance into heaven as implied by the concept of purgatory.

Opponents of the concept of purgatory contend that Jesus' promise to the thief who was crucified with him on Calvary: "Today, you shall be with me in paradise" (Luke 23:43), gave an unmistakable picture that eternal reward in heaven comes instantaneously after passage from this life on earth. After all, they continue, there is not one passage in all of the Bible that refers specifically to purgatory. As a result, they feel that heaven awaits the soul—immediately.

Why are young people "confirmed" in the Church?

Those Christians who were baptized as infants are given an opportunity to confess publicly their faith. This act of confession before the assembled congregation is called "confirmation" since it is an affirmation of the faith into which they were baptized.

Confirmation is a traditional high point in the lives of young people who become members of the Roman Catholic, Lutheran, Eastern Orthodox, and Anglican denominations. More recently, other communions—the Methodists and Presbyterians in particular—have encouraged the service of confirmation.

The tradition is a carry-over from the Jewish ceremony of Bar Mitzvah involving boys at age 13. Christian youngsters of about the same age have completed several years of instruction in the basic teachings of the particular denomination they seek to join.

Roman Catholic and Eastern Orthodox Christians regard confirmation as a sacrament through which the Holy Spirit comes in a special way to strengthen young people who are now "soldiers of Christ."

Why do some Christians accept seven sacraments?

According to Roman Catholic and Eastern Orthodox teachings, Christ gave seven sacraments to the Church. Sacraments are ceremonies by which the Christian comes into intimate personal contact with Christ and receives his grace in a special way.

These Christians believe that Christ himself instituted all seven sacraments, although some in a more general sense than others.

The seven sacraments are: baptism, Holy Communion,

confirmation, penance, extreme unction (now called "anointing of the sick"), ordination, and marriage.

Why do most Protestant denominations subscribe to only two sacraments?

While agreeing that most of the seven sacraments endorsed by the Roman Catholic and Eastern Orthodox denominations are of benefit to Christians everywhere, most Protestants contend that only two—baptism and Holy Communion—were really instituted by Christ. They cannot accept that confirmation, ordination, penance, matrimony, or anointing of the sick (extreme unction) have any biblical basis as "sacraments." This status is reserved for baptism and Holy Communion only.

Why are the Ten Commandments numbered differently among various denominations?

Christendom is divided on the proper numbering of the Ten Commandments given to Moses on Mt. Sinai. The books of Exodus (20:1-17) and Deuteronomy (5:6-18) present the text of the commandments, but Roman Catholic and Lutheran theologians endorse one system of numbering, while the Episcopal, Eastern Orthodox, and the majority of Protestant denominations accept another numerical designation.

The difference centers upon two of the commandments—the first and the last. Roman Catholics and Lutherans list the first commandment as: "You shall have no other gods before me. You shall not make yourself a graven image. ... " The rest of the Christian Church divides this into two parts, making the first part commandment number one and the second, about graven images, commandment number two. The designation of a separate command regarding graven images was made by leaders of the Reformed movement following the German Reformation who wished to strike out against the alleged evils of statues—aids to worship commonly used by Roman Catholics.

In order to make the final number of the commandments total ten, Catholics and Lutherans separate Exodus 20:17 and label: "You shall not covet your neighbor's house" as the ninth commandment and "You shall not covet your neighbor's wife, or his manservant, or his maidservant . . . " as the tenth. The other denominations choose to combine these two sentences into one commandment.

Why did the Roman Catholic Church publish an "Index of Forbidden Books"?

In 1559, Pope Paul IV began a tradition of compiling a list of books known as the *Index Librorum Prohibitorum* ("Index of Forbidden Books"), which consisted of those writings the Church hierarchy felt were blasphemous or profane in content. These books were "off limits" to Catholic readers. Sometimes the books contained perceived errors in dogma or severe criticism of the Church. At other times, the books were banned because of their blatant references to sex, especially if such descriptions involved active participation by clerics. One of the more famous examples is the collection known as the *Canterbury Tales* written by Geoffrey Chaucer in the 1300s. In the years that followed, the "Index" included the total works of Dumas, Balzac, and Stendhal.

Much criticism was levied against the action of the Church which forbade its members from reading certain books. Consequently, many years after the "Index" was established, Pope John XXIII, in 1962, allowed new authors who were being considered for inclusion on the list, a chance to justify their writings.

While the original reason for framing such an "Index" was to protect the Roman Catholic faithful from heresy or immoral literature, the action sometimes was counterproductive. It seems as though the inclusion of a book on the "Index" was priceless publicity. The result often was larger gross sales.

In 1966, without any great fanfare, the Catholic Church ceased publishing the "Index."

Why do Roman Catholics abide by "canon law"?

Faithful members of the Roman Catholic Church must not abide only by the Ten Commandments and the "Golden Rule"; they must also follow the teachings imposed by the several hundred "canon laws" which are universally binding upon all Catholics.

A "canon law" is a rule imposed by the Church designed to help a Christian lead a life pleasing to God. Although these laws do not appear in Holy Scripture, per se, they were written in order to direct the faithful in decisions about specific areas of living.

One canon law, for instance, states that anyone who has been bound by a previous marriage that has ended in divorce is not free to marry in the Church as long as that former marriage partner is still alive.

The first 20 canon laws were published at the Council of Nicaea that met in 325. Later, other canon laws emerged based upon the opinions of influential bishops and popes.

Pope Pius X called for the codification of the list of canons on March 19, 1904, and the final product was a volume known as the *Codex Iuris Canonici* ("Code of Canon Law") promulgated by Pope Benedict XV on May 27, 1917. On January 25, 1983, Pope John Paul II promulgated the new Code of Canon Law implementing the new orientations and decisions of the Second Vatican Council.

Chapter 3

The Water, the Bread, and the Wine

INTRODUCTION

From the beginnings of the Holy Christian Church, the followers of Jesus have incorporated into their worship three of the most common substances known to us—water, bread, and wine. Water is used for baptism; bread and wine for the Holy Communion.

Traditionally, baptism has served as the method of initiation into Church membership. Holy Communion gives the assurance of the forgiveness of sins through a reenactment of the last supper shared by Jesus and his apostles on the night before the Crucifixion.

The materials used in baptism and Holy Communion are basic, and the rituals are quite simple. Nevertheless, methods of administering baptism and Holy Communion are carried out differently by the various denominations. In addition, denominations differ, sometimes dramatically, in the interpretation and significance placed upon both baptism and Holy Communion. Some Christians, for instance, consider them only as *symbols* of the faith. Others teach that God, himself, is present in a special way in the water, the bread, and the wine.

While there have been attempts to establish a unified theology in these rituals (regarded as "sacraments" by some), most scholars have long since concluded that any thoughts of unification are mere pipe dreams. The current array of practices and beliefs, they feel, is not a negative attribute, but is proof that the Christian Church is mature enough to accept a diversity of opinion.

Why are water, bread, and wine used in baptism and Holy Communion?

Three of the most common items shared by most civilizations—water, bread, and wine—have been used by the Christian Church in the administration of baptism and Holy Communion. These "elements," as they are known in ecclesiastical circles, are used as a means of allowing people to approach God without suffering any "consequences."

According to biblical teaching, human beings cannot come face-to-face with God and live (Exodus 33:20). Christians believe that God has given to the Church both baptism and Holy Communion through which God approaches people without overwhelming them. These physical elements, then, are the means whereby God bestows grace upon the faithful.

Why do Christians baptize their members?

Baptism is one of the many traditions of the Christian Church that have their roots in the customs of the Jews. Several times in the Old Testament, the healing power achieved by immersion in water is portrayed. One of the more striking examples is that of the Syrian military leader Naaman who was suffering from leprosy. The Prophet Elisha suggested that he dip himself in the Jordan "seven times" (II Kings 5:14), and he was cured.

In the New Testament, baptism is first mentioned when the cousin of Jesus, John the Baptist, ordered believers to be cleansed of their sins through "the baptism of repentance" (Mark 1:4). To be a real Jew, John proclaimed, it was necessary to undergo cleansing: moral and ritual. When Jesus submitted to John's baptism, a link was established between him and John.

Later, Jesus hinted at the need for baptism when he said to Nicodemus: "Unless one is born of water and the Spirit, he cannot enter the kingdom of God" (John 3:5).

Then, at the conclusion of his ministry on earth, Jesus commanded his disciples to baptize the peoples of all nations in the name of the Father and of the Son and of the Holy Spirit (Matthew 28:19).

Throughout the history of the Christian Church, baptism has been used as an "initiation" into its fellowship. Today, the simple act of baptism is observed universally by all Christians, although the teachings about baptism and the manner in which it is carried out differ from one denomination to another.

Why is water the only element used for Christian baptism?

Water is the only proper element to be used in a Christian baptism because:

1. it is the element used in the New Testament when John the Baptist was baptizing at the Jordan River and when he baptized Jesus;

2. it is the only element mentioned by Jesus which is to be used for Christian rebirth (John 3:5);

3. it is the most "natural" element that should be used to signify a cleansing of sin;

4. it is the most readily available element throughout the world.

Why do some Christians insist on baptizing in flowing rivers?

The Bible records the story of Jesus' baptism, performed by John, in the flowing waters of the Jordan River (Mark 1:9-11). Since this rite was conducted in a moving river, rather than in a quiet pond, a few groups within the Protestant denominations insist on continuing that tradition and in reenacting Christ's baptism as precisely as possible. This means conducting baptisms outdoors in flowing, not stagnant waters. Such baptisms are always performed in rivers deep enough for the total immersion of the person to be baptized.

Those who live in the northern half of the United States with its frigid temperatures, freezing water, and other problems attendant on cold winters, wait until the spring of each year to conduct their baptisms.

Why do some Christians baptize infants?

The Book of Acts (16:15, 33) reports the baptism of entire households of people at one time. The earliest explicit mention of infant baptism does not appear in the Early Church until the second century, and then only in conjunction with the presence of an adult sponsor. St. Augustine was one of the earliest Church leaders to defend this practice around the start of the fifth century.

Within a few short years, primarily through the persuasive writings of St. Augustine, baptism of infants became obligatory for most Christians rather than permissive as it had been. Today, the majority of Christian denominations, including Methodists, Presbyterians, Roman Catholics, Lutherans, Anglicans, Eastern Orthodox, and Congregationalists, practice infant baptism.

Those who promote infant baptism argue that the Bible

does not prohibit such a practice. They feel that baptism always presumes the context of the Christian community—both adults and children. They believe, also, that the benefits of baptism rest in the working of the Holy Spirit who is able to enter the heart and soul of a child as much as those of an adult.

Why do some Christians baptize only adults?

Some denominations, such as the Baptists, Assemblies of God, and the Brethren, reject the practice of baptizing infants who are not old enough to speak for themselves. They believe, instead, that the candidate for baptism should have reached an age of accountability (approximately 14 years old) and should demonstrate some evidence of a personal conversion experience through a marked change in social behavior or through one of the "signs of the Spirit" "speaking in tongues" (discussed in Chapter 2).

The insistence on adult baptism (sometimes called a "believer's baptism") is observed even if persons were baptized as infants and now wish to affiliate with one of these denominations. Such candidates for membership, therefore, must be rebaptized, since they are now able to speak for themselves.

Why do some Christians immerse those they baptize?

The biblical verse usually cited as proof that immersion is the only proper method of baptizing is the one by St. Paul which states: "We are buried with him [Jesus] by baptism into death . . . " (Romans 6:4). Another support for this practice rests on the fact that the word "baptize" (from the Greek *baptizo*) means to "cleanse" or to "dip." On top of this, some authorities argue that the earliest form of baptism in the Church included immersion of the candidate for membership.

This issue was the focus of heated debate in colonial America when the Rev. Roger Williams, a clergyman of the Church of England (Episcopal) preached a dogma contrary to that held by his own denomination. Williams insisted that immersion is necessary for a true baptism. He and his followers (called "Baptists" by their critics because of their demand for baptism by immersion) were severely persecuted by their neighbors and other members of the Church. They endured as much as humanly possible, until they were forced to leave their homes in Plymouth, Massachusetts. They formed a new religious community in Rhode Island, and called their new place of sanctuary "Providence."

The practice of immersing candidates for baptism was adopted in 1708 by a group of Christians of Schwarzenau, Germany, known as the "Brethren" in some circles, and as "Dunkards" in others. The name "Dunkard" was derived from the German word *tunken* which means to "dip." A particularly unique practice of immersion was adopted by this group. It is known by the term "triune immersion"—a procedure in which the believer is immersed not just once, but three times: in the name of the Father, and of the Son, and of the Holy Spirit. Today, the Dunkards have almost 250,000 members.

Why are some babies baptized by immersion?

In the Eastern Orthodox Church, as well as in a few other fellowships, infants are baptized by immersion. Those who observe this practice believe that immersion is necessary for a valid baptism, and that all (young and old alike) should be baptized. They are unwilling to wait (as do some Christians) for someone to reach the age of accountability before being baptized.

A priest who immerses babies makes certain that he protects them from possible drowning by placing his hand firmly over the nose and mouth of the infants before immersing them in water.

In the Eastern Orthodox tradition, babies are baptized 40 days after birth, which is the period of time that elapsed between the birth of Jesus and his presentation in the temple (Luke 2:22f).

Why do some clergymen baptize by pouring or sprinkling water on the head of the candidate?

Not all Christian denominations practice baptism by immersion. To the contrary, the vast majority of Christians (Roman Catholic, Lutheran, Anglican, Methodist, and Presbyterian, just to name a few) administer baptism by pouring or sprinkling water on the head of the candidate for Church membership.

The two methods are used interchangeably by these denominations. If a clergyman prefers pouring, he cups the water in the palm of his hand and pours it over the head of the youngster or the adult, generally three times, while saying: "I baptize you in the name of the Father, and of the Son, and of the Holy Spirit." If he chooses the method called "sprinkling," he dips his fingertips into the water and literally shakes droplets onto the head of the candidate while saying the same words.

Regardless of the method employed—pouring or sprinkling—the amount of water used is of little importance. What is important is the fact that water is used in the name of the Triune God.

Why is an eyedropper sometimes used in a baptism?

Unusual circumstances sometimes dictate unusual methods of doing things. Baptisms are no exceptions.

Sometimes, when a baby is born and complications arise, the infant is placed in an incubator. If conditions are serious enough that there is fear the young child will not survive, a clergyman will administer baptism by filling an eyedropper with water and, reaching into the incubator, will let three drops fall on the baby's head.

Although this rather unorthodox method is used, the baptism is just as valid in the eyes of that clergymen's denomination as if it were conducted in church.

Christian practice allows any believer to baptize another; consequently, Christian nurses are often trained to perform baptism in emergency cases.

Why are "godparents" often present at baptisms?

At their children's baptism, parents promise to teach them the Ten Commandments, the Lord's Prayer, and the Apostles' Creed. They also pledge to bring them to the church and to raise them in the Christian faith. Alongside each set of parents often stand two other adults—a man and a woman—who share in these vows. They are called "godparents."

The origin of this tradition has been traced to a time of persecution in the Early Church when believers were sometimes put to death because they worshiped a God different from the one sanctioned by the government. To make sure that children who lost their parents would not grow up without proper instruction, as early as the second century fellow members of the Church vowed to take upon themselves the responsibility of raising such children in the Christian faith.

Technically speaking, the obligation of godparents ends when a youngster receives the rite of confirmation (generally at about 13 or 14 years of age). Nonetheless, a special bond continues to exist between the godparents and their "godchild" throughout their years together on this earth.

Why must godparents at a Roman Catholic baptism also be Catholic?

According to the teachings of the Roman Catholic Church, a non-Catholic Christian cannot be a godparent at a Catholic baptism, since the godparent is the representative of the community of the Catholic faithful and becomes the guarantor not only of the Christian faith but also of the Catholic faith of the Child.

Most other denominations in the Christian Church do not insist that the godparents be members of that particular denomination, since their belief is that baptism is the method whereby the child is made a member of the Church at large, not of a specific denomination.

Why are godparents not present at modern baptisms as they were in years past?

While people consider it an honor to be asked to serve as godparents (called a "sponsor" in some denominations), their presence at the ceremony today is merely symbolic. Except for some rare instances among remote and backward nations, Christians are not in fear of losing their lives because they follow their faith. Consequently, the need for someone to insure that a child will be raised in the Christian faith has all but disappeared. In addition, our modern society is so mobile that there is little reason to believe that a godparent will be around to see that a child receives Christian instruction.

Why do Christians celebrate Holy Communion?

Almost every Christian denomination celebrates Holy Communion in one form or another. Although the teachings about it vary, most believers consider Holy Communion as a reminder that Jesus died for their sins and left them this legacy as a means of assuring them of the forgiveness of sin. It is also regarded by most Christians as the one act which links one believer to another as members of the "Body of Christ" [the Church]. Hence, the term Holy "Communion."

Christians teach that the Holy Communion was instituted by Christ during the "Last Supper" which he celebrated with his apostles. The earliest written account we have of this instance in Jesus' life comes from the pen of St. Paul:

> The Lord Jesus on the night when he was betrayed took bread, and when he had given thanks, he broke it, and said, "This is my body which is for you. Do this in remembrance of me." In the same way also the cup, after supper, saying, "This is my blood. Do this, as often as you drink it, in remembrance of me." For as often as you eat this bread and drink the cup, you proclaim the Lord's death until he comes (I Corinthians 11:23-26).

Other references in the New Testament are in Matthew 26:26-29, Mark 14:22-25, and Luke 22:17-20.

Questions regarding Jesus' Last Supper are answered also in Chapter 1.

Why is the Holy Communion sometimes called the "Eucharist"?

The term "Eucharist" comes from the Greek word

eucharisteo, meaning "I rejoice." This designation for Holy Communion is used universally within the Church, although its most common usage is among the liturgical denominations—Roman Catholic, Lutheran, Eastern Orthodox, and Anglican.

While some people have traditionally looked upon the reception of Holy Communion as a solemn occasion (since it is a reminder of Jesus' death on Good Friday), most Christians hold that the spirit behind the sacrament is one of gratitude and joy in which they are assured that their sins are forgiven. For them, this is a cause for celebration and rejoicing—just as the term implies.

Why do Christians differ in their understanding of Holy Communion?

Although Holy Communion is held in high esteem by the majority of Christians, there is precious little written about it in the New Testament. We know only that during the meal known as the "Last Supper," Jesus broke bread and gave it to his disciples with the words: "Take, eat; this is my body" (Matthew 26:26); he did the same with wine, saying: "Drink of it, all of you; for this is my blood of the covenant" (Matthew 26:27-28). Then Jesus commanded them to continue this practice "in remembrance of me" (I Corinthians 11:24).

In the centuries that have passed since these words were uttered, Christians have raised questions as to what Jesus actually meant when he said these words. Attempts to interpret Jesus' words have resulted in a variety of teachings about Holy Communion which fall, generally, in three areas:

1. The teaching of "transubstantiation" which says that the bread and wine mysteriously turn into the body and blood of Jesus.

2. The teaching of "symbolism" which emphasizes the

belief that the bread and wine are only representations of something which Jesus did nearly 2,000 years ago.

3. The teaching of the "real presence" which says that the bread and wine do not change, but still contain the real body and blood of Jesus.

These three positions are explained more fully in the next three questions and answers.

Why do some Christians believe in "transubstantiation" during their celebration of Holy Communion?

Some Christians, namely the Roman Catholics and Eastern Orthodox, plus some Lutherans and Anglicans, believe that the bread and wine used in the Holy Communion become the real body and blood of Christ at the moment of consecration by the officiating clergyman. They take literally the words of Jesus at the Last Supper when he blessed the bread and said: "This is my body," and gave thanks and said of the wine: "This is my blood" (Matthew 26:26–28).

St. Thomas Aquinas (1225–1274) attempted to explain this mystery in his classic work *Summa Theologica* when he said that the "accidents" of the bread and wine do not change, but the "substance" does. By "accidents," he referred to the physical properties of the elements such as the quality, color, and taste, which continue to exist and remain the same insofar as our senses are concerned. The "substance," on the other hand, refers to what the elements truly are. Before the consecration, they were bread and wine; after the consecration, they are the body and blood of Christ.

This mysterious occurrence is called "transubstantiation" (meaning: the "act of changing the substance").

Why do some Christians believe the elements used in Holy Communion should be thought of only as symbols?

Certain Christians (including the majority of Baptists, Presbyterians, Methodists, and some Anglicans) believe that the bread and wine used in Holy Communion are merely symbols of the body and blood referred to by Jesus during the Last Supper. To support this view they use the reference by St. Paul, I Corinthians 11:23-26, where Jesus tells his disciples: "Do this in *remembrance* of me." Remembrance, they believe, means that the bread and wine are to be looked upon as "memorials," as reminders and symbols. They see no reason why anyone must accept the teaching of "transubstantiation" or of the "real presence" held by the majority of Roman Catholics, Lutherans, Eastern Orthodox and Anglicans.

This "memorial" approach to Holy Communion was introduced by Ulrich Zwingli (1484-1531), a contemporary of Martin Luther, who felt that the Reformation had not gone far enough in ridding the Church of some of the Roman Catholic teachings—including the dogma of Holy Communion—which some of the people found offensive.

Why do some Chistians accept the theory of the "real presence" of Jesus' body and blood in the Holy Communion?

A teaching held by the majority of Lutherans, many Anglicans, and some other Protestants states that when Jesus consecrated the bread and wine at his last supper by saying: "This is my body" and "This is my blood," he declared that those who participated that evening, as well as those who would continue the tradition, did indeed partake of his body and blood. At the same time, that which is consumed remains bread and wine. This view differs, slightly, from the dogma of "transubstantiation" which declares that the bread and wine miraculously change to the body and blood of Jesus at the time of consecration on the altar.

The theology of the "real presence," as it is sometimes called, was described by the reformer Martin Luther (1483–1546) who said that the bread remains bread, and the wine remains wine, but the body and blood of Jesus is "in, with, and under the bread and wine."

Today, many theologians feel that those who insist on debating the issue are only "splitting hairs," since the differences between the dogma of the "real presence" and the traditional Roman Catholic teaching of "transubstantiation" are so slight.

Why were some of the first Christians who shared the Holy Communion accused of being cannibals?

Because Christianity, during its formative years, was an illegal religion in a world dominated by the Roman Empire, Christians were careful to whom they spoke about their beliefs. Consequently, those who were not members of "the Way" (the name given to the first Christians) remained uninformed as to the teachings of the Christian faith except through what they could gather via rumor and hearsay.

One of the most confusing of the Christian teachings must have been the gossip regarding the service of Holy Communion which was a part of every worship service. When the outsiders learned that the assembled faithful were "eating the body of Christ and drinking his blood," they interpreted this in a *literal,* rather than a *spiritual* sense. This sounded like cannibalism, pure and simple.

Such an accusation only fueled the fires of hatred already felt for the Christians by those loyal to the Roman government. Only when some of these same accusers were instructed in the Christian dogma were they able to understand what was actually happening during the sharing of Holy Communion.

Why do most Christians prefer to use unleavened bread during Holy Communion?

When Jesus initiated the sacrament of Holy Communion at his Last Supper (which was the Passover *Seder* meal), he used unleavened bread (Matthew 26:26). This was (and remains) the custom of Jews who celebrate Passover. The practice commemorates the hasty exodus of the Jews from Egypt who "took their dough before it was leavened" (Exodus 12:34). Most Christians prefer to continue to observe this tradition through the celebration of the Holy Communion.

The unleavened bread is generally pressed into small wafers (measuring approximately one inch in diameter) marked with an appropriate Church symbol such as a cross. Each communicant, then, receives a wafer as the clergyman repeats the words: "The body of Christ." In many circles, the communicant responds with an "Amen."

Why do some Christians choose to use regular bread during Holy Communion?

The most common type of bread used in Holy Communion throughout the Christian Church is unleavened bread. However, some denominations—the Methodist, Presbyterian, and Baptist, just to name a few—will occasionally use regular (leavened) bread for two practical reasons:

1. Convenience. Leavened bread is simply easier to find.
2. Taste. Some people prefer the more familiar taste of leavened bread to the rather strange taste of an unleavened wafer.

Why is the bread sometimes placed in the mouths of the communicants?

Most clergymen, when distributing the elements of the Holy Communion, prefer to place the bread into the outstretched hand of the communicant; others insist on placing the bread directly into the mouths of the communicants. This latter, unusual (and somewhat awkward) method of distribution has its roots in a problem that arose in the Early Church.

Some of the new converts to the faith believed the unleavened bread (called the "host") which was transformed into the body of Christ contained some mysterious power. During the Holy Communion they broke the portion of the consecrated bread in half and ate it. They saved the remainder to ward off evil spirits, believing that it would bring them good luck for as long as they kept it in their possession.

To discourage this practice, clergymen placed the bread into the open mouths of congregants—a way of making certain that the entire portion of bread would be consumed. Clergymen who follow this tradition today believe that it is a way of preventing what they consider a desecration of the sacrament.

Why do some churches offer Holy Communion every Sunday?

Some churches within Christendom—especially the Roman Catholic and Eastern Orthodox—celebrate Holy Communion at the conclusion of each Sunday morning worship. This practice is in keeping with the tradition established in the Early Church when the sacrament was offered each time the faithful met for worship. Some Christians, in fact, are convinced that the worship service is not complete unless Holy Communion is shared.

Why do some churches choose *not* to offer Holy Communion each Sunday?

The Bible does not command that Holy Communion be offered every Sunday, although the Early Church followed that practice as did the Church during the time of Martin Luther.

The Protestant Reformation which was promoted through the teaching and preaching of Luther and others emphasized the preaching of the word of God in lieu of the sacraments. Partly as the result of a rebellion against the practices of the Roman Catholic Church, the reformers offered Communion less frequently. In addition, the Communion service became unnecessarily long, and the people urged that it not be offered each week.

Today, as a result, some churches—particularly the Lutheran and Anglican—will offer Holy Communion once or twice each month. Many of the remaining Protestant denominations will offer it three or four times a year. At the same time, there is a growing trend among all denominations to increase the number of times that Holy Communion is offered. Some Lutheran and Anglican churches, for instance, now include it at each Sunday morning worship.

Why are some Christians required to announce their intention to partake of Holy Communion at least 24 hours before Sunday morning worship?

Christians in German settlements have traditionally announced their intentions to receive the sacrament of Holy Communion at least 24 hours before Sunday morning worship. The announcement is made either in person or by telephone call to the pastor. The pastor then informs the person of the obligation to prepare mentally and spiritually for the receiving of the bread and wine. The preparation may include prayers and readings from the Holy Bible.

On occasion a pastor may be aware that the announcing communicant is engaged in an activity that is contrary to the command of God, such as living in adultery. If so, the pastor will counsel with his parishioner and may forbid the person to share in the Holy Communion until such time as a new life-style is forged.

This custom of announcing for Holy Communion is not commonly observed today.

Why do some people "register" for Holy Communion?

"Registering" for Holy Communion is an outgrowth of the German custom of announcing an intention to partake of the sacrament 24 hours before Sunday morning worship. Instead of announcing to the pastor in person the intention to share in the Eucharist, the communicant will sign a "Communion card" and hand it to an usher when approaching the altar railing for the bread and the wine.

Registration for Communion is a means whereby the individual church can record the number of times a member communes each year. Most congregations expect members to commune at least once a year if they are to be considered active members and eligible to vote on congregational matters. The Communion cards provide a record of Communion participation.

Why is a "ciborium" used during the Holy Communion?

A "ciborium" is a chalice-shaped vessel with a lid that is used to hold the sacramental bread of the Holy Communion. During the distribution of the sacrament, the officiating clergyman carries the ciborium in one hand and, with the other, lifts from it the wafers or pieces of bread to be given to the communicants.

At the conclusion of the service, the consecrated bread remains in the ciborium until the next time Communion is offered.

The ciborium was introduced into the Christian Church during the Middle Ages.

Why is the bread used during Holy Communion often called the "host"?

The "host" is a term used to describe the bread that is distributed during Holy Communion by Roman Catholics, Lutherans, Eastern Orthodox, and others who accept the teaching that the consecrated bread contains (or actually becomes) the body of Christ. According to their interpretation of the Eucharist, the bread is that element which carries with it (i.e., serves as a host for) the body of Jesus.

Why is red wine traditionally used during Holy Communion?

Red wine was probably the kind used by Jesus at the Last Supper, since this was the wine used by most of his contemporaries during the Passover observances. Red wine was described later in the Talmud (the great library of authoritative Jewish tradition completed in the fifth century) as superior. Today it is traditionally served at Passover Seders.

The red color is symbolic, also, of the blood shed by Christ for his followers. In fact, one of the charges against the first Christians was that of cannibalism, because outsiders heard that participants in Holy Communion were "drinking the blood of Jesus."

Ironically, similar charges were levied against Jews over

the centuries. They were accused of murdering Christians' children and drinking their blood at the Passover Seder. As late as this century, in Messina, New York, such an accusation was made, and the rabbi of the town was questioned when a little Christian girl disappeared at Passover time. When the girl was found unharmed the next day, the town mayor apologized publicly. Accusations of this nature, of course, were always proven purely libelous and unfounded.

Why must some clergymen drink all of the wine at the conclusion of the service of Holy Communion?

At the conclusion of a service of Holy Communion in the Roman Catholic Church, the officiating priest must drink all of the wine remaining in the chalice (the cup which holds the consecrated wine). His reason for doing this is in keeping with the Catholic teaching on the Eucharist which says that the wine becomes the real blood of Christ. Once the wine has been consecrated, it remains the blood of Christ even after the service has been completed. Therefore, as a practical matter, it is much easier for the priest to consume the wine rather than store it, subjecting it to the possibility of spoilage.

This practice of consuming all the wine is not limited to Roman Catholics. Eastern Orthodox and other Christians who accept the dogma of the "real presence" of Christ's body and blood in the bread and wine of the Communion often make certain that not one drop of the wine remains after the celebration of the sacrament.

Why is water sometimes added to the wine during the Holy Communion?

Just prior to the consecration of the elements for Holy

Communion in many liturgical churches—e.g., Roman Catholic, Lutheran, Eastern Orthodox, and Anglican—the officiating clergyman adds some water to the wine. This gesture symbolizes the biblical account of Jesus' sacrifice on the cross when both blood and water came from his side wounded by one of the Roman soldiers (John 19:34).

Water is added to the wine a second time, after the distribution of the elements, when the priest or pastor consumes the remaining wine. The water in this instance is added solely for purposes of cleansing the vessel, making certain that none of the wine remains in the chalice.

Why do some Christians serve grape juice instead of wine during Holy Communion?

In many parts of the world, especially in the southeastern section of the United States, many members of the Baptist, Methodist, Presbyterian, and others of the more "conservative" denominations choose to abstain from using alcoholic beverages throughout their lives. Even at the service of Holy Communion, they will not drink wine.

When sharing in the Lord's Supper, these Christians will use grape juice instead of wine as used by Lutherans, Roman Catholics, Eastern Orthodox, and Anglican denominations. They feel that grape juice may be used because this is the closest they can come to using wine without drinking an alcoholic beverage.

As to the report that Jesus drank wine during the Last Supper with his disciples, this is not taken literally by those who are opposed to the use of alcoholic beverages. They believe that when the Bible says Jesus drank wine, it actually means a nonalcoholic beverage.

Why is a chalice used in many churches during Holy Communion?

A chalice (from the Latin *calix,* meaning "cup") was the vessel used in the distribution of the wine for Holy Communion in the Early Church. This tradition is maintained today by the majority of Roman Catholics, Eastern Orthodox, and Anglicans, as well as by many Lutherans and other Christians. The chalice (often called the "common cup") symbolizes the unity of those who commune.

Fearing that disease might spread from one communicant to another, from the ninth century until 1969, the Roman Catholic Church allowed only chalices made of metal to be used during the Holy Communion. Bowing to the realization that metal is no more sanitary than other substances, the Roman Catholics now allow chalices to be made of a number of materials including wood and stone.

Why are individual glasses used by most Protestant denominations during Holy Communion?

In America, especially, people were concerned that disease might spread from one communicant to another if the "common cup" were to be used during Holy Communion. As a result, many of the Protestant churches adopted a policy of serving the wine (or grape juice) in small, individual cups each holding approximately one-quarter ounce of liquid.

The use of individual glasses at Holy Communion is primarily an American practice. Protestants in Europe, for the most part, still use the "common cup."

Why do most Protestants take Communion while seated in pews instead of approaching the altar?

In most Protestant congregations during the distribution of the bread and wine (or grape juice) at Holy Communion, the assembled body is served while sitting in the pews. This is in contrast to the practice of the liturgical churches in which the communicants approach the altar to receive the elements of the sacrament.

Three reasons have been cited for receiving Holy Communion while being seated:

1. It is an outgrowth of the revolt in the sixteenth century against the Roman Catholic teaching and the importance it placed upon the centrality of the altar in church.

2. It takes much less time to distribute the elements.

3. It allows the entire congregation to wait until everyone has received the elements and consume them at the same time, a factor which enhances Christian unity.

Why do some churches have "closed Communion"?

The Roman Catholics, Lutherans, and Eastern Orthodox teach that the sacrament of Holy Communion should be given only to those who are confirmed members of their denominations or to those who understand and believe the official teaching of their denominations regarding the presence of Christ in the bread and wine. This practice of excluding all others is often called "closed Communion." The restriction stems from the warning of St. Paul:

Whoever . . . eats the bread or drinks the cup of the Lord in an unworthy manner will be guilty of profaning the body and blood of the Lord. . . . For anyone who eats and drinks without discerning the body eats and drinks judgment upon himself (I Corinthians 11:27-29).

The denominations that practice closed Communion are of the opinion that people who approach the altar of the Lord in order to receive the bread and wine must be aware of what is taking place. Were they to partake of the Eucharist without realizing that the body and blood of Christ are present in the bread and wine, they would, as St. Paul wrote, eat and drink judgment upon themselves. In the eyes of these denominations, it would be better for uninformed persons not to partake of the sacrament at all. Some clergymen, in fact, will purposely pass by those who are known to be members of other denominations and will not give them the bread or the wine.

Closed Communion has another—perhaps more positive—dimension. In each case, the communicants may safely assume that the others sharing the bread and wine with them are of the same theology. The Communion, then, is not just between the individual communicants and their Lord, but reaches out to others who have approached the altar with them.

Why do some churches practice "open Communion"?

For every denomination that practices "closed Communion," there are two that embrace a concept known as "open Communion."

Open Communion is common among the Baptists, Presbyterians, Methodists, and the majority of Protestant denominations. It is an outgrowth of the teachings of the Swiss reformer Ulrich Zwingli (1484-1531) who believed that no one should judge those who sincerely desire to commune at the Lord's table. After all, he noted, Jesus did say: "Come to me, *all* who labor and are heavy laden, and I will give you rest" (Matthew 11:28). The Communion should, therefore, be open to all who seek the assurance of God's forgiveness of sins.

Why does a clergyman sometimes wash his hands during the Holy Communion?

Another carry-over from the tradition established by the Jews is the symbolic washing of hands by the celebrant of the Holy Communion.

In ancient times, when offering a sacrifice to God, the priest would wash the blood from his hands before partaking of the sacrificial meal. Likewise, after the consecration of the bread and wine that has now become the body and blood of Christ—a stark reminder of Jesus' sacrifice on Good Friday—the priest or pastor dips his fingers into a bowl of water on top of the altar, or pours water from a vessel over his hands as a symbolic cleansing.

This custom is still observed in most liturgical churches. Because they regard this gesture as only symbolic, most Protestant churches do not carry on this tradition.

Why is "Worldwide Communion Sunday" becoming so popular?

Although it is not an official part of the Church year, the first Sunday in October is observed by most Christian denominations as "Worldwide Communion Sunday."

Normally, the sacrament of Holy Communion is celebrated within a closed environment of a congregation (especially among the more conservative liturgical churches that practice "closed Communion"). On this day, however, there is a greater sense of unity among participating congregations. Some churches conduct joint Communion services. In a number of major cities in the United States a community-wide service of Holy Communion is conducted in a large church or in a public meeting place.

The rise in popularity of this special observance is, in part, due to the renewed emphasis upon ecumenism that was fostered through the Second Vatican Council in the 1960s. Many consider this as evidence that there is a strong desire among Christians to accentuate those elements that unite them rather than those that divide them.

Chapter 4

Public Worship

INTRODUCTION

It is eleven o'clock, Sunday morning. In a large cathedral in Boston, a priest robed in brightly colored vestments solemnly approaches an ornate altar carved out of solid marble. A choir intones an ancient chant. The sweet-smelling fragrance of incense fills the air. A bell sounds. Nearly a thousand of the faithful kneel on thin, padded benches at their pews. The priest holds high a small wafer, whispering to himself: "The Body of Christ." These are Christians at worship.

At that precise moment, in a rural village of eastern Tennessee, less than 50 people gather in a circle inside a tar-covered shack. They are shaking with excitement. One speaks in a strange language. Another "interprets" what was spoken. The rest stand with arms outstreched and palms turned skyward. They are shouting "Praise the Lord!" and "Amen!" These, too, are Christians at worship.

Public worship for Christians has a variety of forms. It may be formal or free, stoic or emotional, depending upon denominational tradition or geographic setting. In each instance, the service of worship involves a body of Christians who share an appreciation for one form of expression over another.

The methods of community worship for Christians vary

121

as much as their theology. The following questions survey some of the differences and similarities.

Why is Sunday the generally accepted day of worship for Christians?

Isn't it strange that Christians who believe in the Ten Commandments seem openly to violate one of them? After all, God said: "Remember the sabbath day, to keep it holy" (Exodus 20:8). The Sabbath was the seventh day of creation and the seventh day of the week, yet most Christians worship on Sunday, the first day of the week. Why the change?

Obviously, there was no intent on the part of the Church to contradict the commandment of God. But the Early Church recognized Sunday as the day of worship because it was on a Sunday that Jesus rose from the dead. Since the resurrection of Jesus is the focal point of the Christian faith and the confirmation of all that Jesus taught, the first Christians gathered to celebrate this event on the first day of the week (Acts 20:7 and I Corinthians 16:2).

Undoubtedly, another important reason why early Christians worshiped on Sunday was to distinguish themselves from the Jewish community to which many of them belonged before their conversions.

Today, with the exception of the Seventh-Day Adventists, Christians hold Sunday as their day for public worship.

Why do Seventh-Day Adventists insist on worshiping on Saturday instead of Sunday?

Although most Christians worship on Sunday, the Seventh-Day Adventists (who trace their beginning to the early 1840s and number about 400,000 today) choose to worship on Saturday instead of Sunday, as is the habit of most Christians.

The Adventists believe that God's command: "Remember the sabbath day, to keep it holy" referred to the seventh day of the week, since it was on the seventh day that God rested at the conclusion of his creation of the universe. They believe, too, that the Early Church was in error when it started a tradition of conducting worship on a day other than that set aside by God.

Why do Christians follow the liturgical year as their "calendar for public worship"?

Many Christians, particularly those belonging to the Roman Catholic, Episcopal, Lutheran, and Eastern Orthodox denominations, follow a calendar for public worship called the "liturgical year." This calendar was created by leaders of the Early Church as a guide for worship throughout the year. It listed dates and "seasons" which highlighted the life and teachings of Jesus, plus reviewed the dimensions of the ideal Christian life.

The liturgical year contains prescribed readings from the Holy Scriptures and prayers that are meant to be used on a particular Sunday in every liturgical church throughout the world. In theory, Christians are able to attend public worship at any church that follows the liturgical year and hear the same readings, pray the same prayers, and listen to a sermon based upon the same theme as used in the worship conducted in their home parish.

Those clergymen who follow the liturgical year claim that these ancient guidelines compel them to preach on a variety of subjects within the course of a year, whereas they might be tempted to concentrate solely upon subjects with which they may be more familiar or in which they hold a personal interest.

Why do some Christians choose not to follow the liturgical year?

While the essence of worship in the Roman Catholic, Lutheran, Episcopal, and Eastern Orthodox churches is centered upon the themes imposed by the liturgical year, the bulk of Protestantism chooses not to be bound by the prescribed Bible readings and prayers set aside for the specific days and seasons.

Harry Emerson Fosdick, renowned minister of the Riverside Presbyterian Church in New York City, used to say that every sermon, every reading from the Bible, and every prayer used in public worship should speak to a genuine need of the people at that moment in time. To Fosdick, imposing the ancient themes of the liturgical year on today's Christian is restrictive at best.

The late Donald Turbin, a minister at various Methodist churches in Michigan, once said: "I cannot become excited about some of those themes that were so important to Christians 2,000 years ago. There is so much more that the Bible has to offer us today. To follow the so-called 'liturgical year' would bind my hands as a preacher as well as those of my people."

Why does the liturgical year contain "seasons"?

In addition to the major festivals, the liturgical year contains a variety of "seasons" during which Christian worshipers may reflect upon specific events of Jesus' life or upon dimensions of the ideal Christian life.

The festivals and seasons of the liturgical year are as follows:

Advent, which begins four Sundays before Christmas and reminds us of Jesus' first coming into the world and of his second coming on the Day of Judgment.

Christmas, which celebrates the birth of Jesus.

Epiphany, a reminder of the visit to the Christ Child by the Wise Men and a symbol of Christ's manifestation to the Gentiles.

Sundays after Epiphany (also called "Sundays in Ordinary Time"), signifying Christ's public ministry and his working in our souls.

Lent, the 40 days before Easter. This is a time for personal reflection often accompanied by some sort of fast or intensified prayer life.

Easter, the feast of the Resurrection of Jesus from the dead.

Ascension, celebrated 40 days after Easter and recalling Jesus' ascending into heaven.

Pentecost, the celebration of the giving of the Holy Spirit to the Christian Church.

Trinity, a reminder of the Church teaching about the Triune God—the Father, the Son, and the Holy Spirit.

Sundays after Trinity (sometimes called the "Sundays after Pentecost" or "Ordinary Time—after Pentecost"), that encompass the second half of the liturgical year and stress the ideal Christian life.

Why do some Christians follow a "liturgy" as their form of worship each Sunday morning?

The word "liturgy" comes from two Greek terms: *leos,* meaning "people" and *ergon,* meaning "work." The two words used together represent a public work of any kind, not just something religious. Liturgy, then, is merely a term for an order to follow for the public.

In the strictest sense of the word, every program of worship is a "liturgy." However, when the Christian Church refers to *the* liturgy, it speaks of a formal structure of worship which has been used by Christians since the first century.

Why is the order of worship always the same in the liturgical churches?

The churches that endorse the order of worship known as the "liturgy"—particularly the Roman Catholic, Lutheran, Episcopal, and Eastern Orthodox—follow the same pattern each Sunday. The pattern which was molded by 2,000 years of Church history begins with a public confession of sins and concludes with the distribution of Holy Communion.

Those denominations which observe this particular order of worship are convinced that nothing anyone could add or subtract from it would improve it.

The liturgy used each Sunday consists of the following:

Confession of sins—a general confession in which the people say that they have sinned in "thought, word, and deed."

Pronouncement of absolution—assurance by the pastor or priest that those who confess their sins and are truly repentant will be forgiven.

Acknowledgment of God's authority—through chants, hymns, and prayers, the congregation praises God.

The reading of God's word—including selected readings from the Old Testament, from one of the epistles, and from one of the Gospels.

A hymn of praise.

A sermon—usually an exposition of one of the three lessons prescribed for the particular Sunday in the liturgical year.

The offering—an opportunity for the worshipers to support the work of the Church, as well as to offer their lives to God.

The prayers of the Church—when the congregation prays for the Church at large, for the nation, and for local concerns.

The Holy Communion—when the people receive the bread and wine which contains (or represents, as the case may be) the body and blood of Christ. This part of the worship includes the great prayer of praise and thanksgiving known as the "Eucharistic Prayer" or "Canon." It is the consecratory prayer which enshrines the words of Jesus at the Last Supper.

Why do some Christians choose not to follow the historical liturgy?

Dr. John Wheeler, a Baptist minister, missionary, and professor of theology offers the following explanation:

> Just as each person has a unique personality—with likes and dislikes—so, too, each congregation is unique in its expression of worship. Therefore, it is not unusual for any body of people to say, in effect, 'We prefer this order of worship.' In the real sense of the word, this is how the liturgy began. Christians who gathered for worship in the Early Church adopted a style of worship which was comfortable for them. Should we not be permitted to do the same?

As a result, one may attend a service of public worship on Sunday morning at a church of a particular denomination that uses an order of worship entirely different from that used by another congregation of the same denomination in another part of town.

Why is the "collect" prayed in the liturgical worship?

The "collect" is a type of prayer that developed in the fifth century for the purpose of gathering or "collecting" the private petitions of individuals into a simple prayer uttered aloud by the clergyman. Today, this tradition has been altered somewhat. Instead of collecting specific prayer requests from the worshipers, the pastor or priest reads a prescribed prayer adopted by both Roman Catholics and Protestants that follows the emphasis of that particular Sunday in the liturgical year. The "collect" is prayed during the portion of the liturgy when the people acknowledge God's authority.

The form of the "collect" is generally the same each week. The name of God is given in the salutation. This is followed by the authority of God that would enable him to answer the petition(s), the specific request, and the conclusion.

A typical "collect" is the one prayed on Christmas Eve:

Father,
you make this holy night radiant
with the splendor of Jesus Christ our light.
We welcome him as Lord, the true light
    of the world.
Bring us to eternal joy in the kingdom
    of heaven,
where he lives and reigns with you and
    the Holy Spirit,
one God, for ever and ever. Amen.

Why is the offering a part of Christian public worship?

Unlike other religions that obtain their financial support through "dues," congregations of the Christian Church (both liturgical and nonliturgical) incorporate the donation of money into the order of worship. This tradition is maintained for two reasons.

First, St. Paul ordered the congregations in the first century: "On the first day of the week, each of you is to put something aside and store it up, as he may prosper, so that contributions need not be made when I come" (I Corinthians 16:2).

Second, the giving of financial support for the work of the Church is, in itself, an act of worship. For Christians, worship is two-dimensional. God speaks to them through the reading and preaching of the Word, and they have the opportunity to express to God their thankfulness for the blessings they have received. Giving a portion of their income is one way they show their thankfulness.

Underlying the offering is the prayer of all Christians that they are willing to offer their entire lives with their joys and sorrows, pains and sufferings, in an act of worship every day throughout the coming week.

Why does a clergyman face the altar when leading the congregation in prayer?

The altar, which is a part of every church building in which the historic liturgy is used in public worship, represents Almighty God. Therefore, when the clergyman and the people are praying to the Lord, they all face the altar. When the word of God is given to the people as in the pronouncement of forgiveness for sin or in the reading of the Holy Gospel, the clergyman faces the assembled congregation.

In churches which do not follow the historic liturgy, often the altar is replaced by a small table sitting in the front of the church that is used to hold the bread and wine (or grape juice) for the Holy Communion.

Why do Christian churches traditionally offer prayers for heads of state?

The Christian Church has traditionally offered prayers for the rulers of the nations ever since the Roman emperor, Constantine (272?–337) recognized Christianity as a legal religion. Consequently, most Christian services of worship will include a prayer for the president or ruling monarch of the nation in which the congregation is located. Many include also prayers for the governor and legislature of the local state or province.

This particular tradition, however, caused concern during certain periods of history. For instance, during the Revolutionary War, some Anglican churches in America were questioned for their habit of praying for the King of England (who at that time was deemed to be the official head of the Anglican Church).

Today, the customary petition on behalf of a head of state is that he or she will govern according to the will of God.

Why did some American Christians once refuse to pray for the President of the United States?

During the Civil War, the southern people of the United States omitted from their church services the customary prayer for the President of the nation. At New Orleans, Brig. Gen. Benjamin Franklin Butler, who served as federal military governor of that city from May 1 until December 16, 1862, ordered all Christian churches of the city to offer a prayer on behalf of President Abraham Lincoln as part of their Sunday services as long as the Union troops occupied the city.

At St. Paul's Episcopal Church, when the Rev. Elijah Guion chose to omit this prayer, he was seized by federal soldiers who had been posted at various churches to enforce this order. As the soldiers marched down the aisle of the church to arrest the minister, the women of the congregation threw their prayer books and hymnals at them. This came to be known as the "Battle of the Prayer Books."

Why do churches often have "chancels"?

A "chancel" is that area of a church building that contains the altar and from which the clergyman conducts the service of public worship. Its designation comes from the Latin *cancilli*, meaning "lattices" or "crossbars," since the chancel area was formerly enclosed with protective lattices. This was a subtle reminder that this section of the church was reserved for ordained clergy. As a carry-over of this tradition, an altar rail surrounds many chancels today.

Although chancels are a standard part of the liturgical church buildings, many nonliturgical congregations have adopted their use.

In some Christian denominations, the Roman Catholic as an example, altar rails are being eliminated as marking too great a separation between the clergy and the faithful. Churches are being designed to show more forcefully the unity of the worshiping assembly and the importance now placed upon the fact that *everyone* shares in the worship.

Why are chancel areas elevated above the main floor of the church building?

The chancel area in which the altar sits and from which the clergyman conducts the Sunday morning worship is most often elevated a few feet above the main floor of the church building for two reasons. First, the altar is the center of worship in these churches and, as such, is placed on the highest level of the building.

The second reason is more practical than theological. While worshipers are seated in their pews, it is difficult for them to see that which is in front on the same level. Therefore, in order that all may see what is happening, the chancel is raised as would be a stage.

Why is the liturgy sometimes called the "Mass"?

The name "Mass" probably comes from the Latin word *missa*, meaning "dismissal." In the Early Church, the singing of a hymn entitled *Ite Missa Est* signaled that the Holy Communion—the final portion of the liturgy—was over.

Although the term "Mass" is associated primarily with the Roman Catholic Church today, its use was encouraged by Martin Luther, the German Reformer of the sixteenth century. Through the influence of later reformers such as Ulrich Zwingli and John Calvin the term was discarded as an attempt to demonstrate the distinction between the Roman Catholic and the Protestant churches.

Why is it considered a sin for Roman Catholics to miss public worship on Sunday (or Saturday evening)?

According to Christian teaching, a sin is a deliberate violation of God's will. This may involve a sin of "commission" in which persons do something wrong, or a sin of "omission" in which believers fail to do what is expected of them. Failure to take part at Mass on Sunday morning or Saturday evening (the Church has always considered sundown, Saturday evening, as the beginning of the day of worship) is a sin of omission, because Catholics eliminate themselves from receiving the special benefits made available to them.

One of the more popular books of Roman Catholic instruction, *A Catechism of Christian Doctrine*, says that the fruits of the Mass include "the blessings that God bestows . . . upon the celebrant, upon those who serve or assist at it, upon the person or persons for whom it is offered, and also upon all mankind, especially the members of the Church and the souls in purgatory."

Why is there a service called a "black Mass"?

Two kinds of worship services—both drastically different in scope and purpose—are called "black Masses."

One "black Mass" (also called a "Requiem Mass") is a Mass offered for the dead. In this solemn service, the priest traditionally wore black vestments, symbolic of the sadness felt by family and friends at the departure of a loved one.

The other "black Mass" is not conducted by Christians at all. On the contrary, it is a parody of the historic Mass conducted by those who claim to be worshipers of Satan. In this "Mass," the Lord's prayer is recited backward, and the service is pervaded by mockery of the Christian faith and teachings.

Why are sermons a part of the public worship?

The sermon holds an important place in public worship, especially in the denominations of the Protestant tradition. Sermons may be brief (from five to 10 minutes in length) or long (with some lasting over an hour).

The sermon is the focal point of most nonliturgical church services, while it is somewhat less important in those congregations that follow the historic liturgy.

The purpose of the sermon varies with the church and with the individual clergyman. In the liturgical churches, for example, the sermon (sometimes called a "homily") is a discourse based upon one of the prescribed readings from Holy Scripture for that particular Sunday in the liturgical year. The portion of the Bible used as basis for the sermon is called a "text." The task before the clergyman delivering this type of sermon is to relate that particular portion of God's word to the people.

Sermons may not always be based on Scripture, however. One of the popular Protestant preachers, Harry Emerson Fosdick, used to equate the writings of Shakespeare and other famous authors with the Bible. Those who follow in his pattern usually begin with a subject of importance to their listeners and, if appropriate, apply some Scriptural references for added support.

Why are sermons not preached at some services of public worship?

Not all worship services have sermons. Some ancient forms of morning worship (called "Matins") and evening worship (called "Vespers") have only scripture readings, prayers, and one or two hymns. These services are designed for quiet meditation and contemplation. Sermons would not lend themselves to such an atmosphere.

For the main worship on Sunday morning, however, a sermon is expected to be delivered.

Why is Matins conducted?

From the Latin word *matutinae* ("of the morning") comes the term designating the service of prayer, chants, and readings from the Bible known as "Matins," used primarily by the liturgical churches (Roman Catholic, Lutheran, Eastern Orthodox, and Anglican).

In the Early Church, Matins used to be an evening worship (since sundown constituted the start of a new day) held regularly on Saturdays and on nights preceding festivals. It was always followed by a service of Holy Communion. Later it developed into a lengthy service read in prescribed choruses and largely restricted to monasteries. The leaders of the sixteenth-century Reformation simplified the service and returned it to its original order, making it an early morning worship.

The purpose of Matins is to offer an opportunity to praise Almighty God. Its prayers seek grace, guidance, and strength for the work of the day.

Why is Vespers conducted in the evenings?

"Vespers," a derivative of the Latin *vespera* ("evening"), is a rather late entry into the worship pattern of the liturgical churches that quite possibly did not appear until the sixth century. Vespers is an evening service which made provision for prayers and readings from the Holy Bible, not for the incorporation of Holy Communion.

Basically, the prayers, readings, and chants of Vespers review God's mercies and are geared to lift the hearts of the worshipers, now free from work, in praise and thanksgiving for the blessings given them by the Lord during that day.

Today, Vespers is a popular form of public worship on Sunday evenings for college students who appreciate not only the comparative informality of the service, but also the fact that the hour of worship is much more appealing than that of the early morning service.

Why does a Christian sing the "Magnificat" at Vespers?

The "Magnificat" or the "Song of Mary" is often sung at the conclusion of Vespers. The song gets its name from the initial words of the Latin text: *Magnificat anima mea Dominum* ("My soul magnifies the Lord"). The words are said to have been spoken by the Mother of Jesus when she visited her cousin Elizabeth, announcing that she would give birth to the Christ child.

Some scholars believe that the "Magnificat" was really the song of Elizabeth in response to the good news given by her cousin. The debate notwithstanding, the text is an acceptable hymn of praise sung at Vespers during which the worshiper chants:

My soul proclaims the greatness of the Lord,
my spirit rejoices in God my Savior
for he has looked with favor on his lowly servants.

From this day all generations will call me blessed;
the Almighty has done great things for me,
and holy is his Name.

He has mercy on those who fear him
in every generation.

He has shown the strength of his arm;
he has scattered the proud in their conceit.

He has cast down the mighty from their thrones,
and has lifted up the lowly.

He has filled the lowly with good things,
and the rich he has sent away empty.

He has come to the help of his servant Israel
for he has remembered his promise of mercy,
the promise he made to our fathers,
to Abraham and his children for ever.*

Why would a Christian sing the "Nunc Dimittis" at Vespers?

An alternative response to the "Magnificat" at Vespers
is the chanting of a 2,000-year-old prayer called the "Nunc
Dimittis" (from the Latin meaning "Now, you dismiss"). Its
text is recorded in the Gospel of Luke (2:29–32).

When Jesus was presented to the Temple 40 days after
his birth, one of the most delighted people present was a
devout man named Simeon, who was promised by the Holy
Spirit that he would not see death before he had the opportunity to see the Lord's Christ. When Mary and Joseph
showed him the young child and placed him into his arms,
Simeon was overjoyed, and spoke the words which today
compose the "Nunc Dimittis":

Lord, now you let your servant go in peace;

---

*Copyright © 1970, 1971, 1975 by International Consultation on English
Texts.

your word has been fulfilled;
my own eyes have seen the salvation
which you have prepared in the sight of every every
   people:
a light to reveal you to the nations
and the glory of your people Israel.*

This response was added to Vespers in the sixteenth century by the German Reformers as a reminder that the Christian has nothing to fear in this life or the next.

Today, many Christians regard the "Nunc Dimittis" as a tender prayer of parting and peace at the close of the day.

Why would a worshiper carry a "missal" to Sunday morning worship?

It is not uncommon for Roman Catholics who participate at Mass on Sunday morning (or Saturday evening) to carry with them a book that contains every prescribed reading and response for the celebration of the historic liturgy throughout the year. The book is called a "missal," a term from the Latin: *liber missalis* or "the book of the Mass."

The missal was introduced into the Roman Catholic Church in the tenth century as an aid for the people who participated in the public worship. It is used still to this day.

When used to its fullest extent, the missal is regarded by many as a "treasure." To them, it is a living instrument of *Christian knowledge,* a *prayerbook* that teaches how to pray, an *introduction to the Bible,* and a book of *liturgical culture.* According to Dr. Anthony Buono, a Roman Catholic theologian from New York, "The missal is a sure guide to true Christian spirituality and real Christian living."

---

*Copyright © 1970, 1971, 1975 by International Consultation on English Texts.

Why is "Compline" no longer a popular order for worship?

When St. Benedict (in 530) introduced the order for worship called "Compline," Christians were in the habit of gathering for worship at nearby locations at various hours throughout the day. "Compline," from the Latin *completa* ("completion") was the name given to the service that marked the completion of the daily worship schedule. The brief devotional (about 20 minutes in length) came at the close of the day, immediately before retirement at night.

Today's highly mobilized society, in which churches are often miles away from home, has created a life-style that makes the observance of Compline impractical. Although Compline is available for use by worshipers in the liturgical tradition, and contains such classic chants as the "Nunc Dimittis" and "Salve Regina" ("Hail, Holy Queen"), its lack of appeal has relegatèd its use chiefly to monastic communities.

Why do Christians chant in public worship?

Christians who celebrate worship with the historic liturgy recite the prayers through a type of singing called the "chant" (from the Latin *cantare*, meaning "to sing").

The people maintain this rather ancient tradition for three reasons: One, the melodies help keep the congregation "together" in their responses. Two, words accompanied by a tune are easier to remember. Three, the chant is a unique style of music unheard in contemporary society except in worship; it is another means of setting the divine service apart from anything else in the Christian's experience.

The chant has its roots in the worship practice of the Early Church when the congregations commonly responded in unison to the leader of the service. In Antioch, the worshipers adopted the practice of antiphonal singing, with one group answering the other.

As a protest against the accepted style of worship by the Roman Catholic Church, some of the sixteenth-century reformers—Ulrich Zwingli and John Calvin in particular—eliminated the chant from Sunday morning worship. Other reformers such as Martin Luther appreciated the qualities of the chant and urged its use in public worship.

Why are chants often called "Gregorian chants"?

Pope Gregory the Great, who died in 604, was most influential in preserving the ancient form of liturgical response called the "chant." He was so impressed by its effect on the orderly response at worship that he ordered his scribes to preserve the musical settings in manuscript form. He formed a choir school in which he instructed men and boys in the proper intonations and uses of these unique melodies. The chants became increasingly popular throughout the Church. Notations on the manuscripts allowed other congregations to adapt them quite easily to their services of worship.

In honor of the man who did so much to promote this style of liturgical music, we refer to the chants as "Gregorian Chants."

Why do some Christians choose not to chant during public worship?

Many Protestants—especially those of the Calvin or Zwingli traditions (such as the Presbyterians, Baptists, and Methodists)—choose not to incorporate the chant at their Sunday morning services of worship for two reasons.

First, some feel that the chant is identified too much with the Roman Catholic service. In keeping with their Protestant heritage, they would rather speak the responses in worship than chant them.

Second, many are of the opinion that chanting is something that belongs to a bygone ara. It is not contemporary music; hence it should not be considered as a part of contemporary worship.

Other Protestant denominations disagree with this stance, however, Today, Lutherans and Anglicans, along with the Eastern Orthodox, use chants at each service of public worship on Sunday morning, as well as at other divine services such as Matins and Vespers.

Why do Christians sing hymns?

At every service of Christian worship on Sunday morning, congregations gather for the purpose of hearing the word of God and singing hymns. The word "hymn" is a Greek word meaning "song of praise of gods or heroes." The earliest mention in the New Testament of such singing is the record of the hymn sung by Jesus and his apostles immediately following the Last Supper (Matthew 26:30).

The Early Church made use of the psalms of the Jewish religion and specifically Christian hymns such as the "Magnificat" (Luke 1:46–55), "Benedictus" or "Song of Zechariah" (Luke 1:68–79), and the "Nunc Dimittis" (Luke 2:29–32). It also made use of other texts, such as those found in St. Paul's letters (e.g., Ephesians 5:14, I Timothy 3:16 and 6:15f).

It is very probable that hymns were used in the liturgy from the first. St. Paul, for example, admonishes his hearers to "sing psalms and hymns and spiritual songs with thankfulness in your hearts to God" (Colossians 3:17).

Originally, however, only the words of Holy Scripture were allowed to be set to music. One of the earliest Christian hymns is mentioned in a letter of Clement of Alexandria (150–215) entitled: "Bridle of Colts Untamed." Unfortunately, we have no record of its text or music.

Hymns set in the language of the people were not sung at public worship until some German reformers of the sixteenth century (such as Martin Luther) encouraged their use. At the same time, John Calvin (who founded the Presbyterian Church) maintained the established practice of singing only words of Holy Scripture.

A more vibrant impact of emotionally-based hymns was introduced in America through the so-called "gospel hymns" of the movement known as the "Great Awakening" that swept the American colonies during the middle of the eighteenth century and through "spirituals" sung by black slaves who were brought to the United States from Africa.

One of the more recent developments in hymn singing uses guitars and other contemporary instruments for accompaniment. Oddly enough, many of the young people who have adopted this modern expression of praise insist that all of the folk music be set only to biblical texts—a demand made by worshipers in the Early Church.

Why are "spirituals" a part of the historically black churches in America?

The unique type of hymn associated with historically black congregations in America is called a "spiritual." The spiritual is a type of expression unique to the United States which had its beginning during the pre-Civil War days when slaves on southern plantations were not allowed to gather for Sunday morning worship. Although many were converted to Christianity by local clergymen, the slaves were forbidden to assemble for worship for fear that they might use these occasions as opportunities to plan rebellions or mass escapes.

The slaves, then, expressed their praise to Almighty God by singing while working in the fields. Usually one of the slaves would intone a word of praise, and those within hearing distance would repeat it.

Often these songs expressed the feelings of frustration and loneliness of the slaves. Consequently, many reflect the sadness of the slaves' plight, comparing their status with those of the Jews who were held captive by the Egyptians.

Today, spirituals have become part of worship in nearly every Christian denomination. Songs such as "Were You There?" and "Deep River" are now sung in both historically white and historically black congregations.

Why do some hymnals have odd-shaped notes?

A rather odd style of notation appears yet today in some contemporary hymnals, especially in the Southeastern United States. The style is the result of an effort by musicians of the eighteenth and nineteenth centuries to teach the tunes of church hymns to people of limited musical training. The notes, for example, not only appeared at different levels on a music staff, but were shaped differently in order to indicate tone association.

Fa, for example, was a triangular notehead (▷); *sol* was round (◖); *la* was square (◻); and *mi* had a diamond shape (◈).

Many of America's favorite hymns, such as "What Wondrous Love" and "Amazing Grace" were preserved in this manner through the widely-used hymnal entitled: *Southern Harmony and Musical Companion* published in 1853 by William Walker, affectionately known as "Singin' Billy."

Why do Christians call the "Doxology" the "Old Hundreth"?

One of the most popular hymns in the Christian Church is the "Doxology" (a word from the Greek *doxa*, meaning "praise" and *logia*, "speech"). The text is often referred to as the "Old Hundreth," because it is based upon the words of Psalm 100:

> Make a joyful noise to the Lord, all lands!
> Serve the Lord with gladness!
> Come into his presence with singing!

Poet Thomas Ken (1637–1711) paraphrased these words into the familiar modern adaptation of the psalm:

Praise God from whom all blessings flow.
Praise him, all creatures here, below.
Praise him above ye heavenly hosts.
Praise Father, Son, and Holy Ghost.

The reference to the Trinity—Father, Son, and Holy Ghost—was added by Ken to the words of the psalm so that it might conform more to basic Christian theology.

Some contemporary hymnals still list the "Doxology" as number 100 in the book in keeping with the tradition of calling this hymn the "Old Hundreth."

Why were women once forbidden to sing in church choirs?

Prior to the twentieth century, women did not ordinarily sing in church choirs. This function was reserved for men and boys.

The prohibition against women singing in choirs was related directly to the admonition of St. Paul: "The women should keep silence in churches. . . . For it is shameful for a woman to speak in church" (I Corinthians 14:34–35).

Taking this command literally, Church hierarchies (particularly those of the Roman Catholic, Anglican, and Eastern Orthodox traditions) reserved the choir section in the church building (normally an area alongside the chancel) for men and boys, some of whom were so dedicated to serving the Church through music that they submitted to castrations in order to maintain a soprano-like quality to their singing.

In the twentieth century it generally became a common practice for women to sing in choirs in most denominations. However, it wasn't until the Second Vatican Council (called by Pope John XXIII in 1962) that the Roman Catholic Church officially permitted women to sing in church choirs.

Why do men and women sometimes sit on opposite sides of the church during public worship?

In some churches throughout Europe and the United States, the men of the congregation sit on the left side of the sanctuary and the women on the right side. It is a custom quite possibly promoted by the Early Church that had its roots in Judaism.

In the Jewish tradition dating back about 3,000 years, women were separated from men during worship in the Temple. The purpose was to separate the "pure" from the "impure." Women were considered impure during the days of their menstrual period (Leviticus 15:19–32). Men were considered impure if they suffered from certain skin diseases. Since many more women than men were considered impure at any given time, the area set aside in the Temple for the impure was commonly called the "Women's Court." As a carry-over of this tradition, some churches still separate the men from the women at worship.

In Puritan America, another justification was introduced for the separation of the sexes during Sunday morning worship. In an effort to prevent young men and women from "casting eyes of flirtation upon one another during the reading of the Sacred Scriptures," they were made to sit on opposite sides of the sanctuary.

Why do some Christians prohibit musical instruments in their worship?

Some church groups will not allow instrumental music as a part of their pattern of worship. They feel that since no instrumental music accompanied the worship of the first Christians, they should continue in this tradition. Some congregations emphasize this teaching so strongly that they incorporate this belief into their official titles. Hence, throughout the nation one may see a sign identifying a house of worship as the "United Church of Christ without Instrumental Music."

The man chiefly responsible for the modern stance of those who prohibit instrumental music in church was the sixteenth-century reformer Ulrich Zwingli. His ultraconservative approach to the Christian faith caused him to promote the concept that merriment and the "party spirit" were dangerous to the Christian, since they laid the groundwork for Satan and his angels. Music was, according to Zwingli, a product of this type of environment. Therefore, to use instrumental music, even in worship, would run contrary to the Puritan practice of abstaining from frivolity.

Some authorities suggest that the custom of excluding music from the worship is a carry-over from the Hebrew tradition of eliminating music as an expression of mourning for the destruction of the Temple in the year 70. This rationale, however, was never expressed by Zwingli as far as we know.

Why would a worshiper shout "Hallelujah!" in church?

In a fundamental Baptist church on Sunday morning it would not be unusual to hear members of the congregation interrupt the pastor's sermon with shouts of "Hallelujah!" The injections are responses by the worshipers as a sign of gratitude for the blessings from God.

"Hallelujah" (or "Alleluia") is a Hebrew word meaning "Praise the Lord." The word appears in the Bible, most often in Psalms (especially Psalms 111–117) and in the book of Revelation (19:1,3,4,6). According to Christian teaching, the word is to be used not only by God's people here on earth but also by the souls who are in heaven.

"Hallelujah" is a word used not only in nonliturgical congregations, but also in the Roman Catholic, Lutheran,

Anglican, Eastern Orthodox, and other churches that follow the historic liturgy in their worship.

The use of the word in the liturgy was initiated by Pope Gregory the Great (540–604) and was to be sung after the reading of the second lesson (the epistle for the day). This practice is still observed each Sunday in liturgical churches except during Lent when the emphasis is placed upon the suffering and death of Christ and the mood of the worshipers is more solemn. The word is sung again after sundown the Saturday before Easter; hence that day is often called "Hallelujah Saturday."

Why would one Christian hug or kiss someone during Sunday morning worship?

During a prescribed few minutes within the liturgical worship, people informally greet one another with handshakes, hugs, or kisses, while saying such things as: "The Lord be with you," or "God bless you." This gesture of affection is known as the "passing of the peace" and is designed to bring worshipers closer together as well as emphasize the fellowship Christians share with each other.

The "passing of the peace" was a standard part of public worship in the Early Church which, for one reason or another, disappeared in the middle ages. It was revived in the middle 1960s, and is now an accepted part of the worship by many Roman Catholics, Lutherans, and Anglicans.

Why would someone "walk the sawdust trail" during worship?

A person who walks to the front of a congregation in order to tell those assembled that he or she has now accepted Christ as a personal savior is often referred to as one who has "walked the sawdust trail."

The term is a product of a phenomenon in American

Church history known as the "traveling evangelist"—a preacher who travels from town to town, pitches a tent, and conducts revival services characterized by enthusiastic preaching and singing.

At most revivals, the evangelist offers an "altar call," during which those in the audience who wish may walk down the center aisle separating the rows of chairs to the front of the tent in order to relate their conversion experience to anyone who will listen. In the past, this aisle on which such persons walked was often covered with sawdust, much like an aisle found in circus tents. Consequently, those who offer similar testimony today, even in the most contemporary of church buildings, are said to "walk the sawdust trail."

Why do some Christians bring live snakes to church?

In what some consider a rather macabre way of demonstrating their faith, certain Christians who live in the Southeastern United States bring live, poisonous snakes to church. While other members of the faithful look on in stark amazement and terror, these believers allow the snakes to crawl over their bodies as a way of showing that God will protect them from all harm.

Members of the Dolly Pont Church of God in the Grasshopper community, northeast of Chattanooga, Tennessee, for example, were reported by the Associated Press in 1981 to fondle snakes, coiling them about their heads in a roped-off portion of the church during the service.

Later that same year, a participant in a snake ritual conducted at another church was bitten and, within hours, died from the snake's venom. Several of the victim's family remained with the body awaiting a miraculous resurrection, since, as one of them claimed: "God would not let one of his faithful die because of this." Their hopes vanished after 24 hours, and the body of the victim was buried.

Events such as these are not representative of common Christian practice. Most Christians shy away from fondling poisonous snakes in church for two reasons:

1. It is dangerous.
2. It is inconsistent with Christian theology.

On the second point, Dr. Raymond W. Albright, former Professor of Church History at the Episcopal Theological School in Cambridge, Massachusetts, said: "This type of demonstration, although performed by sincere souls, is actually contrary to one of the basic warnings of the Bible— 'You shall not tempt the Lord your God'" (Matthew 4:7).

Why do some women cover their heads in church?

Some Christian women will never enter a house of worship unless they have covered their heads with some sort of material. They take literally the words of St. Paul: "The head of every man is Christ, the head of a woman is her husband. . . . Any woman who prays or prophesies with her head unveiled dishonors her head—it is the same as if her head were shaven" (I Corinthians 11:3-5). The covering they wear may be a shawl which covers the entire head or it may be merely a small napkin or handkerchief used as a symbol of modesty.

Some authorities argue that the real reason behind St. Paul's words lay in the fact that some of the early converts to Christianity were not the most righteous of women. In fact, some were prostitutes who were punished by having their heads shaved. In the event that one of these women accepted Jesus as her savior, she should not be chastised because of her former way of life. Therefore, for all women, the covering was worn so that no one could identify the woman with a "checkered past." At least during the time of worship, she could escape the ridicule of her neighbors.

Why do some Christians attend worship seven times a day?

The Psalmist wrote: "Seven times a day I praise thee" (Psalm 119:164), and most sixth-century monks took this literally. The result was a practice established by St. Benedict around 530 that spread to monastic communities throughout the world. Benedict's plan was to arrange and adapt a series of specific worship services for different hours of the day, in line with the admonition of the Psalmist.

During these seven visits to church, eight services were made available (two of which—Matins and Lauds—were normally combined into one):

Matins—read at midnight or later. Meditation is on the divine word.

Lauds—at dawn when nature awakes. Praise is given to God as creator.

Prime—at the beginning of a day's work. Characterized by supplications for grace.

Terce, Sext, and *None*—at 9:00 A.M., 12:00 P.M., and 3:00 P.M. respectively. All three emphasize petitions to God.

Vespers—at the close of the day. A service of praise and thanksgiving, reviewing God's mercies.

Compline—before retirement at night. The worshipers commend themselves into the safe hands of the Lord.

In the liturgical churches, these services gradually developed into a structured manner of worship called the Divine Office, the Breviary, or the Liturgy of the Hours. It is a second public prayer of the Church (in addition to the Mass or the Lord's Supper), and each clergyman above the order of deacon is obliged to recite it daily in private or with others.

The new Liturgy of the Hours, reformed by the Second Vatican Council, has altered the traditional schema. Prime is omitted; Matins completely restructured; and the other hours slightly restructured. Matins is now called "The Order of Readings"; Lauds is "Morning Prayer"; Terce, Sext, and None are parts of "Daytime Prayer" (as "Midmorning," "Midday," and "Midafternoon"; Vespers is "Evening Prayer"; and Compline is "Night Prayer."

These worship services are generally conducted only in monasteries today, although Lauds and Vespers have become more popular in some congregations.

Why would a worshiper want to sit on an "anxious seat" during worship?

The "anxious seat" is a name given to a special bench introduced by Charles G. Finney, a lawyer-turned-preacher who lived in the 1820s during the period of history known as the "Great Revival." Finney, a Presbyterian, employed unusual dimensions in his Presbyterian church services, such as praying for sinners by name. In the front of the churches that he visited in western New York was a designated bench on which all sinners and those struggling with the problems of conversion were invited to sit. These were the "anxious ones" who awaited some sign from heaven that their prayers were answered. Hence the name "anxious seat."

Today, in some rural churches, especially in the Carolinas and surrounding states, churches of various denominations incorporate an "anxious seat" as part of their furnishings.

Why are "Jesus Festivals" a popular form of public worship?

Some people—especially teenagers—would rather worship in the outdoors at a "Jesus Festival" than attend services at one of the elaborate cathedrals of the world.

A "Jesus Festival" is the name given to a type of religious gathering that became popular in the late 1970s during which hundreds, sometimes thousands of people congregate for two or three days at an outdoor campground for one purpose—to praise the name of Jesus Christ. The atmosphere is one of zealous celebration of the new life in Christ, punctuated with emotional songs and testimonials.

The leaders of the "Jesus Festivals" are often popular evangelists whose preaching stirs the participants to greater and greater heights of enthusiasm. Yet the movement is neither the product of an evangelist nor the result of a highly organized church body. Instead, it is an outgrowth of the desire of lay people who seek a simple, sincere, and fundamental expression of their faith. In short, it is another dimension of the current trend in various walks of life to "return to the basics."

While a lot of singing and preaching is heard at a "Jesus Festival," there is little theological or philosophical debate. According to those who attend them, one of the purposes of a "Jesus Festival" is to escape from such things.

Chapter 5

Prayer and Private Worship

INTRODUCTION

"Worship" has been described as any act of communication between individuals and their God. For Christians, worship may be public—normally inside a church building along with fellow believers—or may be a private affair by which they attempt to communicate with God by word or deed those things dearest to their heart.

Public worship generally involves one hour a week in a formal setting on Sunday morning; private worship (often called "private devotions") can occur at any time or any place. For this reason, most of the Christian's worship is private.

Central to private worship for Christians is prayer—a personal conversation with God. They borrow from the traditions of both the Old and the New Testaments for their prayer life. Most Christians are quite familiar, for example, with the Psalms of David in the Old Testament. Very often children in Sunday school memorize, word for word, entire Psalms such as number 23: "The Lord is my shepherd. . . . " Christians also follow the New Testament example of Jesus who prayed often to his heavenly Father and who taught the most famous of all Christian prayers—the "Lord's Prayer" (Matthew 6:9-13).

In addition to prayer, some Christians feel that other

acts of personal expression are necessary. These expressions of devotion can involve anything from a silent, informal confession of sins, to an almost ritualistic self-abuse of the body. Some invest a significant amount of time and money in order to journey to sacred shrines in faraway lands.

This chapter is about different forms of prayer and private worship. Some of the questions and answers show striking similarities to the traditions of other religions; others reveal unique practices that may appear strange to the outsider. A few of the questions point out differences of opinion among Christians about the particulars of prayer and private worship.

Why do Christians pray?

Christians pray following the example and the injunction of Christ. Jesus lived his whole life in communion with his Father in heaven. He also specifically resorted to more fervent prayer at important occasions of his public ministry, e.g., before his baptism (Luke 3:21), on the occasion of many of his miracles (Luke 9:16), both before and after his passion (Luke 22:39-46; Luke 22:32; 23:34; 23:46).

Now seated at the right hand of God the Father, Jesus continues to pray for us (Romans 8:34; Hebrews 9:24; I John 2:1).

At the same time, Christians pray in accord with Jesus' specific exhortation for us to pray always (Luke 18:1), and: "Ask, and it will be given you; seek, and you shall find; knock, and it shall be opened to you" (Luke 11:9).

Ultimately, Christians pray to remain in touch with God. As John Cardinal Newman (1801-1890) indicated, Christians pray, because prayer is to the spiritual life what the pulse and breathing are to physical life.

Why do Christians divide prayer into four main kinds?

Christians divide prayer into four main kinds according to the purposes for which they pray:
1. to *adore* God as creator and Lord;
2. to *thank* God for his many favors;
3. to *ask* God to bestow his blessings;
4. to *atone* for sins committed against God.

Why do Christians pray in private in addition to praying in public worship?

Christians pray in private in accord with the specific words of Jesus:

> When you pray, go into your room and shut the door and pray to your Father who is in secret; and your Father who sees in secret will reward you (Matthew 6:7).

Why do Christians not always obtain what they pray for?

Christians do not always obtain what they pray for either because they have not prayed with the proper dispositions (which include devotion, humility, resignation, confidence, and perseverance), or because they have unwittingly asked for something that God sees is not for their good at that moment. In the latter case, their prayer obtains a different benefit for them from Almighty God.

Why do Christians pray "in the name of Jesus"?

Jesus told his apostles: "If you ask anything of the Father in my name, he will give it to you" (John 16:23). Thus,

Christians pray in the name of Jesus, because they believe that the promise given the apostles applies also to them.

The word "name" in New Testament times meant "character." Christians believe, consequently, that effective prayer is that which is prayed according to the "character of Jesus." It's another way of constantly praying: "Thy will be done."

Prayer in the name of Jesus is the method, also, by which most Christians witness to their faith. It is a way of saying to all who might overhear their prayers that they are, indeed, members of the Christian community.

Why do most Christians fold their hands when they pray?

Folded hands in prayer is a relatively new gesture by Christians. It was introduced in Roman Catholic monasteries and in colonial America as a way of avoiding fidgeting during long prayers intoned by the leaders of worship.

Folded hands may take the form of interlocking fingers or merely placing the palms together while pointing the fingers skyward.

In the Early Church, Christians seldom, if ever, folded hands during prayers. Instead, they turned their palms upward and held their arms raised as if to "catch the blessings from Almighty God."

Why do most Christians bow their heads in prayer?

A bowed head is a sign of humility, as when a servant would bow his head before an earthly king. In the same manner, most Christians bow their heads in reverence toward God, as the Psalmist declared: "The sacrifice acceptable to God is a broken spirit; a broken and contrite heart, O God, thou wilt not despise" (Psalm 51:17).

Why do Christians often bow or kneel before the altar in a church?

Bowing and kneeling are signs of humility and servitude. Bowing of one's head or kneeling before the altar while offering a private prayer in a church or a chapel is common practice among both Protestants and Roman Catholics.

The altar holds special significance for Christians, particularly those of the liturgical churches—Roman Catholic, Lutheran, Eastern Orthodox, and Episcopal. The altar is the place where God and the faithful meet in the exchange of gifts. God gives his people the body and blood of Christ through the Holy Communion; the people give God their gifts of prayer, praise, and thanksgiving. Hence, Christians bow or kneel before the altar as an expression of their humility before God and in grateful appreciation for the gifts of grace given them through the sacrament of Holy Communion.

Christians who believe in the Real Presence of Jesus in the Eucharist have an added reason for kneeling before an altar. They offer adoration to Jesus who is present in the tabernacle on the main altar which contains the consecrated elements of the sacrament.

Why do some Christians stand during prayer?

President Abraham Lincoln often attended New York Avenue Presbyterian Church in Washington, D.C., along with his close friend, photographer Matthew Brady. During the portion in the worship for prayer, the President stood, while the other worshipers followed the custom of the day and remained seated. The sight of the six foot, four inch

President standing while others sat was a strange sight. When one faithful church member asked him why he stood for prayer, our 16th President responded: "When my generals come into the Oval Office, they stand for their commander-in-chief. Isn't it proper, then, that I stand for *my* commander-in-chief?"

Standing is a sign of respect, just as a soldier stands to salute a flag, and a gentleman rises when a lady enters a room. Likewise, many Christians follow the insight of President Lincoln and stand out of respect for God during prayer.

Why is it customary for Christians to close their eyes during prayer?

Prayer demands complete concentration. Any disturbance can cause the mind to wander, thus breaking the communication process with God. In order to concentrate on the petitions they are offering to their heavenly Father, Christians most often close their eyes so that visual disturbances may be eliminated.

In some Roman Catholic monasteries, priests and monks have been known to pray continually for two to three days without ceasing and without ever opening their eyes, even while they were eating. After this exercise, certain monks have reported seeing visions of the saints, of the Virgin Mary, and of Christ himself.

Why do some Christians pray through saints?

Since we are sinful humans, some Christians feel that God will listen to the requests brought to him by those saints who are already in heaven before he would listen to ours. Consequently, it is not unusual for certain Christians—especially those of the Roman Catholic and Eastern Orthodox traditions—to offer prayers to God through the Virgin

Mary, one of the apostles, or any one of the hundreds of saints canonized by the Church.

The New Testament reveals that intelligent, aware beings who once lived on earth are in direct communication with God. In the Gospel of Matthew, for instance, Jesus promises his disciples that they will sit with him by judging the 12 tribes of Israel (Matthew 19:28); in Luke—in the parable of Dives and Lazarus—a dialogue is held between the occupants of heaven and hell (Luke 16:19-31); the Book of Revelation pictures the saints of God standing before the heavenly throne (Revelation 6:9).

Those who pray through saints have often testified about abundant blessings that have resulted from their prayers through the saints.

Why do some Christians refuse to pray through saints?

While Roman Catholic and Eastern Orthodox Christians often pray through saints, the bulk of Protestants feel that this practice runs contrary to their interpretation of the Bible. This was, in fact, one of the ideas emphasized by the reformers of the sixteenth century who taught the concept of the "individual priesthood of all believers." They stressed that any Christian could approach God in prayer without any intermediary. They pointed to the words of St. Paul in the New Testament: "There is one mediator between God and man, the man Christ Jesus" (I Timothy 2:5).

Why do some Christians pray the "Stations of the Cross"?

In order to note Jesus' last hours on earth, Christians—especially Roman Catholics—perform an act of private worship known as the "Stations of the Cross" during which they stop at 14 locations inside the church, each marked by a cross and each representing a specific event as Jesus walked to the place of his crucifixion on a hill called "Golgatha." At each "station" a prayer is offered. Though there are no required prayers, suggestions have been prepared by various authors.

The custom of walking the 14 stations of the cross was originated in the fifteenth century by the Friars, and was, in turn, taken up by other groups.

The 14 stations are:

1 – Jesus is Condemned to Death
2 – Jesus Carries his Cross
3 – Jesus Falls for the First Time
4 – Jesus Meets his Mother
5 – Simon of Cyrene Helps Jesus Carry his Cross
6 – Veronica Wipes the Face of Jesus
7 – Jesus Falls the Second Time
8 – The Daughters of Jerusalem Weep for Jesus
9 – Jesus Falls the Third Time
10 – Jesus is Stripped and Receives Gall to Drink
11 – Jesus is Nailed to the Cross
12 – Jesus is Raised Upon the Cross and Dies
13 – Jesus is Taken Down from the Cross
14 – Jesus is Laid in the Sepulcher.

Nowadays, Christians stress the resurrection of Jesus more than they do his death. Thus, it has become customary to conclude the Stations with a reminder of the resurrection. Some Christians even go so far as to add a fifteenth "Station"—the Resurrection.

Why do some Christians pray the "Ave Maria"?

"Ave Maria" is the Latin phrase meaning "Hail, Mary." It is an expression of praise that has its roots in the greeting voiced by the angel Gabriel to the young Virgin Mary when he told her that she would bear the Son of God: "Hail, O favored one, the Lord is with you" (Luke 1:28). The complete text of the "Ave Maria" is: "Hail, Mary, full of grace. The Lord is with thee. Blessed art thou amongst women, and blessed is the fruit of thy womb, Jesus. Holy Mary, Mother of God, pray for us sinners now and at the hour of our death. Amen."

Roman Catholics, traditionally, have included this prayer in their private devotions. However, many Protestants, including some of the sixteenth-century Reformers, prayed the "Ave Maria" throughout their lives. Even Martin Luther once praised Mary as the greatest woman who ever lived.

In the eyes of many Christians, Roman Catholics in particular, Mary is the model Christian, particularly in her faith and love. Her life consisted simply in being fully committed to God's will. Today many shrines and churches are dedicated to her honor.

Why do some Christians refuse to pray the "Ave Maria"?

Although the prayer "Ave Maria" is popular among Roman Catholics and other Christians, most Protestants refuse to include the prayer in their private worship for two reasons. First, many regard the prayer as being "too Catholic"; they feel that they do not wish to be identified in any way with the Roman Catholic Church. Second, some feel that Mary was exalted far out of proportion, especially in 1950 when Pope Pius XII declared that Mary was taken into heaven body and soul at the end of her earthy life.

Why do some Christians pray the "Rosary"?

A Rosary is a string of beads used primarily by Roman Catholics (as well as by some Episcopal and Lutheran

Christians) as an aid in offering prayers to the Virgin Mary. The Rosary contains sets (typically five or 15) consisting of one large bead followed by 10 smaller ones. In their private devotions, Christians run their fingers over the beads, using each one to mark a specific prayer. They pray the Lord's Prayer at the touch of the larger bead, then 10 "Ave Marias" with the smaller ones. A "Gloria Patri" ("Glory Be to the Father") concludes each set.

The term "Rosary" comes from the Latin *rosarius,* meaning "a garland of roses." An early European legend tells about its origin. As a monk was deeply concentrating in uttering repeated "Ave Marias," he received a vision of the Virgin Mary looking at him. As he continued to utter her praises, the Virgin seemed to gather rosebuds from his lips, one for each time he spoke her name. She then wove these rosebuds into a garland which she placed atop her head. This was the first "Rosary."

Forms of the Rosary were used as far back as the twelfth century by monks and nuns of the Church. Pope Pius V (1504–1572) established the formula for the Rosary as it is used today.

Why is the Rosary prayed for "penance"?

After Christians confess their individual sins to a priest in the Roman Catholic or Eastern Orthodox Church, they may be given instructions to pray the Rosary a certain number of times as an act of "penance."

Penance, which is viewed as a sacrament in both the Roman Catholic and the Eastern Orthodox traditions, originated as a development of the idea that repentance for sins included not only an inward feeling of contrition but also an outward act of humiliation—similar to the Old Testament manner of expressing sorrow by wearing sackcloth and sprinkling ashes over one's head.

Today, penance normally includes a more "positive"

action such as increased prayers for forgiveness and praise to God. The Rosary is but one aid in the offering of such prayers.

Why do Christians say "Amen" at the end of prayers?

Most Christians end their private and public prayers with the word "Amen." "Amen" is a word adopted by Christians from the Jews, and means "Yes!" or "So be it!" The word appears for the first time in the Bible in Numbers 5:22.

Most people of the Early Church were unable to read; in keeping with the Hebrew tradition, worshipers would listen to the leader of the service as he read an entire prayer. At its conclusion, the assembled congregation responded in unison: "Amen!"

Today, in some of the more "expressive" Protestant congregations, worshipers interject shouts of "Amen!" during the preaching of the sermon as a sign that they agree with what the preacher is saying.

Why do some Christians pray for souls in "purgatory"?

The Council of Trent (1545–1563) addressed the subject of souls in a place called "purgatory" and declared: "The Catholic Church . . . [teaches] that there is a purgatory, and that the souls detained in it are helped by the prayers of the faithful." Earlier, the Council of Florence (1438–1445) had said that those in purgatory " . . . are benefited by the suffrages [prayers of intercession] of the living faithful, namely the Sacrifice of the Mass, prayers, alms, and other works of piety."

In II Maccabees 12:46 (a book considered canonical by

the Roman Catholic Church) comes the advice: "It is therefore a holy and wholesome thought to pray for the dead that they may be loosed from sins." In the Gospel of Matthew (12:32), Jesus states: "Whoever speaks against the Holy Spirit will not be forgiven, either in this world or in the world to come." The inference here is that sins can be forgiven even after death. Since these souls are still alive and can be forgiven of sins, Roman Catholics believe that their prayers will help those in purgatory.

Why would Christians want to "confess their sins"?

A central practice among Christians is the "confession of sins"—an act of admitting that they have fallen short of the ideal Christian life through their misdeeds. Christians believe that the first step in having sins forgiven is the willingness to admit that they are sinful beings.

The Church recognizes two kinds of confession: *public* confession in which individual Christians join others gathered for worship in acknowledging that they are sinners, and *private* confession in which they articulate this fact through a prayer to God or through a conversation usually with an ordained clergyman.

Public confession is quite general, and Christians admit to having sinned against God in thought, word, and deed. Private confession, on the other hand, is much more pointed, and specific sins are revealed.

Why do some Christians avoid private confession altogether?

The confession of specific sins to another person privately, be he a member of the clergy or a lay person, is something that is foreign to many Christians who feel that they need no other human being to hear a recitation of wrongdoings.

Another objection to private confession on the part of many Protestant Christians is that this is a practice they consider solely for Roman Catholics. They object to adopting any Roman Catholic practice. This opinion continues in spite of the fact that Martin Luther and other reformers participated in and urged private confession throughout their lives.

Perhaps the greatest objection to private confession of specific sins comes from the feeling that, in spite of the clergyman's pledge to the contrary, the content of one's confession may be revealed to outsiders.

In the popular compendium, *The People's Almanac,* Michael Medued relates that once, when President John Kennedy (a Roman Catholic) entered the private confession booth, his familiar voice was recognized by the priest.

"Good evening, Mr. President," said the priest.

"Good evening, Father," answered the President, who quickly arose and walked out.

Why can Christians who confess their sins to a clergyman be confident that their secrets will not be revealed?

The best reassurance of the confidentiality of confession is the penalty a priest or a pastor would suffer if he violated a confidence. Roman Catholics teach, for example, that the priest who dares break the seal of confession directly, remains under excommunication. The same holds true for many Protestant clergymen. Pastors and priests are forbidden to mention anything that transpires in a private confession, even in a court of law.

Why do many Christians insist on three dimensions to the confession of sins?

On the surface, it may appear that the acknowledgment of sins or the state of sin to God is all that is required for forgiveness. However, many Christians believe that a meaningful confession involves three dimensions:

1. *Contrition*—a sincere remorse for the sin;
2. *Confession*—a verbalizing of the wrongdoing;
3. *Satisfaction*—atonement for the sin through prayer or good works.

Most Protestants insist upon the first two dimensions; Roman Catholics demand that satisfaction [penance] be included in confession of sins.

Why must a "mortal sin" be confessed?

In the eyes of Roman Catholics and other Christians, a mortal sin is a grievous offense against the law of God. It is an act which cuts sinners off from God's love, rejects Christ, is a detriment to their fellow humans, and a source of disruption in the universe. Such sins include: refusing to worship God; hating or seriously injuring the reputation of another; adultery; stealing; lying; drunkenness; refusing to help someone in serious need.

Since mortal sins could cause persons to fall away from their loyalty to God, Roman Catholics are strictly obliged to confess each mortal sin within a year of committing it.

Why does a clergyman offer "absolution" for sins?

Absolution is the formal action of a pastor or a priest as he pronounces forgiveness of sins by Christ to those who merit it. This authority is derived from the New Testament which announces that Christians receive the grace of forgiveness when pronounced by the clergyman as though it were given by Jesus Christ himself (Matthew 16:19-20).

Why are there different forms of absolution?

When a pastor or priest announces the forgiveness of sins, he may offer one of two forms of absolution—*indicative* or *precatory*.

Through *indicative* absolution, the sinner is forgiven by the pastor or the priest who speaks in God's stead. The words spoken are: "I absolve you of your sins."

Precatory absolution, on the other hand, is effected when a pastor or priest merely pronounces forgiveness upon those who repent. Precatory absolution can be bestowed (pronounced) upon an individual in a confession booth or to an assembled congregation.

Traditionally, Roman Catholics use the indicative form of absolution, while Protestants, who play down the position of the clergyman in this role, use the precatory form.

Why do some Christians insist on performing some form of penance for forgiven sins?

Although the nearly universal dogma of the Christian Church includes the belief that Jesus died for all sins and that specific sins, once confessed, are forgiven, some Christians feel the need for some form of retribution. They feel compelled to perform some act of personal devotion, such as reciting a specific number of prayers or doing some work of charity. They feel that the penance will impress upon them the seriousness of their sin and assist them in avoiding the temptation to commit it again.

Penance should not be regarded only as a "payment for sin." Instead, as the Right Reverend Herbert Edmondson, retired Bishop of Haiti of the Episcopal Church, says: "Penance should be a means of 'completing' the process of confession and forgiveness. I, therefore, encourage my people to conduct some sort of private devotional—such as reading Psalm 51—in response to the blessing of forgiveness they have just received."

Why do some Christians make use of indulgences?

Some Christians, especially members of the Roman Catholic Church, believe that after sins have been forgiven there still remains temporal punishment for those sins which must be remitted. The Bible gives examples of such remission (punishment): Adam and Eve were forgiven their sin, but in punishment for it were cast out of paradise. The Israelites in the wilderness who worshiped the golden calf were forgiven, but in punishment they never saw the Promised Land.

In the Early Church such punishment was remitted by public penance. In time, indulgences were substituted for this public penance. Indulgences draw on the merits of Christ and those of the saints.

In an indulgence, the Church makes use of its power as minister of Christ's redemption. It not only prays but also grants (by an authoritative intervention) to the faithful who are suitably disposed the treasury of satisfaction which Christ and the saints won for the remission of temporal punishment.

A *partial indulgence* is a release from some of the temporal punishment due to sin; a *plenary indulgence* is a remission of all such punishment.

In order to gain a plenary indulgence (total remission), one must do the work or say the prayer and fulfill the following conditions: (1) receive the sacrament of penance; (2) receive Holy Communion; (3) pray for the intentions of the Pope; and (4) be detached from sin, including venial sin.

There are also other ways of gaining partial indulgences: (1) by prayer to God; (2) by giving ourselves or our goods to others; and (3) by renouncing some permissible gratification.

Why were numbers of days or years formerly affixed to partial indulgences?

The number of days or years formerly affixed to partial indulgences meant that the punishment remitted was equal to the remission that would have been gained by doing public penance for the designated days or years. However, people came to believe that the time indicated meant time spent in purgatory. Hence, the Roman Catholic Church has eliminated all reference of time in the case of partial indulgences.

Why do some Christians object to any imposed penance for sins?

Protestants, in general, oppose any penance dictated by a pastor or a priest to an individual as a part of the confession and forgiveness of sins. This attitude was promoted by the sixteenth-century Reformers who preached that sins, once forgiven by Christ, require no further actions on our part. Martin Luther, especially, preached the concept that human beings are justified by faith, not by works.

Why do some Christians fast as a part of their private worship?

Abstinence from eating and drinking has been practiced in numerous societies as an outward sign of personal devotion toward one's God. Some Christians, also, incorporate some sort of fast—complete or partial—for a set length of time as an act of devotion.

The Christian's concept of fasting stems from the Jews who fasted during specific times such as the Day of Atonement (Leviticus 16:29, 31; 23:27, 29, 36).

Jesus engaged in fasts, but seemed to express neither strong approval nor disapproval of them. He did urge that if fasting were to be done, it should be to the glory of God rather than as a show for others (Matthew 6:16–18).

There is some evidence of fasting in the Early Church (Acts 13: 2–3; 14:23), but it seems not to have had as much emphasis then as it had with some of the more fundamental Protestant churches around the turn of the century that encouraged members to engage in prolonged fasts to the point at which some nearly died of starvation.

Why do some Christians conduct a partial fast by refusing to eat meat on Fridays?

A rather mild form of fasting for Christians began in sixteenth-century England as an act of private devotion. On Fridays, members of the Church were asked to abstain from eating meat as a gesture of grateful love for Christ who suffered and died for them.

Friday has always been a day overcast by a spiritual cloud for the Christian. It was on Friday that Jesus was crucified, died, and was buried. Consequently, some Christians consider each Friday as a memorial of that "Good Friday," just as Sunday is a memorial of the first Easter. The small sacrifice of refusing to eat meat on Friday is one way to remind believers of the supreme sacrifice made by Christ for them.

The so-called meatless Fridays were initiated by the Church in England for reasons more economic than spiritual. In 1548, during the second year of the reign of King Edward VI, with the urging of the Church, Parliament ordered all subjects to abstain from eating meat on Fridays and encouraged them to eat fish as a substitute in order to support the fishing trade.

Roman Catholics continued this practice until the early 1970s when the Church declared that this partial fast was no longer mandatory, but could be observed on a voluntary basis (except for Ash Wednesday and Fridays of Lent which are still days of abstinence from meat).

Why do some Christians begin and end their prayers with the "sign of the cross"?

Making the "sign of the cross" at the start and conclusion of prayers by Christians dates back to the second century, and was mentioned by Tertullian (160–225) who called it the "sign of the Lord." Early Christians used the sign before and after the prayers they recited upon rising in the morning and before retiring at night.

During the persecution of the Early Church by the Roman Government, fellow believers used the sign as a source of identification, by quickly touching the forehead, the breast, one shoulder, then the next. Even when noticed by a member of the Roman army, its intent was unknown to them.

Today, Roman Catholics, Eastern Orthodox, some Lutherans, and Episcopalians incorporate the sign of the cross as a regular part of their prayers. Most Protestants, however, refrain from using it.

Why is the sign of the cross sometimes made three times?

Members of the Eastern Orthodox Church, as well as some Roman Catholics, Lutherans, and Anglicans, make the sign of the cross three times as an added symbol for the

Holy Trinity—the Father, the Son, and the Holy Spirit. While making these signs, the worshiper will often verbalize the "Trinitarian invocation" by saying: "In the name of the Father [sign], and of the Son [sign], and of the Holy Spirit [sign]."

Why is the sign of the cross made with three fingers?

When making the sign of the cross during their prayers, believers normally join the thumb and the first and second fingers of their right hand together, symbolizing the three persons of the Trinity—the Father, the Son, and the Holy Spirit. The remaining fingers joined together and folded in toward the palm of the hand symbolize the two natures of Jesus—God and man.

Why do most Protestants refuse to make the sign of the cross during prayers?

Although the sign of the cross has been used by Christians since the days of the Early Church, most Protestants avoid making the sign of the cross for two reasons. First, the cross is a reminder of the cruel death of Jesus; they would rather emphasize his resurrection from the grave. Second, and perhaps more to the heart of the matter, many Protestants remain cautious about any kind of association with the Roman Catholic Church. They feel that by merely copying a tradition so strongly identified with the Roman Catholics they risk losing their distinction as Protestants.

In spite of this reluctance on the part of Protestants in the past to use the sign of the cross, a modern trend among some Protestants—especially Lutherans and Episcopalians—is to include it as they begin and end their prayers.

Why do some Christians punish their bodies as an act of private devotion?

Throughout the history of Christianity there have been stories about believers who subject themselves to physical abuse—at their own hands—as an act of penance for sins they committed. They base their practice on the claim of St. Paul:

> The desires of the flesh are against the Spirit, and the desires of the Spirit are against the flesh; for these are opposed to each other to prevent you from doing what you would (Galatians 5:17).

The most spectacular appearance of self-torture took place in Northern Europe in 1349 during the outbreak of the Black Death, when Christians beat themselves with whips and drove nails into their hands and feet (similar to the wounds that Jesus suffered during his crucifixion). They theorized that if their blood mingled with Jesus' blood, and if their bodies showed the wounds (the "stigmata") of Christ, the plague would come to an end, and their sins, indeed, would be forgiven.

Self-mortification of the body has been practiced in practically every religion known to humankind. Self-flagellation, for example, is present in the Muslim world today. Some Jews used to allow themselves to be flogged 39 times with a leather strap as they confessed their sins on Yom Kippur (the "Day of Atonement"). Although this is rarely practiced today, some Jews symbolically beat their breasts while relating their sins. Some of the more famous Christians, such as the sixteenth-century Reformer Martin Luther, are on record as having beaten their bodies to states of unconsciousness as an act of contrition.

Today, self-punishment of the body is rare, although thousands of people still gather in San Fernando in the Philippines every Good Friday to watch hundreds of young men beat themselves with whips in memory of Jesus' suffering. The ritual culminates in two men being nailed to heavy wooden crosses which they have dragged to the outskirts of town, in vivid portrayal of the crucifixion.

Why do some Christians insist on giving ten percent of their earnings to the Church as an act of private devotion?

In the Book of Genesis (28:22), Jacob vowed to give one-tenth of his earnings to the Lord were God to protect him. This was the start of a tradition called "tithing," which some Christians believe should be followed as a part of their personal expression of gratitude for the blessings they received from God. Some denominations—such as the Seventh-Day Adventists—insist that their people tithe as a condition of membership.

Christians who tithe look upon the distribution of the money in one of two ways. Some feel that ten percent of their earnings should go to the Church only. Others feel that this amount should be divided among the Church and other charitable organizations such as the United Way or the Red Cross.

Why do some Christians make use of blessings?

Christians have traditionally made use of blessings—of God, of persons, of places, and of things. By such blessings, God is praised, and earthly creatures are dedicated to his greater honor and glory while fulfilling their particular functions.

These blessings are usually done in the name of the Church. In the cases involving persons, places, or things that are blessed, they all receive honor inasmuch as they are a part of the Body of Christ on earth (the Church). The act of blessing always implies that the newly bestowed honor and glory is made possible only because of the relationship of that person or thing so honored with Christ's Church.

Why do worshipers gather for prayer at Fatima on the 13th day of each month?

The tiny Portuguese hamlet of Fatima is located about 70 miles northeast of Lisbon. It marks the place of one of the most talked-about miracles of modern day.

On May 13, 1917, three young children—Lucia (age 10), Francisco (age 8), and Jacinta (age 7), were tending sheep on a hillside just outside the village. Suddenly, they saw a flash of light, and there appeared to them "the most beautiful lady we ever saw." The children were told by the lady not to tell anyone of their vision, but to return to that spot on the 13th day of the next six months and to pray a Rosary daily for the end of the War (World War I).

On June 13, the children returned and were told by the lady in the vision that two of them (Francisco and Jacinta) would soon join her in heaven, but that Lucia would remain on earth for a while.

Jacinta could keep the secret no longer. She told some of her friends and relatives about the vision. As a result, on July 13, a large group of people awaited the children's return home, and prayed their Rosaries. By now, many of the townspeople were calling the children "liars." The lady in the vision, however, promised them a miracle in October.

On October 13, an estimated 80,000 people joined the children on the hillside in the rain and prayed their Rosaries. When a flash of light appeared, the onlookers knew the "beautiful lady" was speaking to the children, although only the youngsters could see her. The lady asked that a shrine be built there in her honor.

Soon after, the sun appeared to approach the earth with great velocity, while dashing wildly around the sky. The rain stopped instantly. The people fell to their knees in awe and wonder. The sun stopped its descent, spun three times, and headed back toward heaven. When the people looked at their previously rain-soaked, dirty clothes, they marveled at the fact that they were now clean and dry. Truly, they thought, the children were telling the truth.

Less than two years later, Francisco died; a few months later, Jacinta joined him in death, just as the beautiful lady of the vision had predicted. Lucia became a nun in 1934 and still resides in a cloistered convent of the Carmelite Order.

In response to the request of the "lady," a chapel was built in her honor on the exact spot of the vision. Today, thousands of worshipers each year visit the national shrine of Our Lady of the Rosary of Fatima at the Cova da Iria. The crowds are the largest, of course, on the 13th of each month.

The basic message of the lady to the world was to repent for sin and to pray for the conversion of Russia.

Why do the sick visit the water at Lourdes?

Each year, over three million people visit Lourdes, in France. Of these, 500,000 are sick and await a miracle. Although thousands of people have reported cures, only 63 have been verified as "miracles" by the Church.

It all began on February 11, 1858, on the outskirts of the little town of Lourdes, in the foothills of the French Pyrenees. A 14-year-old peasant girl named Bernadette Soubirous was gathering firewood with two other children when she heard a sharp noise from a grotto nearby.

"I lost all power of speech," said the girl, "and there came out of the grotto a colored cloud, and soon after a lady, young and beautiful." The lady appeared to be 16 or 17 years old.

Young Bernadette started to pray her Rosary, but her arm became paralyzed. The lady in the vision made a sign, and the paralysis went away. When Bernadette told her friends about her vision, they called her an "imbecile."

Although forbidden by her parents and legal authorities to return to the spot, Bernadette went back again and again. More visions appeared to her. During one, she was told to drink and bathe in the water. Since there was no water in the area, she dug into the gravel. A bubbling pool arose from the hole she dug, and within 24 hours became a full stream. Because of Bernadette's testimony and the presence of the water, others believed her. Of the thousands who came to the "healing waters," seven were cured of illnesses in the first year.

Bernadette Soubirous later became a nun and died in 1879. She was canonized as a saint by the Roman Catholic Church in 1933.

On August 15 (the Feast of the Assumption of Mary), 1983, Pope John Paul II visited the shrine at Lourdes, the first Supreme Pontiff to do so.

Why do some Christians refuse to pray with those who are not Christian?

Since Christians believe that all prayer should be in the name of Jesus, some feel that they should not participate in praying with non-Christians who would not use the name of Christ. In the opinion of these Christians, not only would the prayer be invalid, but also such an action might be interpreted by the outsider to the effect that there is no difference between the Christian and the non-Christian.

Most Christians, however, are not so "parochial" in their prayer life. When a non-Christian offers prayer at a public meeting, for example, they often say to themselves: "In the name of Jesus. Amen."

Why do some Christians believe that God hears only the prayers of Christians?

If a valid form of prayer for the Christian is only that which is prayed in the name of Jesus, it would follow for some that other prayers are "invalid." Some go so far as to conclude that God hears only Christian prayers, nothing else.

In early 1982, the President of the Southern Baptist Convention seemed to believe this to be the case. He drew lusty criticism from the press and even members of his own denomination when he declared that God does not hear the prayer of the Jew. Later, under pressure from a variety of sources, he tempered his remarks.

Even so, there are those Christians who would endorse his statement. As we have seen, some carry their conviction so far as to refuse to pray with anyone outside of the Christian community.

Why is the "bidding prayer" used in worship?

By the ninth century, one of the more popular forms of prayer was the so-called bidding prayer which invited the members of a congregation to offer their prayers for a series of specific causes. The feeling behind this type of prayer was that the power of prayer would be greatly enhanced were an entire group to pray at one time for a specific request. Traditionally, the prayer asks for the blessings of the Lord upon the rulers of government, for the clergy, for people of the Holy Christian Church, and for those souls who have departed this life.

During the bidding prayer, the prayer leader asks the congregation to think of a particular person or cause. The group prays silently about this subject for a moment or two. Then, the leader utters a prayer especially written for this petition. The congregation responds to each petition with an "Amen."

The bidding prayer is used most often on Good Friday, although it may be used on other occasions as well. In the Roman Catholic Mass, a slightly different form of this prayer is now obligatory as a result of a declaration by the Second Vatican Council.

Why does a clergyman sometimes offer a "secret prayer" during worship?

In some denominations, after a clergyman consecrates the bread and wine of Holy Communion, he traditionally offers a silent prayer asking for the blessing of God upon the bread and wine as well as upon those about to receive it. This prayer was first used in France in the middle of the eighth century and, until 1964, was always given in silence, thus the designation "the silent prayer," because its content was known only to the clergyman.

Today, however, it is the custom of the clergyman to recite the prayer aloud. The prayer may be one of the prescribed prayers of the Church or one that is "original."

Why do some Christians pray at fixed hours each day?

The practice of reciting prayers at fixed hours of the day or night is not uncommon among most organized religions. Christianity, too, has those who feel it necessary to establish certain times for prayer. St. Paul, for example, prayed at midnight while imprisoned (Acts 16:25), and others such as Cornelius, were described as devout people who "prayed constantly to God" (Acts 10:2). As we have seen in Chapter 4, this practice of praying at fixed hours in the Christian Church is called the "Divine Office."

The monks of Palestine, Egypt, and France were the first to organize a complete Office during the fourth century in which prayers were to be prayed at three and four hour intervals, day and night. Later, St. Benedict (480–550) arranged the Offices in fixed detail which he called *Opus Dei*, meaning "The Work of God."

As in monasteries, many Christian households set aside certain times for prayer and private meditation. This practice makes it less likely for conscientious believers to allow this dimension of their spiritual life to be sidetracked by the pressures of the day.

Why do Christians often join hands while praying with one another?

Often when Christians gather for prayer, they form a circle and join hands. While this practice is never mentioned in the Bible, it has existed in Christian communities since the ninth century. The joining of hands is a reminder that Christians are bound to each other through their faith in Christ.

Some authorities claim that this custom originated as a gesture to show everyone in the group that no one was holding a weapon, thus insuring the safety of the rest. It is the same tradition from which our custom of "shaking hands" originated, showing to the person we are meeting that we have no weapons and mean no harm.

Chapter 6

Marriage and Divorce

INTRODUCTION

The sight and sound of a "Just Married" automobile procession—horns blowing, white streamers flowing from the lead car—make people turn and look. The bride and groom may be unknown to the spectators, but everyone senses the importance of the occasion. A new "community" of two individuals is in the making.

There are many ways of viewing a marriage. The sociologist is interested in marriage as a social institution. The lawyer considers it a contract involving rights and responsibilities of people in society. The psychologist is concerned with the effect of the union upon the personal development of the couple and their future offspring. The Christian Church has its own approaches toward marriage.

Although the elements involved in the marriage ceremony are generally the same among all Christian denominations, each has special emphases. Roman Catholics, for instance, most often insist that a marriage ceremony must be conducted by an ordained priest. Protestants generally recognize any marriage performed by a legal representative of the state, be it a clergyman or a lay professional such as a judge or a justice of the peace.

Some of the traditions associated with the marriage ceremony are deeply rooted in Christian symbolism; others can be traced back to medieval pagan practices which have little to do with religion.

Marriages, unfortunately, are not made in heaven; they are contracted on earth. As humans, Christians make mistakes as do others in society, and must suffer the agony of divorce. In America, nearly 50 percent of those who promise to live together until death do them part stand on opposite sides in a divorce court. The Church has been forced to deal with this reality.

In Puritan America, divorce was an "unforgiveable sin"; it spelled doom, especially for the woman who, according to the wagging-tongued gossips, "was unable to keep a husband content." For them the Church offered very little comfort. Today, both society and the Church are reexamining their positions.

According to the traditional teaching, Christian marriages are ordained of God, to be held in honor by all, and designed to be life-long unions. In the event such a union fails, and a divorce follows, the Church responds in a variety of ways.

Most churches are much more tolerant toward divorce than were the Christians of Puritan America, and their clergymen have few reservations about conducting marriage ceremonies for divorced people who want to remarry. The Roman Catholic Church, with few exceptions, still considers marriage as a life-long commitment and refuses to endorse a second marriage for anyone who is divorced.

This chapter takes a look at some of the modern day attitudes of the Christian Church toward marriage and divorce.

Why does the Church promote premarital chastity?

The Church has always regarded premarital chastity as the Christian "ideal," not because sexual intercourse is something impure, but because it is the symbol of a permanent union between one person and a life-long partner.

The act of intercourse is regarded by nearly every Christian denomination as the fullest expression of love which should take place only when there has been a public, total commitment of one to another in a marriage ceremony.

Why are "banns" published before a wedding?

Public announcements made during feudal times in Europe were called "banns." Today, the term is used exclusively for announcements that two people purpose to enter the holy estate of matrimony. It carries the request that friends and neighbors pray for their new union.

The banns used to be posted in a public place such as the doors of the village church or on a bulletin board in front of the town hall. In modern times, these announcements usually appear in church bulletins or in local newspapers.

A typical publishing of the banns reads like this:

Mr._____and Miss_____purpose to enter the holy estate of matrimony on_____. They request your prayers on their behalf so that their marriage may be to the glory of God and in harmony with his will.

Charlemagne (742–814), often dubbed the "first Christian emperor in the West," may have been responsible for the issuance of the banns, since he ordered inquiry before all marriages in his domain in order to avoid consanguinity between the prospective bride and groom. The practice of issuing banns at least seven days before the proposed marriage was endorsed by the Synod of Westminster in 1200 and the Lateran Council of 1215.

Why do most clergymen insist on premarital counseling for couples about to be married?

In their attempt to curb the alarming rate of divorce in today's society, most Christian clergymen insist that a couple meet with them in one or more sessions for premarital counseling. Through these sessions the pastor discusses the obligations the man and woman have toward each other in their new community. Among the subjects covered in these sessions are the spiritual, financial, psychological, and sexual aspects of marriage.

Why is Jesus regarded as the third party at a Christian wedding?

The late Roman Catholic Archbishop, Fulton J. Sheen, used to stress that Jesus was the third party at a wedding—coining the phrase "three to get married." He did so to indicate that Christian marriage partakes of the mystical marriage of Christ and his Church. In the words of St. Paul:

"Husbands, love your wives, as Christ loved the church and gave himself up for her. . . . For no man ever hates his own flesh, but nourishes and cherishes it, as Christ does the Church" (Ephesians 5:25-29).

Why do Christians generally feel that marriages should be performed by an ordained clergyman?

The service of matrimony centers upon two people pledging their love and devotion to each other in the company not only of family and friends but also of God. Therefore, to the Christian bride and groom marriage is much more than a secular arrangement; it is a union for which they and their friends seek the blessings of Almighty God.

Most Protestants recognize marriages performed by any ordained clergyman. Roman Catholics insist that marriages be conducted by a priest.

Why do Roman Catholics insist that a marriage ceremony be conducted by a priest?

In the eyes of Roman Catholics, marriage is a sacrament of the Church. As such, it should be conducted by an ordained priest. In marriage, as in any other sacrament, Roman Catholics regard the priest as Christ's instrument. A wedding ceremony, therefore, conducted by someone other than a priest is not considered as "valid" in some Roman Catholic circles.

Even though in the case of marriage it is the partners who give the sacrament to one another, the presence of the priest as a witness is needed for validity, according to the law of the Roman Catholic Church.

Why is the bride "given away" by her father?

Traditionally, the clergyman asks during the wedding ceremony: "Who gives this woman to be married to this man?" The father of the bride, who has escorted her down the aisle, responds: "I, her father."

In biblical days, daughters were considered the "property" of their fathers until they became married; then they were the "property" of their husbands. Therefore, the father "gave" his daughter to the man he deemed suitable for her. Although most people would not accept this ancient concept, the tradition remains as a way for the bride to honor her father at the ceremony.

Why were brides instructed to "obey" their husbands as part of their marriage vows?

St. Paul wrote to the church in Ephesus:

Wives, be subject to your husbands, as to the Lord. For the husband is the head of the wife as Christ is the head of the church, his body, and is himself its Savior. As the church is subject to Christ, so let wives also be subject in everything to their husbands (Ephesians 5:22-24).

The tradition in the Christian home has generally endorsed the concept that the husband is the head of the household, serving as final authority on all matters. When the bride, then, chose to enter into the holy estate of matrimony, Christian pastors of past generations insisted that she understand that her role was one of submission.

Even in these modern times, many Christians accept what some refer to as a "dominant-submissive relationship." At the same time, they remain aware of the added important dimension for husbands given by Paul:

Husbands, love your wives, as Christ loved the church and gave himself up for her. . . . Husbands should love their wives as their own bodies. He who loves his wife loves himself (Ephesians 5:25-28).

While wives are subject to their husbands' authority, husbands must regard the welfare of their wives as being more important than life itself. Obedience by the wife, in the opinion of these Christians, instills a greater responsibility upon the husband.

Those who adhere to a literal interpretation of St. Paul's guidelines feel free, even today, to include the word "obey" in the wedding vows taken by the bride.

Why do most couples today prefer to eliminate the word "obey" from the marriage ceremony?

The word "obey" clearly indicates a subservient role on the part of one who makes such a promise. In modern America especially, the growing conviction on the part of both the bride and the groom is that marriage involves a partnership requiring a "give and take" attitude. The word "obey," they feel, carries with it the same chauvinistic approach encouraged by those who lived centuries ago when wives were the "property" of their husbands.

Why does the bride stand on the left side of the groom?

This tradition follows the pattern practiced in the days of old when the husband feared that his wife might be captured by enemy soldiers or former rivals.

As the bride stands at the altar, she remains at the groom's left side and she remains on the left side as the couple recesses down the aisle. In this manner, the man's right arm (his sword arm) remains free to protect her.

Why does a "best man" stand next to the groom at weddings?

Witnesses to marriages have always been a part of the ceremony. In fact, witnesses used to be present not only at the exchanging of the vows but during the consummation of the marriage as well.

Normally, the witnesses consist of a "maid (or matron) of honor" and a "best man." This unique designation of the male witness has its roots in ancient times when enemy warriors were known to capture young brides just prior to a wedding. In order to prevent this from happening to his bride, a clever groom would ask the biggest man—or the "best" man—of the community not only to be his witness but also to ward off all those with evil intent.

Why does the bride receive a wedding ring?

The wedding ring given to the bride at Christian weddings is actually a pagan tradition that has been incorporated into this religious observance. In more primitive societies, men kidnaped women from other tribes and villages for their wives and bound them with fetters around their wrists and ankles as reminders that they were now the property of their captors. Later, although this barbaric practice had ceased, a ring placed upon the finger of the bride became a symbol of the woman's submissive relationship to her new husband.

At first, the Christian Church refused to be a part of this tradition, and the use of the ring in the marriage ceremony was not permitted until the start of the ninth century.

In 800, Pope Nicholas first made reference to the contemporary Christian interpretation of wearing a wedding ring. No longer, he said, was it to be a mark of servitude, but a symbol of "the eternity, constancy, and integrity of life." As the ring is a circle, said the Pope, with no beginning and no ending, so a Christian marriage is to last for as long as the two are on the face of this earth.

Why is the wedding ring placed on the bride's left hand, third finger?

Roman and Greek anatomists believed that a vein and a nerve led straight from the heart to the third finger (the fourth finger if we count the thumb) of the left hand. This, according to the ancients, was the "healing finger" with which physicians stirred their mixtures of drugs so that any improper mixture would be made known to them "in their hearts" before being given to their patients.

The third finger, while the most prominent of all, is the weakest—unable to be stretched independently. Its use during the ceremony traditionally symbolizes that the bride's role in marriage is to be that of a servant and, thus, to work in harmony with her husband.

As late as the sixteenth century, the groom recited the Trinitarian formula as he placed the ring on the finger of his bride. He first touched the ring to the tip of the thumb with the words: "In the name of the Father . . . ," then moving it to the forefinger said: ". . . and of the Son . . . ," then to the middle finger, saying: " . . . and of the Holy Spirit." Finally, he placed it on the third finger, saying: "Amen."

Today, most grooms place the ring directly onto the third finger, left hand, with the words: "Receive this ring as a token of wedded love and faithfulness" or their equivalent.

Why do most grooms also receive wedding rings during the marriage ceremony?

In contrast to the ancient philosophy that the wedding ring reflected a subservient role by the bride in a marriage, today's Christian weddings often include an *exchange* of rings—one for the bride and one for the groom.

The groom's ring is a constant reminder to him that the marriage is one designed to last until death. It also is a statement that this marriage involves a "binding to each other" in lieu of the dominant-submissive roles endorsed earlier by the Church.

Why do brides wear wedding veils?

The bride's wedding veil is the result of a tradition borrowed from the Jews. The custom is said to be related to the incident in the Book of Genesis where Abraham's servant, Eliezer, is sent to find a wife for Isaac, and finds Rebekah. When Isaac comes to meet her for the first time, Rebekah says: "Who is the man yonder, walking in the field to meet us?" and the servant replies: "It is my master [Isaac]"(Genesis 24:65). Whereupon Rebekah takes her veil and covers herself. According to the Chief Rabbi of England, J. H. Hertz, in his commentary on the Pentateuch, Rebekah acted in line with Eastern etiquette, noting that it was not necessary to cover her face in the presence of Eliezer who was a servant.

Some authorities believe that this custom might have resulted from the Roman tradition whereby the bride wore a full-length veil, which was later used as her burial shroud.

In the Orient, a bride's veil is opaque, designed to serve as testimony that she is willing to approach the wedding ceremony blindfolded, with complete faith and trust in the man who is to become her husband.

Why is the bride's veil raised during the wedding ceremony?

The Bible tells the story of Jacob—one of the Patriarchs of the Hebrews—who fell in love with a young girl named Rachel (Genesis 29:16–20). However, according to Hebrew practice in those days, her older sister, Leah, had to marry first. Jacob, therefore, struck a pact with Laban, the father of the two sisters, to work seven years without pay in order to be given Rachel's hand in marriage.

After seven years had passed, Jacob was told by Laban that his new bride would be awaiting him in his tent after sunset. When Jacob went to his tent that evening, his bride lay in his bed in the darkest corner of the tent. The next morning, at daybreak, Jacob saw the face of his bride for the first time. It was Leah!

The story relates how he stormed after Laban, who had

cheated him out of the woman he wanted. Laban demanded that Jacob work seven more years without pay if he wished to marry Rachel. Only then would he release Rachel to him as his bride. Jacob agreed.

The lifting of the veil is a carry-over from this story. In this way, the bridegroom can be certain that the girl he chose to marry is, in fact, the girl he is marrying. This is why the bride's veil should be raised just before the exchanging of the wedding vows.

Why do the bride and groom often hold lighted candles at the wedding ceremony?

As single adults, the bride and groom were independent creatures who spent most of their time developing their individual personalities. Now that they have pledged themselves in marriage to one another, their lives are intertwined with that of their partners in wedlock. As Jesus put it: "They are no longer two but one" (Matthew 19:6).

Symbolizing this unique blending of personalities, the bride and groom often carry lighted candles that they bring to a single, unlighted candle that stands before the altar. As the words of Jesus from the Gospel of Matthew are read by the clergyman, the man and woman light the single candle with the flames of the ones they have been holding. After the new flame is lighted, the individual candles are extinguished. This is the couple's public witness that their two lives are now one.

Why do brides wear white during the wedding ceremony?

White has traditionally been the color representing purity. In the Christian Church, young girls are encouraged to remain virgins until the day they marry. White, therefore, signifies that the bride has kept herself pure for her husband.

White wedding gowns are proper, of course, for a first marriage. Women who are remarrying are usually advised by a pastor or priest to wear a dress or gown of a color other than white.

Why aren't paraments (altar hangings) changed to white for weddings?

The purpose of the liturgical colors reflected in the paraments that hang from the altar is to demonstrate the mood of the season of the Church year. (Note: See the section specifically dealing with paraments in Chapter 8.) While many feel that a particular color on the altar might better complement those of the dresses worn by the bride and her attendants, any effort to change these colors would not be in harmony with the prescribed purpose of the paraments.

Why do some clergymen ask during the wedding ceremony: "If anyone can show just cause why these two should not be joined together, let him speak now, or else forever hold his peace"?

In the days of King Arthur, adventuresome young men were selected to serve the king as knights. As part of their training, the candidates went off to wage war against the enemy. Normally this training lasted for a full year.

Prior to his departure, the candidate became engaged to a local maiden, and carried her scarf into battle as a symbol of his devotion for her. Throughout his year of training he dreamed of the day when he would return to be married.

At the marriage ceremony itself, the officiating person asked publicly if anyone could prove that the young bride had been unfaithful while her betrothed was away. If some-one responded with a "Yes," the ceremony was halted immediately. If investigation proved the accusation correct, the girl was banished from the community to live forever in shame.

Today, some ministers who include these words in the ceremony confess they do not know what they would do were some former boy friend or girl friend to come forth to challenge the ceremony. For this reason, alone, many cler-gymen have chosen to omit this question from the cere-mony.

Why do some churches prohibit the use of secular music at weddings?

A wedding conducted by a Christian clergyman in church is no less a religious service than Sunday morning worship. Consequently, some churches and clergymen are steadfast in their refusal to allow anything but religious music as a part of the ceremony. Even some of the more traditional wedding songs such as "O Promise Me" and "Because" are forbidden at the service because they give no glory to God. Instead, many pastors and priests encourage couples to choose hymns or solos more appropriate for the occasion. Among those religious songs most requested are "O Perfect Love" and "The Wedding Prayer."

Why do guests at a wedding throw rice at a couple following the ceremony?

God instructed Adam and Eve: "Be fruitful and multiply" (Genesis 1:28). This was the first command by the Creator to the world's parents. In line with this command, wedding guests toss rice at the couple as they leave a church follow-ing the wedding ceremony. In pagan times, rice and other grains were symbols of fertility. Throwing grain upon the heads of the newly married couple was a way for the guests to express their wish for a fruitful union. They believed that the fertility of the seeds might be magically transferred to the young man and woman on whom they fell.

Today, tossing rice is a way of wishing the couple a long and happy marriage as well as the blessing of many children.

Why are shoes tied to the back of the car of a bride and groom?

For centuries, shoes have served as an emblem of possession. Casting a shoe on a piece of land meant to take possession of it. Even the Psalmist has God saying: "Upon Edom I cast my shoe" (Psalm 60:8).

The passing of a shoe from one man to another concluded a transfer of property. It was the symbol that a legal procedure was completed.

In ancient times, a woman was considered chattel. When her parents "transferred" possession of her to her new husband, a shoe was given as a token of good faith that the property had properly changed hands. It indicated that the parents had relinquished all rights of dominion over their daughter who now belonged to a new master.

Shoes being dragged behind the car of the bride and groom who are leaving for their honeymoon are symbolic of this ancient gesture.

Why are weddings traditionally not conducted during "Holy Week"?

Although most Christian churches have no explicit prohibition against holding a wedding during the seven days between Palm Sunday and Easter (the period known as "Holy Week"), weddings are traditionally not performed at this time. This is a period generally set aside by Christians for serious introspection. The spirit of fun often manifested at wedding celebrations, some believe, is not appropriate during this rather somber period in the Christian calendar.

Why do many Christian Churches discourage "mixed marriages"?

Many Christian Churches discourage "mixed marriages"—i.e., marriages between people of different denominations. This attitude is most prevalent in marriages between Roman Catholics and non-Catholics, because in many cases it gives rise to grave (though not insoluble) difficulties, especially regarding the rearing of children.

In a mixed marriage a certain division is introduced into the living cell of the Church, as the Christian family is rightly termed. Thus, the fulfillment of the Gospel teachings regarding the family becomes more difficult because of deviations in matters of religion.

The Roman Catholic Church, for example, desires that its members should be able to attain perfect union of mind and full common life in their marriages. However, since human beings have the natural right to marry and beget children, the Roman Catholic Church now deals with these situations with pastoral concern.

Why does the Roman Catholic Church make special arrangements for mixed marriages?

The Roman Catholic Church recognizes the natural right of persons to marry free from any undue pressure. Thus it makes special arrangements for mixed marriages (i.e., those between a Catholic and a non-Catholic):

1. Catholics and other Christian ministers should do all they can to prepare couples for a mixed marriage.

2. The couple are urged to develop a common life of prayer in the home.

3. The couple are urged to come to an agreement before marriage about the religious education of the children—in order to avoid pressure from relatives later.

4. Both parties should provide religious values for the children.

5. The non-Catholic should be advised that the Catholic is to make the following promise: "I reaffirm my faith in Jesus Christ and, with God's help, intend to live that faith in the Catholic Church. I promise to do all in my power to share the faith I have served with our children by having them baptized and reared as Catholics."

6. The Catholic party must give consent in the presence of a Catholic priest, although the bishop can permit the ceremony to be performed by the minister of the non-Catholic party.

Why may some marriages be "annuled"?

An "annulment" of a marriage is a declaration by the Church that no marriage bond ever existed between a bride and a groom. Normally, an annulment is granted if one partner deceived the other in order to become married.

The most striking example of deception would be if one of the partners were still married at the time of the wedding, and failed to inform his bride of that fact.

The Roman Catholic Church still accepts as grounds for annulment the fact that one of the partners intended never to have any children. The reason behind this is that the Catholic Church regards procreation as one of the essential purposes of marriage. Persons who reject this purpose are actually rejecting marriage as the denomination understands it. Hence, they never really contract a sacramental (i.e., Roman Catholic) marriage.

It must be noted, however, that the Catholic Church

also allows other grounds for annulments, such as fear for one's safety and impotency.

Why do some Christians consider divorced persons as still married?

In the minds of some Christians, especially Roman Catholics, once a man or a woman takes a vow of marriage, he or she makes a life-long commitment. Therefore, a person remains married until death separates him or her from the other.

In spite of the fact that a divorced person may have completed all of the legal steps necessary for a divorce, he or she is still considered married. Remarriage by either party is totally unacceptable, and it is viewed as an adulterous relationship—a mortal sin. (See the next question for the reasoning behind this conviction.)

Most Protestants, however, would not agree with such a rigid stand. They are inclined to accept the fact that two people have agreed to terminate a marriage through the legal channels of a divorce.

Why are divorced people who remarry considered by some Christians as "living in sin"?

When a man and a woman exchange wedding vows before the altar of the Lord, they pledge to remain husband and wife for as long as they live. Jesus addressed this subject when he said: "What therefore God has joined together, let no man put asunder. . . . Whoever divorces his wife, except for unchastity, and marries another, commits adultery" (Matthew 19:6-9).

Some Christians interpret this command as absolute law, to be applied in every circumstance regardless of the situation at hand. Simply stated, they feel that divorcing one person and marrying another (except for unchastity) is the same as living in open adultery (or "living in sin").

Why did the Roman Catholic Church at one time excommunicate those who were divorced and had remarried?

Even though civil law may permit remarriage of a divorced person—Roman Catholics included—such a union is viewed by the Catholic Church as no marriage at all, but rather an adulterous relationship. If a man or a woman lives in such a "state of sin," he or she has chosen to withdraw from the fellowship of those who truly confess their sins and are repentant of them. The Catholic Church, then, felt it had no alternative but to pronounce the guilty parties "excommunicated"—i.e., withheld from receiving the sacrament of Holy Communion and removed from the other rights that flow from fellowship in the Church.

On November 10, 1977, after involved consultation with his advisors, Pope Paul VI agreed to lift the penalty of excommunication for Roman Catholics who elected to marry after obtaining a divorce.

Why does the Roman Catholic Church allow married people to separate in lieu of obtaining a divorce?

The Roman Catholic Church realizes that there are good reasons for married people not to live with one another. Since full-fledged divorce is out of the question, this denomination allows such married people to separate and live apart from one another. For all intents and purposes they live as divorced people—with the essential exception that they cannot remarry (or legitimately have sexual relations with anyone else).

Why is the attitude of the Church toward divorced persons changing today?

Society's attitude toward divorced persons has changed considerably over the past few decades. Whereas the divorced were often shunned by the remainder of the community, and failure in marriage was linked to failure as a person, modern society no longer considers divorce as the "unforgiveable sin."

Throughout this change, the Christian Church has been slow to endorse radical change in its attitude regarding divorce. The Roman Catholic Church, for example, automatically placed remarried divorced persons under the ban of "excommunication" until 1977.

Today's Church, however, appears to reflect society's changing attitudes toward the divorced through less rigid pronouncements. This new posture of concern and prayerful approach is the theme of a statement issued by the Rev. Richard P. Fenske, a Lutheran pastor, who formed the "Divorce Clinic" in Columbia, Maryland:

> The role of the Church is not to condemn people for getting a divorce, not to judge who is to blame, and not to ignore them; rather it is to be a family to those involved, and to expect them to grow by using divorce as the raw material coupled with the grace of God to develop new strengths.

Pastor Fenske's concern is shared by other Christians as well. Today's Roman Catholic Church, for instance, hosts parish committees of "Widows and Divorced Catholics" that are geared toward dealing with this complex issue. Through such committees, the Catholic Church attempts to attend to the spiritual welfare of these people and to bring them into the circle of love and concern offered by the Church.

Why do some churches still prohibit remarried divorced persons from sharing in the Holy Communion?

Bishop Cletus F. O'Donnell of Madison, Wisconsin responded to Pope Paul VI lifting the ban of excommunication for remarried divorced Catholics in 1977 by saying:

> The Church cannot recognize as valid and sacramental those second marriages after a divorce unless there has been a determination by a Church tribunal on behalf of the Church Community that the persons involved are free to marry. Lifting the burden of excommunication does not of itself permit those who have remarried after divorce to receive the sacraments of Penance or Holy Communion.

Bishop O'Donnell is not alone in this attitude. Other spokesmen for a variety of Protestant denominations declare that in order to receive Holy Communion, persons must approach the body and blood of Christ with contrite hearts, truly repentant of their sins. In the strictest sense of the word, they promise God that they will work in an honest attempt to commit their sins no more.

If Christians once made the vow to live with another until death departed them and then they forsake that vow by marrying another, they live in a "state of sin" and cannot honestly confess to God that they are attempting to change their way of life. They are, therefore, withheld from Holy Communion *for their own sake.* As St. Paul warned:

> Whoever . . . eats the bread or drinks the cup of the Lord in an unworthy manner will be guilty of profaning the body and blood of the Lord. . . . Any one who eats and drinks without discerning the body eats and drinks judgment upon himself (I Corinthians 11:27, 29).

Why are some Christians more prone to accept divorce when one of the partners is not baptized?

While Christians, in general, seldom endorse the dissolvement of any marriage, even Roman Catholics may accept the divorce and remarriage of a person who has been divorced by a partner who refused to be baptized.

This practice is called the "Pauline Privilege" and is based on St. Paul's words in First Corinthians (7:12-15). It concerns only a marriage between nonbaptized persons when one of the partners receives baptism after the marriage. If the nonbaptized person refuses to live with the baptized person, the marriage is declared dissolved—only after much investigation, however.

The underlying reason for the privilege is that the marriage of nonbaptized persons, although a valid marriage, is not on a par with the sacramental approach to marriage held by many Christians. Hence, it can be dissolved once one of the partners has become Christian and taken on a new dimension, so to speak. The purpose of invoking the "Pauline Privilege" is to make it possible for the Christian to effect a sacramental marriage.

Why do some clergymen conduct a ceremony for divorce?

Professor Robert E. Elliott of the Perkins School of Theology at Southern Methodist University is one of today's ordained clergymen who have performed a special "service of divorce" for those who wish formally to "untie" the marriage bonds that have held them together. The service is attended not only by the divorcing couple but also friends and family members. Hymns are sung, vows are exchanged, and a special blessing is given to the couple.

The "service of divorce" is certainly not an official

function of any Christian denomination. In fact, most clergymen would refuse to conduct such a service. At the same time, those who have participated in these services have reacted much like Marla Hart of San Jose, California, after she divorced her husband:

> It was as nice as getting married. When you're married, your energies are joined. This ceremony was to separate and claim back the energies. For me it was beautiful and a blessing.

Chapter 7

Festivals and Seasons

INTRODUCTION

Christians, like all human beings, are deeply affected by the rhythm of the calendar. The times and seasons have a profound influence on their business and social lives. Included in these seasons are the festivals and seasons of the Church. The familiar readings from the Bible, the hymns, national customs, legends, and family traditions associated with them combine to paint some of their most cherished memories.

That which Christians refer to as the "Church year" begins four Sundays before Christmas (December 25). This is the season of *Advent* which is a time for the believer to prepare for the coming of the Christ child into the world. *Christmas,* with all of its pageantry and gala celebration, is a time when Christians rejoice at the birth of the one whom they accept as God's Son—Jesus.

Twelve days later (January 6) is the festival of Epiphany that commemorates the visit of the Wise Men to the child Jesus.

Next comes *Lent,* the 40-day period for reflection on the suffering and death of Jesus that concludes with what many regard as the most important day for worship in the year— *Easter,* the celebration of Jesus' resurrection from the dead.

The Feast of the Ascension, observed 40 days after

Easter, recalls Jesus' departure from earth into heaven. Ten days later, the Church celebrates the divine gift of the Holy Spirit on *Pentecost.*

The last portion of the Church year, and by far the longest season, begins around the first week in June and continues to the first Sunday in Advent. This season contains the so-called *Sundays after Pentecost* (also known as *Ordinary Time—after Pentecost*) during which Christians reflect on their relationship with others and their witness to their faith through living.

Although the relationship of these seasons in the Church year to public worship is covered in Chapter 4, the questions and answers presented in this chapter address these major festivals and seasons in much more detail.

Some of these festivals and seasons, we shall note, are observed by only a segment of the Christian population; others are celebrated by nearly all Christians.

Why do Christians celebrate Advent?

Christians set aside the four-week period prior to December 25 (Christmas) as a time for preparing themselves for the coming of Jesus into this world.

The word *advent* is a Latin term meaning "coming" or "arrival." The season reflects this emphasis through two separate but related themes:

1. the coming of Christ into the world as a baby in Bethlehem;
2. the second coming of Christ into the world on the Day of Judgment.

During Advent, the Christian community shares in singing traditional hymns, such as "O Come, O Come, Emmanuel." Some congregations conduct special midweek church services to mark the season.

Originally, Advent was of undetermined length. In the

Early Church it was primarily a period of fasting and worship for those who were scheduled to be baptized on Epiphany (January 6). Centuries later, it developed into the current four-week observance.

Advent took on a somber character in the eleventh century at the urging of Pope Gregory VII. Marriages were prohibited, and joyous celebrations were kept to a minimum. Today, however, Christians reflect a joyful anticipation for the birth of the Christ child.

Why do Christians light four candles during Advent?

A growing custom among Christians is the lighting of four candles set in a wreath made of twigs from a fir tree (the traditional tree of Christmas). The wreath, called the "Advent wreath," is shaped in a perfect circle, representing the eternity of God.

The four candles mark the four Sundays of Advent which immediately precede Christmas. One of the candles is lighted on the first Sunday, and another added each week thereafter. As the light cast by the candles increases each Sunday, Christians are reminded that Christmas draws near.

The candles of the Advent wreath are given the following names:

1. *The Prophecy Candle,* a reminder of the foretelling of Jesus' birth by the Old Testament prophets.

2. *The Bethlehem Candle,* recalling the words of Micah that the Christ child would be born in Bethlehem (Micah 5:2).

3. *The Shepherds' Candle,* a reminder of the first people (shepherds) to worship the baby Jesus.

4. *The Angels' Candle,* lighted on the Sunday before Christmas in remembrance of the angel who spoke to the Virgin Mary at the conception of Jesus and of the angels who

appeared to the shepherds in the fields outside Bethlehem that first Christmas eve.

Why do Christians celebrate Christmas?

Christians around the world celebrate Christmas as the birthday of their Lord, Jesus Christ. The word "Christmas" is a contraction of the phrase "Christ's mass," i.e., a service of worship honoring the Christ child.

Why was Christmas not celebrated by Christians of the Early Church?

Christians of the first century did not celebrate the festival honoring the birth of Jesus—for the same reason they honored no other birthday anniversary. It was the feeling at that time by all Christians that the celebration of all birthdays (even the Lord's) was a custom of the pagans. In an effort to divorce themselves from all pagan practices, the early Christians refused to set aside a date marking Jesus' birth. As a result, the first celebration of Christmas by Christians did not take place until the fourth century.

Why is Christmas celebrated on December 25?

Although Christmas is celebrated on the 25th day of December each year, the exact date of Jesus' birth is unknown. Most biblical scholars agree that the birth, in fact, did not take place in December at all, but probably occurred during the spring of the year. The Gospel of Luke states that the shepherds to whom the announcement of the birth was made were watching their sheep by night (Luke 2:8) which would suggest lambing time (the spring). Only then did shepherds bother to guard their flocks around the clock. In winter, for example, the sheep would have been kept in the corral.

Why, then, the 25th of December? Actually, the date was chosen not by Christians, but by Romans, the traditional antagonists of the Early Church.

Each year as the days became noticeably shorter in November and December, the Roman citizens feared that the earth might be "dying." With the "return of the sun" at the end of December resulting in longer days, the Romans celebrated the "Feast of the *Sol Invictus*" ("Unconquerable Sun") on December 25. Bishop Liberius of Rome ordered in 354 that all Christians celebrate the birth of the Christ child on that day. Scholars believe that the bishop chose this date so that Christians, still members of an "outlaw religion" in the eyes of the Romans, could celebrate the birth of their Savior without danger of revealing their religious conviction, while their Roman neighbors celebrated another event.

Why was the celebration of Christmas once banned in the United States?

As strange as it may seem, the celebration of Christmas was once banned by, of all people, Church leaders. All joyful expression surrounding the birth of Jesus was forbidden in colonial New England owing to the influence of Oliver Cromwell and his Puritan followers who preached against, as they expressed it, "the heathen traditions surrounding this sacred event." No public observance of the season was permitted during Cromwell's reign (1649–1658) outside of possible special church services that would be conducted on Christmas eve.

It wasn't until 1856 that Christmas was made a legal holiday in Massachusetts, the last state to hold out for the philosophy of Cromwell.

Why do Christians wish each other "Merry Christmas"?

The word "merry" is an old English term meaning "blessed," as intended to be used in the famous phrase "merry old England." So, when Christians wish each other "Merry Christmas" around the 25th of December, they are, in fact, wishing their friends and neighbors a "blessed Christmas."

Why was the fir tree selected as the official Christmas tree?

The fir tree was first selected by the Germans as a symbol of Christmas, because it was a tree that symbolized the coming of the Christian faith to Germany.

St. Boniface (680–755) led Catholic missionaries from England to Germany in an attempt to bring the story of Jesus to the then pagan Germans. Boniface was so eager to rid the nation of its idolatry that on one Christmas eve "the Apostle of Germany," as he was called, cut down a sacred oak tree in the city of Geismar. This bold act only infuriated the citizens who threatened to kill the leader of the Christian missionaries.

In an attempt to pacify the crowds, and quite possibly to save his life, Boniface gave the city a fir tree as a replacement for the fallen oak as a symbol of his love for the people and of the faith he preached. Germans, to this day, regard the fir tree as a reminder of their break with pagan traditions.

Why are Christmas trees brought into homes and decorated with bright lights?

A traditional part of the celebration of Christmas throughout the world is for Christian families to bring fir trees into their homes and decorate them with multicolored lights. This custom of Christmas also began in Germany.

As just noted, the fir tree was a symbol of Christmas in Germany, but it was neither cut down nor brought into homes until the sixteenth century. The Reformer, Martin Luther, reportedly was returning home late one Christmas eve through the snow and saw a fir tree silhouetted against the starlit sky.

"What a beautiful sight," said Luther. Later, he attempted to describe the spectacle to his wife and children, but words failed him. So Luther, in his typically impulsive style, went outside, chopped down the nearest fir tree, dragged it into his house, and recreated the scene by decorating its branches with lighted candles.

Luther explained years later that the candles demonstrated the light given to the world through the birth of Jesus. The evergreen of the fir tree, he said, represented the deathlessness of the living God.

Another explanation for the origin of the decorated Christmas tree is put forth by a few observers who claim that in the Middle Ages, a religious play in Germany depicted the Garden of Eden by a fir tree. This so-called "Paradise Tree" was later used in homes. At the same time, a Christmas pyramid was used—a wooden structure with candles and other glittering decorations. In time, the two practices were combined, and the Christmas tree was said to have emerged.

Regardless of its origin, the custom of having a brightly decorated Christmas tree inside a home spread over the world as a result of sailors and merchants who visited Germany around Christmas time. In America, the first record of a Christmas tree in a home is in the December 20, 1821 diary entry of Matthew Zahn who lived in the German settlement of Lancaster, Pennsylvania.

Today, the tradition continues, as Christians decorate their homes with brightly colored balsam firs (the most popular), blue spruces, Douglas firs, or pine trees.

Why did the English Christians refuse to bring Christmas trees into their homes?

While the majority of the Christian world celebrated Christmas with a decorated and lighted Christmas tree, England was unwilling to adopt this German tradition until 1841—nearly 300 years after Martin Luther first cut down a fir tree and dragged it through the snow to his home.

One of the reasons for the delay was political. The bitter aftermath of wars between the two nations lasted far longer than the actual conflicts. (Some of this lingering hostility between England and Germany was reflected by Charles Dickens' reference to the Christmas tree as "the new German toy.") Therefore, the national customs of one country were not eagerly adopted by the other.

In 1841, however, the Prince Consort to the young Prince of Wales ordered a Christmas tree, decorated with bright lights and shiny ornaments, set up in Windsor Castle as a surprise present to the prince who was of German heritage as a nostalgic remembrance of his homeland. This single gesture broke the ice. Within a few years, brightly lit fir trees became regular parts of English family Christmas celebrations.

Why are "Chrismons" hung on trees at Christmas?

"Chrismons" are decorative symbols of the Christian faith that are hung as ornaments on a Christmas tree. One ornament might be shaped as a star, others in the form of a cross, a crown, or a fish (the first symbol used by the Church). In this manner, many Christians feel that they can better incorporate the central meaning of the season into their family celebrations.

The use of Chrismons originated in 1957 through the efforts of members of the Lutheran Church of the Ascension in Danville, Virginia. The term is a combination of the words CHRISt and MONogram.

Today, churches in practically every Christian denomination encourage their members to include Chrismons in their Christmas tree decorations as a visual witness to their faith.

Why is a star placed at the top of Christmas trees?

In many instances, a star is placed atop a Christmas tree as a symbol of the star that appeared at the time of Jesus' birth.

According to both Jewish and Eastern teachings, a new star in the heavens is a divine announcement of a mighty happening. When Jesus was born in Bethlehem, according to the New Testament, a star appeared which caused Wise Men from Persia to follow its path. "And, lo, the star which they had seen in the East went before them, till it came to rest over the place where the child was" (Matthew 2:9).

Why do wreaths hang on doors of Christian homes at Christmas?

A wreath is a symbol of Christmas that Christians hang on their front doors as an indication to all who see it that theirs is a Christian home.

The wreath is a symbol of Christmas that carries with it a message somewhat different from that shared by the other festive customs of the season. The wreath represents the crown of thorns placed on the head of Jesus by the Roman soldiers just before his crucifixion on Good Friday. The wreath is a reminder to the Christian that the purpose of the birth of Jesus into this world was to give his life for all humankind.

Lately, many Christians prefer to think of the wreath in more positive terms. They look at it as symbolic of the "crown of righteousness" and of life given to all believers on the Day of Judgment, as St. Paul indicated:

> Henceforth there is laid up for me the crown of righteousness, which the Lord, the righteous judge, will award me on that Day, and not only to me but also to all who have loved his appearing (II Timothy 4:8).

Why are Christmas wreaths often decorated with bits of holly?

During the Christmas season in many parts of the world, Christians hang wreaths (symbols of the crown of thorns worn by Jesus at his crucifixion) decorated with holly leaves and berries on their front doors as a reminder to passersby that "Christ dwells in this house."

The holly leaves are added because of a story that dates back to the first century which says that the crown of thorns worn by Jesus was mixed with holly. According to the same legend, the holly berries changed from red to white after his resurrection from the dead on Easter morning.

Why are gifts exchanged at Christmas?

The custom of exchanging Christmas gifts began long before December 25 was established as the official date of Christmas. In their celebration of the "Rebirth of the Unconquerable Sun" (known as the Feast of the *Sol Invictus*), Roman parents added to the festivities by giving presents to their children. When the Church adopted December 25 as the date for celebrating the birth of Christ, one of the reasons for this designation was to allow those who were followers of the outlawed Christian faith to observe the event without being conspicuous. Gift-giving provided a part of the cover-up. The tradition remains to this day.

Some Christians equate Christmas gifts with the presents of gold, frankincense, and myrrh which the Wise Men brought to the Christ child.

Why are poinsettias a part of Christmas decorations?

The familiar poinsettia flowers that decorate churches and homes during the Christmas season were once thought to be "imposing weeds" in Mexico where they blossom nearly everywhere. The flower was introduced to the United States by Dr. Joel R. Poinsett, the first American minister to Mexico.

The brilliant crimson leaves offered a stark contrast to the drab winter foliage in the northern parts of the nation and, in the minds of many Christians, provided a perfect symbol of the glorious birth of Jesus among the lowly citizens of this world.

Eventually, the flower became known by its popular name in honor of the man who first brought it across the Mexican border.

Why are lighted candles placed in windows at Christmas?

Aside from the beauty and warmth created by a soft glow of candles in a window, Christians use them as symbols of Christ as the "Light of the World" (John 8:12).

German storytellers describe how the Virgin Mary, accompanied by angels, crossed the countryside on Christmas eve on her way to Bethlehem. They encourage little children to place lighted candles in the windows of their homes to "light the way for the Blessed Virgin," and to indicate to all other weary travelers that this is a home in which they can find shelter if needed.

Why are candlelight services of worship conducted on Christmas eve?

One of the more popular traditions of Christmas eve is the annual candlelight service conducted in houses of worship throughout the world. Toward the conclusion of Vespers, or a more informal service of Bible reading and carol singing, the clergyman will light a large candle in front of the congregation. The large candle represents Christ. Parishioners carry small candles to the front of the church and light them one at a time. After all the candles are lit, the assembled body joins in singing the most famous of all Christmas carols, "Silent Night."

Through this gesture, the people demonstrate that Christ is the Light of the World and that light spreads throughout the land to all who receive him.

Why are songs sung at Christmas called "carols"?

The word "carol" was originally given to a popular dance of the fourteenth century. In time, dancers began to sing to the rhythm of their movements, and the term came to refer more and more to the song accompanying the dance. Such popular carols as "Deck the Halls with Boughs of Holly" and "God Rest Ye Merry, Gentlemen" are tunes that were sung with these dances.

Most of today's Christmas "carols" still reflect that lilting quality of a dance.

Why do Christians sing carols at Christmas?

Of all the customs shared by Christians at Christmas, perhaps none come as close to the heart as the carols of the season. Some of the world's most beloved music tells the story of the birth of Jesus. "Silent Night," "O Little Town of Bethlehem," and "Joy to the World" are but a few of the carols that most believers can sing from memory.

Although the music of the season was normally reserved for the litanies (musical prayers in the Mass), as early as 100 the Bishop of Rome urged his people to "sing in celebration of our Lord's birth." By the fifth century, priests annually strolled around their parishes singing the special songs of the Nativity in Latin.

Why do carolers often travel from house to house singing carols during Christmas?

The familiar sight of people walking throughout the neighborhood and singing Christmas carols is a tradition begun by St. Francis of Assisi who is sometimes called the "Father of Caroling." In 1223, Francis encouraged the people of his parish to sing while presenting their Christmas dramas in church. This was a departure from standard practice, since only ordained clergymen were permitted to sing the hymns of the season. The people were so overjoyed at this chance to sing that they took to the streets after acting out a drama and sang from house to house.

By the sixteenth century, wandering minstrels, called "waites," traveled the English towns, accompanying themselves with bagpipes, drums, and fiddles. They repeated their little "concerts" nightly from Christmas eve until the Feast of the Epiphany (January 6).

Why are bells sometimes pealed on Christmas eve?

Many churches in England and in America observe a tradition begun in medieval times of pealing church bells on Christmas eve. At midnight, the bells are tolled in a prescribed rhythm. First they are slow and mournful, announcing the death of Satan. Then, dramatically, the cadence picks up as a triumphal pealing announces the birth of the Christ child.

Why are Yule logs burned at Christmas?

The burning of a huge log in the fireplace on Christmas day is a tradition followed by many European Christians that was borrowed from the Norsemen who burned a huge oak log called the *Juul* (pronounced "Yool" or "Yule") in honor of Thor, the god of thunder. After Christianity became the accepted faith of many Norsemen, they retained this custom as a part of their Christmas celebration. Later, the Scandinavians adopted the practice and even referred to the season as the "Yule season" or "Yuletide." Lithuanians also continued the practice and they still call Christmas eve the "log evening."

The English added another dimension to the ceremony that is maintained to this day. When the Yule log is brought into the home and placed in the fireplace, a fire is started with a bit of the Yule log remaining from the year before. Before the new log is consumed by the flames, the fire is extinguished, and a portion of the log is saved as a "good luck" charm for the coming year. It is used as a "starter" for the next year's Yule log.

Why is "Christmas" sometimes abbreviated as "Xmas"?

It is not unusual to see the word "Christmas" abbreviated as "Xmas" on signs and in newspaper advertisements around the Yule season. Some Christians object to this abbreviation for the day marking the birth of Jesus. They consider it as another attempt by nonbelievers to rid Christmas of its central meaning.

The abbreviation, however, was never intended to be part of a plot for subterfuge, or even a response to America's zest for economy of words. The "X" is the first letter of the Greek word *Xristos*, meaning "Christ." "Mas" is the abbreviated form of the word "Mass." Put together, the two words mean: "worship for Christ."

Why is "Santa Claus" a part of the Christmas celebration?

"Santa Claus" has been a part of Christmas since the fourth century. The name is actually a corruption of the name of a popular saint called "Nicholas," a member of the first Church council that met at Nicaea in 325.

St. Nicholas, affectionately dubbed "Saint Nick," is the patron saint of Russia and was famed for his generosity in giving what little money he had to those who were less fortunate than he. His feast day was established by the Church as December 6. As a result, boys and girls in Russia, Holland, and Belgium received gifts on this day in his honor.

When the Dutch came to the New World, they spoke of their beloved "Santa Niklaus" to other settlers. Later, his name was contracted to the name by which he is known today throughout America, "Santa Claus," and his feast day was moved by American Christians to December 25 in order to coincide with the tradition of exchanging Christmas presents.

The present day representation of "Santa Claus" as a bearded, red-clothed, pipe-smoking, chubby benefactor is a product of the imagination of Clement Moore, a Professor of Theology at New York Theological Seminary, who wrote the poem, *The Visit of St. Nicholas*, more commonly known as *The Night Before Christmas*, first published in the Troy, New York, *Sentinel*, on December 23, 1823.

Why are stockings hung by the chimney on Christmas eve?

St. Nicholas (after whom America's "Santa Claus" is named) is said to have saved three poor sisters from slavery during the fourth century by dropping gifts of gold to them down through a chimney of the house in which they worked as domestic servants. The gold landed in a stocking one of them had hung there to dry. Hence, today, young boys and girls hang up stockings, hoping that St. Nicholas will drop down gifts for them while they sleep on Christmas eve.

Why do Christians send Christmas cards?

The annual tradition of mailing Christmas cards to friends and relatives began in 1843, in England, when Sir Henry Cole, an artist, designed a card with a Christmas theme that he had reproduced through lithography. His cards were so popular that 1,000 copies were ordered by his friends. Other artists followed suit, and, to this day, people throughout the world wish one another "Merry Christmas" via the postal service.

Many Christians use this custom as an opportunity to witness to their faith by sending or creating cards with bibilical verses relating to the Christmas story recorded in the Gospel of Luke (chapter 2).

In America, the first Christmas cards were printed by an immigrant German printer, Louis Prang, in 1875.

Why do some people celebrate 12 days of Christmas?

The familiar 12 days of Christmas, captured in the famous Christmas song of the same name, comes to us from European Christians of the sixth century. The 12 days are still observed in the homes of many northern Europeans, who believe that the time for celebration should include those 12 days between December 25 (Christmas) and January 6 (Epiphany—the day celebrating the visit of the Wise Men to the Christ child). On each of the 12 days, children of a household receive a gift, the largest and most meaningful being saved for the last day.

Why should Wise Men *not* be a part of the Christmas story?

The common portrayal of that first Christmas in Bethlehem pictures Mary, Joseph, the Baby, shepherds, and three Wise Men at the manger. But, according to the record, the Wise Men never knelt at the manger. The Gospel of Matthew reports that they came "to the house" where the Child was (Matthew 2:11). Most scholars agree that the Wise Men didn't visit the baby Jesus until one or possibly one-and-a-half years after his birth. Several facts suggest this to be the case.

There is no mention of the presence of the Wise Men in the Gospel of Luke where the night of Jesus' birth is described in great detail. What is more, in order to find their way, the Wise Men not only had to sight the new star that appeared in the heavens but also had to interpret its meaning. This would have been time-consuming, and they would have been hard-pressed to reach the manger in time for the birth. Finally, when the Wise Men reached King Herod seeking directions, Herod became so enraged at the possibility of another king arriving on the scene that he ordered all the male children two years and younger to be killed (Matthew 2:16). Had the Christ child been yet an infant, the two-year designation probably would not have been made.

The visit of the Wise Men should not be celebrated at Christmas, but at the Epiphany.

Why does January 1 mean more than just the beginning of a new year for Christians?

January 1 not only begins a new year for Christians, it is also the time for celebration of what is known as the "Feast of the Circumcision."

The Bible speaks of Jesus' parents fulfilling the Jewish law by having the baby circumcised on the eighth day of his life (Luke 2:27). According to the Christian calendar, that would fall on January 1.

The day is important, because the child was officially named during this rite. The Church, however, failed to acknowledge this date as a festival until the sixth century, chiefly because New Year's Day was associated with pagan parades and celebrations. The Church wanted no part of such rituals and did whatever it could to avoid being identified with them.

Today, in all Roman Catholic and in some Protestant churches, the Feast of the Circumcision is a regular part of the Church calendar during which Christians recall the meaning behind the name of Jesus—"God with us."

Why is the visit of the Wise Men celebrated on a day called "Epiphany"?

The visit of the Wise Men to the baby Jesus has been

celebrated by the Church since the fourth century on January 6, a day commonly called "Epiphany." The word comes from the Greek *epiphaneia*, meaning "appearance" or "manifestation." Christians regard the Wise Men's visit as a symbol that Christ was born not for one group of people only, but that he was the "Light of the World" (John 8:12). Consequently, the celebration of Epiphany is sometimes called the "Festival of Lights."

Why do some children put oats in their shoes on Epiphany?

Children in France place their shoes, filled with oats, on the doorsteps of their houses on the eve of Epiphany, so that the camels of the Wise Men may have something to eat while they are "en route to Bethlehem." The next day, they awake to find that the "Wise Men" have left gifts in their shoes.

In a somewhat similar vein, children of Spain, Mexico, and other Latin American countries place their shoes at the foot of their beds on Epiphany eve in anticipation of gifts left for them by the benevolent Wise Men.

Why is Shrove Tuesday celebrated with the Mardi Gras?

The day before the beginning of Lent is called "Shrove Tuesday," a name that comes from the old custom of confessing all one's sins (being *shriven*) prior to the season of fasting and prayer. The day is often marked with gala celebration called a "Mardi Gras," a French term meaning "fat Tuesday." The term reflects the custom of parading a fat ox through the streets of Paris on Shrove Tuesday.

The Mardi Gras is not a Church celebration in the strictest sense of the word. It was an outgrowth of an ancient Roman custom of extensive merrymaking before any period of fast. One might conclude that the Christian uses this celebration as an opportunity to have one final party before the solemn 40-day period prior to Easter.

Why do Christians observe Lent?

Many pious Christians set aside the 40 days which immediately precede Easter (excluding Sundays) as a time of personal reflection and devotion. This period is known as "Lent"—the Anglo-Saxon word for "Spring."

Jewish tradition encouraged a period of preparation for major religious observances. Since many of the early Christians were Jews, it was only natural that they set aside a season for personal reflection before the celebration of Christ's resurrection known as the "Pasch" or "Easter," the major festival of the Church year.

Because of the profound spiritual atmosphere surrounding the Lenten season, a growing number of Christian congregations from nearly every denomination add mid-week church services (usually on Wednesday evenings) as a regular part of the observance.

Why are there 40 days in Lent?

Forty-day periods of fasting commonly accompany the close encounters with God in the Bible. For example, Moses spent 40 days in fasting on Mt. Sinai prior to his receiving the Ten Commandments (Exodus 34:28). Elijah fasted for 40 days on his journey to Horeb (I Kings 19:8), as did Jesus before his temptation by Satan (Matthew 4:2). In line with this "prescription by implication," many Christians observe the 40 days prior to Easter as a season for personal devotion during which, for some, fasting of a sort is included.

The length of the season of Lent has varied down through the years. In the Early Church, it consisted of a 36-

day period of fasting. By the reign of Charlemagne, about the year 800, four days were added, making the total 40 in order to coincide with the periods of fasting endorsed by Moses, Elijah, and Jesus.

Why is the beginning of Lent called "Ash Wednesday"?

Many Christians attend special services of public worship on the first day of Lent called "Ash Wednesday." The name is the result of a tradition in which the pastor or priest burns the palm leaves which have remained from the previous year's Palm Sunday and, after blessing the ashes, uses them to mark a cross on the foreheads of the worshipers with the words: "Remember, man, that you are dust, and to dust you shall return" (Genesis 3:19). The mark is worn on the worshiper's forehead throughout the day as a symbol of their sorrow for their sins.

From biblical times the act of sprinkling oneself with ashes has been a sign of repentance for sin, especially when the sinner is bold enough to approach Almighty God in prayer. When Job, for instance, came to appreciate the holiness of God and his own state of sinfulness, he said: "I had heard of thee by the hearing of the ear, but now my eye sees thee; therefore, I despise myself and repent in dust and ashes" (Job 42:5-6).

The first day of Lent is the time when Christians demonstrate their humility before the throne of God with the mark of ashes.

Why do some Christians eat no desserts at dinner during Lent?

Many Christians use the season of Lent as a period during which they refrain from certain activities that they feel are harmful to their bodies. For some this includes eating desserts; for others it may be the consuming of alcoholic beverages or smoking of cigarettes.

This volunteer abstinence that serves as a reminder of the somber meaning of the season is a carry-over from the biblical record of 40-day fasts by some of God's people who lived on a reduced diet during this period of personal reflection and devotion.

In the past the emphasis was on giving up things for Lent or performing bodily acts of mortification. Some Christians have questioned this negative approach, choosing instead the renewed emphasis on positive piety during Lent.

Why do some Christians read their Bibles more during Lent?

In contrast to those who volunteer to abstain from one or more undesirable habits during the 40 days of preparation for Easter, some Christians prefer to use this period for a more positive course of action such as reading daily from the Bible, offering extra prayers, and performing charitable deeds.

In Washington, D.C., a growing number of Christian congressmen conduct regular Bible study groups and prayer meetings with their staff members during Lent. Some executives of America's largest business corporations hold similar sessions with their employees at this time.

Why are children given palm branches on the Sunday before Easter?

Children who attend church on the Sunday before Easter are often given cut branches from a palm tree as a reminder that the people who stood along the side of the road when Jesus rode into the city of Jerusalem on the

Sunday before his crucifixion threw palm branches on the road as they shouted: "Hosanna to the Son of David!" (Matthew 21:8-9). Hence, this day is called "Palm Sunday."

Many of the children who receive palm branches take them to their homes and drape them over a religious picture or a cross as a daily reminder of the praise given to Jesus as he rode into Jerusalem where he was to meet his death.

In some services of worship, the Roman Catholic and Lutheran as examples, palm branches are given to all participants. They are held in the hand during the reading of the Passion—as a memorial of Christ's triumphal entry and as a sign of his ultimate victory.

Why do some clergymen burn the palm branches not used on Palm Sunday?

The palm branches that are not given to the children who attend worship on Palm Sunday are often burned by the clergyman on Ash Wednesday (the first day of Lent) the following year. The ashes from the burnt branches are used to mark the foreheads of the faithful who attend special services of worship as a symbol of a sorrow for sin.

Why do Christians celebrate Maundy Thursday?

Traditionally, Christians throughout the world observe the Thursday before Easter in commemoration of the time when Jesus instituted the Lord's Supper, sometimes called the "Holy Communion." This day is called "Maundy Thursday" or "Holy Thursday."

The word "Maundy" comes from the Latin *mandatum*, meaning "commandment." On this night, Jesus gave a new command to his apostles to love one another as he had loved them (John 13:34). Also at this time, during the observance of Passover, Jesus commanded them to repeat the custom of breaking bread and drinking wine whenever they met in remembrance of him (I Corinthians 11:23-26).

Why do some Christians conduct a ritual of foot washing on Maundy Thursday?

Some denominations observe Maundy Thursday by encouraging their members to carry basins filled with water from one person to another and wash their feet. Other denominations have the celebrant of the service wash the feet of twelve parishioners. This custom stems from the report in the Gospel of John of how Jesus, just prior to the Last Supper with his disciples, washed their feet (John 13:3-11).

The washing of feet was a common practice in biblical times. Weary travelers who walked dusty roads while wearing sandles were greeted in the homes of their friends by a servant who would wash the dust from their feet. Jesus, through his gesture, demonstrated that he was about to become the servant of all humankind through his death on the cross the next night.

Why do some Christians venerate the cross on Good Friday?

In some churches, one of the parts of the Good Friday worship is the "Veneration of the Cross." This is the result of a tradition established in the fourth century when Helena, mother of Emperor Constantine the Great, was instrumental in finding what many considered the true cross on which Jesus was crucified. It became customary, thereafter, to pay special honor to this cross on each Good Friday.

In time, particles of this cross were sent to different churches so that the cross might be venerated in these locations as well. Still later, when the number of churches increased and it was impossible for pieces of the cross to be supplied for each one, the ordinary crucifix (the symbol of a cross with the crucified body of Jesus) was venerated on Good Friday. The key words of the service were spoken by the pastor or priest: "Behold the wood of the cross on which hung the salvation of the world—come let us adore."

Needless to say, the adoration was and is given not to the pieces of wood or to the crucifix itself, but to the Christ whom they symbolize.

Why are Christians usually somber on Good Friday?

Although Christians trumpet the glory of the resurrection of Jesus throughout the rest of the year, many feel compelled to meditate on the cruel death of their Savior which took place on the Friday before Easter—a day commonly called "Good Friday." In many communities worshipers attend special services—some of which are *tre ore* (three hour) observances, at which the seven statements made by Jesus while hanging on the cross are read and examined.

In some countries local customs have developed about Good Friday. In Durham, England, blacksmiths refused to shoe a horse on Good Friday, since nails are associated with the crucifixion of Jesus. In colonial America, churchgoers sometimes walked barefoot for fear that the nails in their shoes would leave marks on the ground. Today, in practically every town, no Christian schedules a festive occasion. Weddings, parties, and the like would not be considered in good taste.

Why is the Friday before Easter known as "Good" Friday?

It is strange that the anniversary of Jesus' crucifixion is called "Good" Friday. One would expect a negative adjective. The Christian teachings, however, are centered upon life, more specifically the resurrection from the dead to eternal life for Jesus and for all his followers. The sacrificial death on the cross nearly 2,000 years ago atones for sin. The term "Good Friday," therefore, evolves from the emphasis upon the good that came out of evil.

Some theologians feel that the term as we use it today is but a corruption of the designation: "*God's* Friday."

Why do Eastern Orthodox Christians call Good Friday "Great" Friday?

According to the tradition of the Eastern Orthodox Church, there was nothing much "good" about the day on which Jesus was crucified. Instead, these Christians refer to the day as "Great Friday," which places an emphasis upon the victory of God over death that will be celebrated on Easter.

Why do Eastern Orthodox young men walk around the church on Good (or Great) Friday?

On the anniversary of Jesus' crucifixion, six young men of Eastern Orthodox congregations lead the members of the parish in a procession around the church building in remembrance of Jesus' funeral on that day, and carry a flower-bedecked bier called an "epitaphios," symbolic of the burial of Jesus nearly 2,000 years ago.

Why do some school children fly kites on Good Friday?

In the early 1950s, a teacher in a private school in Bermuda demonstrated the story of Jesus' resurrection by giving each of his students a kite to fly on the last day of school before Easter (Good Friday). After each kite was set aloft, he ordered the boys and girls to let go of their kites and set them free. As the kites sailed higher and higher, he told them the story of how the Lord rose from the dead and, 40 days later, ascended to his Father in heaven.

The custom prevails to this day as Christian students in Bermuda traditionally fly kites on Good Friday as a reminder of the Easter story.

Why is the dogwood tree a symbol of Jesus' crucifixion?

According to a legend which began as early as the second century, the dogwood tree was the size of the mighty oak and other trees of the forest until the time of Jesus' crucifixion. The timber of the dogwood was so firm and strong that it was chosen for the cross of Jesus. God, then, cursed the tree so that it would never again grow large enough to be used for such a cruel purpose.

On that day, according to the same tradition, the dogwood became slender, bent, and twisted and its blossoms had two long and two short petals in the form of a cross. In the center of each petal's outer edge were nail prints, brown with rust and stained blood-red. A crown of thorns was at the flower's center to remind the faithful throughout history of the curse of the dogwood.

Why do people march in a parade in Jerusalem on Good Friday?

Each year, in memory of Christ's redemptive death,

pilgrims to the Holy Land gather to watch or to participate in a parade of people who walk the narrow alleyways of the *Via Dolorosa* ("Way of Death") from the praetorium where Jesus was tried and found guilty, to the site of his crucifixion called "Calvary." Many of the people walking this "Way of Death" carry crosses or crossbeams as did Jesus on that first Good Friday. As the faithful conclude their journey, they gather for private devotions inside the Church of the Holy Sepulchre, built on the spot where tradition holds that Jesus was nailed to the cross, died, and was buried.

Why does the Pope walk on bare feet on Good Friday?

On Good Friday the Pope publicly portrays his devotion to God by walking the distance between the Coliseum in Rome and the Forum, visiting the "stations of the cross" on the way. Before beginning his journey, the Pope removes his shoes and all other symbols of authority as an added gesture of humility which says, symbolically, that he is equal with all Christians before the throne of God.

Why is the day before Easter called "Hallelujah Saturday"?

After sundown on the day before Easter Sunday, Christians who observe the liturgical form of worship respond to the reading of the epistle for the day with a chanted "Hallelujah" or "Alleluia" (a Hebrew word meaning "Praise the Lord"). This marks the first time in over six weeks that the liturgy allows this expression to be used, for it is during the six weeks of Lent preceding Easter that the emphasis of worship is upon the suffering and death of Jesus. In this mood the response is not considered appropriate.

At sundown of the evening before Easter, the word is once again made a part of the liturgy to indicate the joyful response of the believer to the resurrection of Christ from the dead. This day, therefore, is often called "Hallelujah Saturday."

Why does the Easter Vigil Service call Adam's sin a "happy fault"?

It was St. Augustine (354–430) who first termed Adam's sin a "happy fault." He did so, thinking not of the sin itself, but of the Redeemer whom it caused God to give us. He reasoned that without this fault, Christ would not have come to this earth. The Church has picked up this theme in the traditional liturgy and extols the "fault" insofar as it brought us so great and loving a Redeemer.

Why do Christians celebrate Easter?

The most celebrated day in the Church year for the faithful is Easter—the festival which commemorates the resurrection of Jesus from the dead. Easter, then, becomes the center of all Christian theology. Christians believe that Jesus' resurrection provided proof that he was the Son of God and has given to all his followers eternal life. "As by a man came death, by a man has come also the resurrection from the dead. For as in Adam all die, so also in Christ shall all be made alive" (I Corinthians 15:21–22).

Why is the celebration of Christ's resurrection called "Easter"?

Like so many traditions and designations in the Christian Church, words used to describe events and festivals come not from religious sources, but from pagan rituals and customs. The name given to the central event of the Christian faith—Easter—is no exception.

The illustrious monk and writer of the medieval Church, the Venerable Bede (673–735), believed the term came from the name of the Teutonic goddess of spring, *Eostre*. He felt the name was chosen because of the time of year during which the feast of the resurrection is always held.

Although this explanation appears dubious to some authorities, no one is able to offer a better one.

Why is Easter so closely associated with the Jewish Passover?

"Out of suffering comes renewal; out of darkness, light." This theme is the keynote of both Easter and Passover celebrated at the same time each year by Christians and Jews respectively.

The celebration of Passover for the Jew serves as a solemn reminder that Israel was a redeemed people, for "when in time to come your son asks you, 'What does this mean?' you shall say to him, 'By strength of hand the Lord brought us out of Egypt, from the house of bondage" (Exodus 13:14).

For the Christian, Jesus offered a new freedom from death. St. Paul wrote: "Death is swallowed up in victory" (I Corinthians 15:54).

The association of Easter with Passover is amplified by the fact that Jesus was put to death on the eve of Passover. Also, the meal that Jesus observed with his disciples on that first Maundy Thursday, and which serves as the basis for the Christian's Holy Communion, was a "Seder"—the special meal which still marks the beginning of the Jewish Passover.

Both Easter and Passover are festivals of spring and, as such, celebrate the rebirth of life, a theme which carries over into the spiritual realm as well.

Why is Easter sometimes called the "Paschal Feast"?

The word "paschal" comes from the Hebrew word meaning "Passover." According to biblical teaching, Jesus rose from the dead on the first Sunday of the Passover (Mark 16:1–8).The "Paschal Feast," then, is a term given to the celebration of Easter.

In commemoration, the French refer to Easter as *Pâques.*

Why is the "Maypop" used to tell the story of Easter?

Roman Catholic missionaries were the first to use a strange looking flower called a "Maypop," that grew on vines in tropical America, to tell the story of Jesus' crucifixion and resurrection. The lobed leaves, they said, represented the hands of the Lord's tormentors; the tendrils were the whips with which he was beaten; the sepals and petals represented the ten disciples—Judas and Peter were absent; in the pistil were shapes of three nails; the five stamens recalled the five wounds; the seedpod was the sponge dipped in vinegar and offered the suffering Christ; and the fringed corona was the halo around the head of the risen Lord.

Today, this flower is still used as a symbol of Easter by residents of Florida and the South.

Why do Christians eat hard-boiled eggs on Easter?

One of the customs of Easter that has grown in popularity over the years is that of eating hard-boiled eggs during the Easter season. Pope Paul V once even acknowledged this tradition in his official Easter prayer when he said: " . . .

eating it [the egg] in thankfulness to you, on account of the resurrection of our Lord." At the same time, the symbol of the egg generated not from Christian observances, but from pagan rituals.

From earliest times, the egg has been a symbol of fertility and immortality. During the rites of spring, the pagan nations included it as a symbol of celebration for the new life promised during the season of planting. The Church only took this ancient sign and applied it as a visual lesson to the resurrection of Christ.

The Easter egg tradition gets its share of "press" each year through the annual custom of children rolling brightly colored eggs down the lawn of the White House. This annual event began during the term of James Madison (1809–1817) at the urging of his wife, Dolley.

Why are Easter eggs colored or painted?

The tradition of painting Easter eggs with bright colors has its origin in a legend that Simon of Cyrene, the man who carried the cross of Jesus to Calvary, was an egg merchant. According to the story, when he returned from the site of the crucifixion, he discovered that all of the eggs in his produce basket had miraculously turned into a variety of colors, adorned with drawings.

Although this may be a delightful tale which developed into an enjoyable practice, there is neither biblical nor sound oral tradition to substantiate it.

Why is the "Easter Bunny" a part of the Easter celebration?

Like the egg, the rabbit has been a symbol of fertility, the observance of which was a part of the Anglo-Saxon mythology and the pagan's celebration of spring.

In a blend of Christian and pagan traditions, the rabbit was adopted as a part of the festival of Jesus' resurrection celebrated during the spring each year.

The custom of a rabbit (or Easter Bunny) leaving colored eggs in the baskets of children who had been good over the past year was brought to America by German immigrants in the late nineteenth century.

Why is a lily the official Easter flower?

The lily, a tall, fragrant plant with long pointed leaves, is the worldwide symbol of Easter because of its shape resembling a trumpet that heralds the resurrection of Jesus.

There are many kinds of Easter lilies. Among the most popular is the Bermuda Easter lily, which blooms early in the season. Chinese and Japanese lilies bloom outdoors normally in June or July, both kinds can be forced to bloom in hothouses in time for Easter.

Why is the picture of a butterfly a part of Easter decorations?

In many Christian churches on Easter morning hang banners with a picture of a butterfly—a symbol of Jesus' resurrection from the dead.

As any school child knows, butterflies have a humble beginning as worm-like caterpillars. While inside their protective cocoons, these creatures are anything but attractive. However, they emerge in time as beautiful butterflies, full of brilliant colors.

The miracle of change is akin to the transformation of Jesus from Good Friday to Easter. A broken body sealed in a grave gave way to the glorified body of the risen Lord.

Why are hot cross buns served on Easter?

During the spring equinox, ancient tribes sought the favor of the gods for a bountiful yield from their newly-planted crop by sacrificing an ox (called a *boun* [thus our word "bun"] by the Saxons). After the ritual, the participants celebrated by eating cakes marked on the top with a symbol of the ox horns. The symbol divided the cakes into four equal parts, thereby making it easy to be divided equally for distribution.

The leaders of the Early Church adapted this custom into their celebration of Easter, with the symbol of the ox horns being now taken as a sign of the cross on which Jesus died.

Later, some believers thought the buns carried magical powers and brought at least one of them into their homes in an attempt to ward off evil spirits. Fishermen sometimes carried one on their boats long after the Easter celebration as a precaution against shipwreck.

Why does Easter appear on different dates each year?

The Council of Nicaea in 325 set the celebration of Jesus' resurrection as the first Sunday after the first full moon following the vernal equinox (March 21). The earliest possible date of Easter is March 22; the latest, April 25.

The dates of Easter for the years 1984–2000 are:

1984 - April 22
1985 - April 7
1986 - March 30
1987 - April 19
1988 - April 3
1989 - March 26
1990 - April 15

1991 - March 31
1992 - April 19
1993 - April 11
1994 - April 3
1995 - April 16
1996 - April 7
1997 - March 30
1998 - April 12
1999 - April 4
2000 - April 23

The dates of Easter, then, become the basis for the dates of the movable feasts of the liturgical year.

Why do Eastern Orthodox Christians often celebrate Easter one week later than most others?

Although most Christians celebrate Easter on the date designated by the Council of Nicaea, the members of the Eastern Orthodox faith observe the festival of Jesus' resurrection one week later on most occasions.

The difference of opinion stems from 1582 when Pope Gregory XIII attempted to upgrade the Julian Calendar that had been worked out by Julius Caesar in 46 B.C. The Julian Calendar was 11 minutes, 14 seconds longer than the solar year, but yearly corrections were not made. By 1580 this difference had totaled 10 days. Pope Gregory tried to rectify this situation by dropping 10 days from the calendar and thereafter adding one day every four years in order to put the calendar on track with what he regarded as the "clock of the universe."

Gregory's calendar, however, failed to consider the relationship of Easter with the Jewish Passover. Since Jesus rose from the dead on the day following Passover, the Eastern Orthodox Church felt that Easter should always follow Passover. Therefore, when the Easter of the Gre-

gorian Calendar falls before Passover, the Eastern Orthodox Church refuses to fall in line with the majority of
Christendom and celebrates the festival of Jesus' resurrection on the following Sunday.

Why do some Christians have their homes blessed during the Easter Season?

Christians have places blessed as a reminder that God is
present in them and they can be of help in the attainment of
salvation. Blessed places have Christ present in them in a
way that is more "grace-laden" than his usual presence in
creation, according to many Christians.

Houses are blessed during the Easter Season because it
is the time of Christ's triumph—a time of Christian joy.
Christians want that triumph and joy to be brought even
closer to the buildings that are closest to them—their
homes.

Why are special worship services conducted on March 25?

March 25 marks the Feast of the Annunciation of the
Lord. On this day, the Archangel Gabriel announced to a
young Jewish girl named Mary that she had found favor with
God and would bear his Son. In the pronouncement to
Mary, the angel instructed that the child be named "Jesus."

When Mary questioned how this could be done since
she was a virgin, the angel replied:

> The Holy Spirit will come upon you, and the
> power of the Most High will overshadow you;
> therefore the child to be born will be called holy,
> the Son of God (Luke 1:35).

The celebration of this special event first took place in

the Church around the year 450, and is observed primarily by Roman Catholics, Lutherans, Anglicans, and Eastern Orthodox Christians.

Why do Christians celebrate Ascension Day?

According to the New Testament, 40 days after Easter Jesus gathered his disciples around him and told them that he must leave and join his Father in heaven. As the disciples were wondering what he meant, Jesus disappeared into a cloud (Acts 1:6–11). Christians believe that Jesus ascended into heaven at this point with the promise to return to the earth on the Day of Judgment.

The importance of Ascension Day varies within Christendom. It is not a popular festival among most Protestant churches; in fact, it's almost forgotten in most denominations. Generally speaking, only those who follow the liturgical year (Lutherans, Eastern Orthodox, Roman Catholics, and Anglicans) stress this event. Roman Catholics consider this day so important that it is a day of "obligation" for participation at public worship.

Why do Christians celebrate Pentecost?

Pentecost is a Greek word meaning "the holiday of fifty days." Fifty days after Easter, Jesus' disciples and a large band of followers gathered to hear St. Peter tell the story of the Lord's resurrection and ascension into heaven. As Peter was preaching, the sound of a mighty wind filled the house; tongues of fire appeared on the heads of the disciples; people from various nations began speaking in strange tongues; and, according to Christian belief, the Holy Spirit was given to the Church. As a result of this phenomenon, 3,000 people were reported converted on that day (Acts 2:1–13). This gift of the Holy Spirit to the Church was the fulfillment of the promise made by Jesus before his ascension: "I will not leave you desolate" (John 14:18).

Like Easter, this festival has been a part of the Church from the very beginning. American Christians, however, tend to regard it as a minor festival, while many Europeans consider it of greater importance than Easter. As a result, attendance at public worship on Pentecost in Europe is higher than at any other time of the year.

Why is Pentecost also called "Whitsunday"?

It is customary in some Christian circles to conduct baptisms on Pentecost in remembrance of the 3,000 who were converted during the first Pentecost. This tradition reaches back to the second or third century when candidates for baptism wore long white robes symbolizing the forgiveness of their sins by God. Consequently, the observance became known as "White Sunday," later shortened to "Whitsunday."

Such European nations as Germany and the Scandinavian countries still continue this practice of scheduling the majority of the year's baptisms for this day, and the festival of Pentecost is often accompanied by family gatherings.

In the Virgin Islands, the day following Pentecost, "Whitmonday," is a legal holiday.

Why is Pentecost called the "Birthday of the Church"?

Christians believe that the gift of the Holy Spirit upon the assembled group who gathered to hear the message by St. Peter was the sign from God that this band of the faithful was now "empowered" to carry out its task of spreading the Gospel of Jesus to the world. With this power came the beginning (or birthday) of what is known today as the Holy Christian Church.

Why do some Christians hang wind chimes outside their homes on Pentecost?

A tradition growing in popularity in the United States involves the hanging of wind chimes outside the entrance of a Christian home. The ringing of the chimes reminds the family that even as the invisible wind is real, so also is the invisible spirit of God which moves over the earth.

Why are confirmations often held on Pentecost?

In many Christian denominations, young people attend instructional classes in the basic teachings of the Church. After they have reached the "age of accountability" (about 14 years old) and have successfully completed approximately two years of study, they receive the rite or sacrament of confirmation, and are made members of that particular denomination. Many Christians feel that the spirit of confirmation parallels closely the significance of the first Pentecost when 3,000 people were converted; thus they schedule their confirmations for that day.

Why is Reformation Day observed in most Protestant churches?

Reformation Day is the anniversary of Martin Luther's posting of the famous 95 theses on the door of All Saints' Church in Wittenberg, Germany, on October 31, 1517. Historians agree that this one act sparked the beginning of the period known as the Reformation.

Until quite recently, many Protestant clergymen used this day as an opportunity to condemn the practices of the Roman Catholic Church. Today, however, a fresh spirit prevails in which Protestant pastors emphasize a more positive note of furthering cooperation among all Christians. Some go so far as to invite Roman Catholic priests into their pulpits to speak to their congregations about the common bond shared by all Christians who believe in Christ.

Why is November 1 especially meaningful to those who have lost a loved one through death?

The Church has set aside one day—November 1—in memory of those who have died in the faith during the year past. On this day the faithful recall the lives of those whom they had loved who have been united with God in heaven. This day is called, appropriately, "All Saints' Day."

Originally, May 13 was selected by the Early Church as the day to remember the departed. When Pope Gregory III (d. 741) dedicated a chapel in the basilica of St. Peter to "all the saints" on November 1, one year prior to his death, he unilaterally established that date as "All Saints' Day."

Why is the night before All Saints' Day known as "Halloween"?

As early as the eighth century, the people of England believed that the souls of the dead left their graves on the night before All Saints' Day and roamed the countryside. No one would walk outside on that night unless he or she wore some sort of grotesque mask in order to frighten away the evil spirits. If any of these brave people dared to walk amid the spirits and remained unharmed, it meant that this person was in league with the supernatural forces. Consequently, were that person to go to a house and ask for food, the homeowner had better not refuse, else the spirits would play a "trick" on him or her. To this day, children of various nations wear masks and travel from house to house on this evening demanding: "Trick or treat."

The night when all the spirits wandered the countryside was the holy or "hallowed" evening. Later, this was shortened to "Halloween."

Why is Thanksgiving Day an "unofficial festival" in the liturgical year?

Although Thanksgiving Day is not an historical part of the liturgical year, America's Christians conduct special services of public worship on this last Thursday in November as a day for giving thanks to God for blessings received.

The observance began when settlers in the New World who survived the winter of 1620 celebrated their first successful harvest in Plymouth, Massachusetts, with Chief Massasoit and nearly 100 braves of his Wampanoag tribe.

The nation as a whole did not observe a special day of Thanksgiving again until November 26, 1789, when President George Washington set aside this one day to celebrate "the great degree of tranquility, union, and plenty which we have enjoyed."

Thanksgiving did not become an annual celebration until Abraham Lincoln in 1863 officially proclaimed the last Thursday in November as "a day of thanksgiving and praise to our beneficent Father." President Lincoln, then, was the first to add this religious dimension to the day.

Ever since President Lincoln's proclamation, American Christians annually give thanks for their blessings of the past year through special services, hymns, and sermons.

Why do Christian churches end the liturgical year with the Feast of Christ the King?

In 1925, Pope Pius XI designated the Sunday before the Feast of All Saints as the day for honoring Christ the King. Thus the kingship of Christ over the hearts of all people becomes a fitting conclusion to the mystery of life of Christ commemorated during the year.

The assigned lessons for this Sunday make it clear that the kingship which is addressed is one that is spiritual, not political, for Christians believe that Christ's kingship is one of love, justice, and peace within the hearts of all believers. (In the reformed liturgical calendar, the Roman Catholic Church has assigned this feast to the last Sunday before Advent.)

Chapter 8

Holy Objects and Symbols

INTRODUCTION

A Christian can worship God at any time and in any place. Unlike some of the other religions of the world, the Christian faith requires no physical object before prayer or public worship can begin. At the same time, the dynamics of Christian worship almost demand some sort of symbolism. An altar, a cross, vestments, and stained-glass windows are but a few possibilities. With few exceptions, Christian churches contain standard objects, symbolic of the beliefs of those who gather for formal services on Sunday morning.

The holy objects and symbols of the Christian faith not only serve to create an atmosphere conducive to public worship but also are treasured as aids to private devotion. Hence, the pious Christian woman may carry a set of beads called a "Rosary" in her purse, and her teenage daughter may wear a small gold cross from a chain around her neck.

The questions and answers in this chapter reveal reasons why some church buildings are constructed as they are; they explain the origin of some of the Christian's most familiar symbols. Not all of these holy objects had their origins in religious circles; some have direct connections with pagan worship. A few, in fact, are of no longer any practical use, yet Christians still hold fast to most of them.

They are, after all, objects of affection which Christians have associated with their worship.

Some of the symbolism presented in this chapter may be peculiar to one denomination exclusively. For the most part, however, the objects and symbols discussed here are those which are accepted by the majority of Christians throughout the world.

Why do churches have steeples?

Though perhaps not so readily appreciated in today's crowded cities, steeples in churches have traditionally had three important functions. First, they house the bells that ring on Sunday mornings reminding the faithful that worship is about to begin. When most people lived in small villages, the bells had to be positioned high enough over other buildings of the village so that the sound would carry. Second, a steeple points to heaven, the focus of every believer. Third, a steeple that towers over other buildings always marks the site of the church, so that even a stranger visiting the town on a Sunday morning would have no trouble finding a house of worship.

Why are bells rung before a church service?

One of the more familiar sounds in most cities throughout the world on Sunday morning is the ringing of bells from inside steeples of Christian churches at the start of public worship. This custom, like so many others in the Christian Church, grew out of pagan superstition.

People once thought that agents of Satan were always poised to tempt God's children. Since popular belief held that evil spirits vanished at the sound of sharp noises, bells were rung before church services in order to rid the building of demons, so that Christians might worship in peace.

Egbert, the eighth-century Archbishop of York, composed a blessing of church bells which contains a reference to this superstition:

> Wherever this bell sounds, let the power of enemies retreat, so also the shadow of phantoms, the assault of whirlwinds, the stroke of lightning, the harm of thunders, and every spirit of the storm winds.

Why are church bells often rung *one hour* before the beginning of worship?

In pre-Reformation Germany, church bells were rung one hour before the start of worship to alert the people to prepare themselves for Mass. This gave worshipers an opportunity to offer preparatory prayers that would put them in the proper frame of mind for the divine service.

This custom prevails in some small villages in America where the bells are sounded not so much to initiate spiritual preparation as to remind the people to dress and get ready for worship that will begin in one hour.

Why are bells sometimes rung *after* church services?

In eighteenth-century England, bells were often rung at the conclusion of the sermon or immediately after the benediction, a custom still observed in some of the more affluent communities of Great Britain. The practice began for a very practical reason. It warned the cooks in the surrounding mansions that the lords and ladies were about to leave church. The servants knew they had better hurry in order to prepare the meal, so that it might come out of the oven at the moment the owners arrived home. This particular tolling, therefore, came to be known as the "pudding bell."

Why are bells tolled for funerals?

The custom of tolling the church bell whenever a member of the particular parish died began in sixteenth-century Germany. The bell was rung one time for each year the deceased lived on earth, thereby informing the townspeople of the age of the departed and, at the same time, summoning their prayers for the person's soul. Since the people of the small German hamlets knew their neighbors so well, it was not difficult for them to discern for whom the bells tolled.

The ringing of the "passing bells," as they were called, were also meant to drive away any evil spirits that might hover over the dying person, ready to pounce on the soul before it left the body.

Why were bells not rung to announce services in the Early Church?

Christians of the Early Church used neither bells nor any other form of audible announcement that worship services were to begin for fear that they would be punished or killed.

Christianity was an illegal religion in the eyes of pagan authorities of different countries for the first five centuries following the resurrection of Jesus. Those caught conducting Christian worship were often severely punished. Therefore, those who dared to worship never "broadcast" the fact with anything such as loud bells; instead, they gathered clandestinely in secret meeting places.

Why do some people kiss religious objects?

Before the start of a church service, devout Christians may kiss their prayer book; at the same time, the officiating clergyman may kiss the stole before placing it around his neck and shoulders. Such Christians are expressing their devotion for the holy object and that for which it stands.

In the Bible, the kiss was a popular symbol of reverence and devotion, not just a romantic expression between a man and a woman. Esau kissed his brother Jacob after a long absence; Aaron kissed his brother Moses; Samuel kissed King Saul; Orpah kissed Naomi, her mother-in-law. In order to fake his loyalty, Judas identified Jesus to the Roman guards by approaching him in the Garden of Gethsemane and kissing him.

This sign of reverence for religious objects can be seen in places other than church. During his Presidential inauguration, for instance, George Washington bent over and kissed the Bible after taking the oath of office, beginning a tradition that has been observed by most of the Presidents who followed him.

Why are relics an aid to worship for some Christians?

Relics are the physical remains (bones or locks of hair) of deceased saints of the Church, or sacred objects with which they came in contact while on earth (e.g., a ring, some clothing, or a handwritten letter). Relics are considered by some Christians to carry with them special blessings and benefits to those who possess or even view them.

In a document entitled *Martyrium Polycarpi* ("The Martyrdom of Polycarp") written in the year 156, the relics of St. Polycarp were described as "more valuable than precious stones and finer than refined gold." Yet the importance of relics became a source of debate in the Early Church. St. Jerome (342–420) warned that the veneration of relics was getting out of hand, and that some people should remember, instead, the Lord for whom the martyrs died.

In spite of Jerome's warning, people still coveted these

relics associated with heroes of the past. History is filled with accounts of soldiers who, in the name of Christ, fought in wars for the sole purpose of bringing to Europe relics from the Holy Land.

During the sixteenth century, the Council of Trent ruled that because the bodies of saints were to be considered temples of the Holy Spirit, the physical remains of their bodies and objects which they touched were not only to be revered but might even be sources for miracles for those who held or viewed them.

Why do some Christians discount the authenticity of certain relics?

By the very nature of the case, authenticity with regard to relics is very difficult to establish with certainty. This is especially true when the relics concern elements stemming from the earliest days of the Church.

Because of the immense fervor associated with them, purported relics have been offered for sale by charlatans who discovered this to be a fast way to make money. Even today, visitors to Jerusalem are warned about those who would sell them portions of the cross on which Jesus was crucified or of the manger in which the infant Jesus was placed on the first Christmas.

One scientist computed that were all the fragments of the "original manger" of Jesus gathered into one spot, there would be enough wood to build a good-sized barn.

Why are relics placed in altars in some churches?

In most altars of the Roman Catholic Church (as well as some of the Lutheran, Episcopal, and Eastern Orthodox churches), is placed a small bit of a bone from one of the saints of the Church. This serves as a reminder to the worshipers of the origin of altars.

At the center of every worship in the Early Church was an altar—a carry-over from the Hebrew use of a special table on which the lamb was sacrificed for the redemption of sins. Worship in the Early Church was almost always conducted in secret, mainly because Christianity was an "outlaw religion." Anyone found worshiping Jesus as Lord was subject to persecution by the Roman government. Therefore, many of the first services of worship were conducted in the catacombs that contained the burial sites of the martyrs who gave their lives for the faith. Their tombs served as the first altars.

Placing a relic in the altar of a church continues this tradition.

Why do some churches have several altars?

The practice of placing several altars in a Christian church, considered by some to be a carry-over of the pagan custom of building "many altars to many deities," is in reality a continuation of the custom of the Early Church of celebrating Mass on the actual tombs of the apostles and martyrs of the faith.

When Christians met for worship in the catacombs— the underground vaults where the dead were buried—the tombs of the departed were scattered throughout each catacomb. In light of this tradition, therefore, in parishes located in major metropolitan areas, such as New York City or Chicago, it is not uncommon to visit a cathedral with several altars, each containing a relic of a saint.

Why do altars have rails around them?

Surrounding most altars in liturgical churches is a railing that separates the chancel—the elevated area on which the altar sits—from the main part of the sanctuary. The rail serves as a barrier to those who approach the altar. The presence of the rail says, in effect: "This is as far as you are permitted to go."

In earlier times, only ordained priests could enter the area between the railing and the altar. This practice is still promoted by the Eastern Orthodox Church. Most Protestant churches have no restrictions, however. Since the Second Vatican Council in 1962, lay people (both men and women) have been allowed in the chancel area in the Roman Catholic Church.

Contemporary liturgists have called for a return to the atmosphere of worship found in the Early Church in which there was no sharp cleavage between ministers at the altar and others in the assembly. This is in keeping with the renewed emphasis on the fact that it is the entire congregation that has gathered for worship—although each member, whether minister or other participant, does so in a way proper to each.

Why were altar rails removed from churches in colonial America?

Puritans in England and in colonial America disliked the use of the altar rail, since they felt that it set the altar apart as something extra sacred. To many of them, this seemed "too Catholic." Consequently, they removed them from their houses of worship. That is why many Protestants to this day have not only abolished altar rails but also downplayed the importance of the altar. While liturgical churches—Roman Catholic, Lutheran, Episcopal, Eastern Orthodox, and others who follow the historic liturgy—have a large altar at the center of the worship area, many Protestant churches use, instead, a small table which is symbolic of the altar, without appearing to be the focal point of worship.

Why is a sanctuary lamp kept burning above the altar?

Many churches—both liturgical and nonliturgical—keep a candle surrounded by glass burning above the altar. This light is supposed never to go out. Before one candle is completely burned, another is lighted from the wick. Its presence signifies that Jesus is the "Light of the World" that never fades (John 8:12).

As already noted, some churches such as the Roman Catholic, have a sanctuary lamp before the tabernacle on the altar to indicate that the consecrated hosts for the Holy Communion are present. It is another reminder of the Catholic teaching that the real body and blood of Jesus are present in the bread and wine.

Why are different colors used on altars at various times of the year?

In keeping with the various themes and seasons of the liturgical year, certain congregatons—primarily those of the Roman Catholic, Lutheran, Episcopal, and Eastern Orthodox Christians—change the colors of the paraments (the altar hangings, pulpit and lectern falls, and stoles which hang around the clergyman's shoulders) to reflect the various emphases of the liturgical seasons. The colors used are violet (or dark blue), white, red, green, and black. Each marks a specific mood for a season:

Violet (or dark blue) is used during Advent and Lent, symbolizing both repentance and the belief that Christ entered this world as King of kings. Its royal color reminds

Christians of the promised victory over eternal death. For this reason, some churches choose to use this color during a specific service for the dead.

White marks the major festivals—Christmas, Epiphany, and Easter. It is the symbol for the purity of the Lord and of his forgiven Christians.

Red is used on days commemorating an apostle (especially a martyred apostle), or a saint, and on All Saints' Day (some churches use white on this day). On those occasions it symbolizes blood shed for the sake of the faith. On Pentecost, it symbolizes the fire that appeared on the heads of the disciples 50 days after Easter (Acts 2:3). Red is also used to designate church anniversaries and national holidays such as Thanksgiving, although some churches prefer to use white for these celebrations.

Green is the color of life. It reflects the emphasis on the "Christian life" on the Sundays between Pentecost and Advent.

Black is used by many congregations for Good Friday and for a "day of humiliation" such as a day of national mourning (caused by an assassination of a President or a declaration of war). It may also be used in services for the dead, although white or violet have become much more popular on these occasions. On Good Friday, red may also be used.

Why are rose-colored paraments sometimes used in Advent and Lent?

In some churches, rose-colored paraments are substituted for violet on the Third Sunday of Advent and the Fourth Sunday of Lent—injecting a note of joy at the halfway point in both seasons in anticipation of Christ's coming and his victory. As a result, the Fourth Sunday of Lent has become widely known as "Rose Sunday."

Why are black paraments not used by many liturgical churches today?

The use of black paraments for Good Friday or for a day of humiliation is not as popular as it once was. Instead, violet or dark blue is often substituted, since many worshipers feel that this color adds a more positive mood to the specific day or season which is in keeping with the emphasis of the Church on Christ's victory over all things.

Why are paraments on the altar changed on the *evening before* the start of a new season in the liturgical year?

The proper time to change the liturgical colors in a church is at sundown on the eve of a particular day or season of the liturgical year. This practice is in keeping with both the Hebrew and the Christian tradition which encourages the celebration of a particular day or event to begin at sundown of the previous day. The Jewish Sabbath, for example, begins at sunset on Friday, and Christmas for Christians begins at sundown on December 24.

Why do so many church altars face east?

St. Thomas à Kempis (1380-1471), the German ecclesiastic and writer, once said that certain Christian practices were "infinitely older than the Church everywhere." Many of today's Christian customs reflect the saint's insight, as we can trace their roots back to pagan rituals.

One such influence of pagan cults was the belief that the source of all life was from the east. Just as the rising of the sun announces new life for the day, so the basis for all life comes from the east. It is not surprising, therefore, that the Early Church predicted that the final judgment would come out of the east. As a sign that the Church was prepared for the second coming of Christ, altars were set in the east wing of the building so that when the faithful prayed, they would face in the direction of the coming of the Lord. Thus, they would be prepared to meet God face-to-face.

Today, the Eastern Church of Greece, as an example, insists that all altars stand in the east of the church. In America, however, this practice is far too impractical, considering the relatively small portions of land on which church buildings must be erected that dictate the architectural designs.

Why do altars have tabernacles?

The word "tabernacle" is derived from the Latin *tabernaculum,* meaning "a temporary shelter or a hut." The tabernacle was the movable tent shrine transported by the Hebrews during their 40 years of wandering in the wilderness.

On the altar of many Christian churches (and on one altar of *every* Roman Catholic church) is a tabernacle—a small compartment that houses consecrated bread which, according to the belief of some Christians, is the body of Christ.

Why do many altars have curtains behind them?

The special curtain that sometimes hangs behind altars is a carry-over from the Hebrew tradition of veiling the "Holy of Holies" from the rest of the Temple. This practice was first mentioned in Exodus (40:21) when Moses brought the ark of the covenant containing the Ten Commandments into the Tabernacle, and set up a curtain in order to screen the ark from the people.

Since the presence of Almighty God is so overwhelming, the Holy of Holies, in which God's spirit dwelled with all of its might and power, had to be shielded from the people.

Although Christian churches do not have a "Holy of Holies" as such, this link with the Hebrew tradition remains.

Why are candles lighted during the service of worship?

With rare exception, candles are always a part of Christian services of public worship. Candles generally are placed on or alongside the altar. Just prior to the beginning of worship, they are lighted by an assistant (usually a teenage boy or girl) called an "acolyte" (from the Greek *akolouthos*, meaning "follower" or "disciple").

Among the Jews and pagans the use of lights had long been regarded as appropriate when people rendered public homage to God or gods. For example, the Book of Esther (8:16) describes a celebration with "light and gladness and joy" commemorating Esther's victory over Haman.

Very probably lights were first used by Christians simply to dispel darkness when the sacred mysteries were customarily celebrated before dawn or in the darkness of the catacombs. It wasn't long, however, before the early theologians recognized the beautiful symbolism of the use of lights.

Light has many qualities that can be applied to God and therefore can easily serve as a symbol for the divinity. It is pure, penetrates darkness, moves with astonishing speed, nourishes life, and illumines everything it touches. It can remind us of the One who is all-pure, all-powerful, vivifier of all things, and the source of all grace and enlightenment.

Furthermore, Christ himself stated: "I am the light of the world; he who follows me will not walk in darkness, but will have the light of life" (John 8:12).

Hence light represents Jesus who came to enlighten

"those who sit in darkness and in the shadow of death" (Luke 1:79). At the same time, the flame of a candle symbolizes love by its warmth and cheerfulness. And as the candle consumes itself in giving light and service to human beings, it inculcates in us a sign of sacrifice and sacrificial love.

Why should altar candles be made of beeswax?

Altar candles are made of a variety of substances, not unlike household candles. Some churches even incorporate electronic "candles" with flickering lights representing flames.

According to tradition, candles used in public worship should be made of beeswax, a substance symbolizing the pure flesh of Jesus while he lived on earth. One ancient writer stated: "The wax, being spotless, represents Christ's most spotless body; the wick enclosed in it is an image of his soul, while the glowing flame typifies the divine nature united with the human in one divine person."

Why are candles normally placed alongside the altar in groups of seven?

Since the candles on or alongside the altar in a Christian church represent the light of Christ, the number seven becomes most appropriate in view of the pattern established in the Bible.

Christians believe that the number seven represents God in both the Old and the New Testament. The seventh day was the one on which God rested from his creation (Genesis 2:2); it was subsequently set aside by Jews as the day of worship. Joshua marched around Jericho seven times as a sign that the power of the Lord would cause the walls of the city to tumble (Joshua 6:1ff). In the book of Revelation, whenever God speaks, his words are accompanied with seven trumpets played by seven angels (Revelation 8:1ff).

Why are the two large candles on top of some altars not lighted during worship?

In many churches, seven candles on each side of the altar are always lighted prior to public worship. At the same time, the two larger candles sitting atop the altar are lighted only when Holy Communion is celebrated.

Although the order for Christian worship known as the "Liturgy" or the "Mass" calls for the offering of Holy Communion at each service of public worship, some churches (especially those of Protestant denominations) elect to offer the "Sacrament of the Altar" only once a month. Only then are the two large candles on top of the altar lighted, signifying that something "extra" is taking place that day.

The only exception to this rule would be if the two candles on top of the altar were the only candles present in church. Then, the candles would be lit for every service as an indication that Christ is the "Light of the World."

Why do some churches have golden domes above the altar?

Anyone visiting an Eastern Orthodox house of worship for the first time notices the huge dome in the ceiling above the altar. The dome is always painted gold, symbolizing the glories of heaven. Near this traditional dome often appears an engraving inscribed with the motto: "Standing in the temple of your glory, we think we stand in heaven."

Why is holy water sometimes sprinkled on people during worship?

The practice of sprinkling holy (or blessed) water on

people, altars, and other objects of blessing dates back to the ninth century. It is symbolic of the blessings of God that are spilled out upon people and objects of worship.

The term given this ritual is "asperges," taken from a chant based on Psalm 51 in Latin: *Asperges me, Domine* ("Sprinkle me, Lord"). As this prayer is chanted, a priest or pastor swings a container called an "aspergillum" or "aspersorium," which lets out tiny droplets that fall on the people and holy objects. The "aspergillum," however, is hardly ever used in modern times and, for the most part, has been eliminated from official Protestant celebrations. It is still used in Roman Catholic worship and has seen a resurgence in the new liturgy as decreed by the Second Vatican Council.

Why is holy water used in some churches?

"Holy water" is the term given to water that has been blessed for specific religious purposes. Holy water is nothing more than common tap water to which a pinch of salt has been added and over which a blessing has been pronounced.

"Blessed water" is placed at the entrances to many Christian churches in a "holy water stoup." Upon entering the church, the worshipers place their hand in the water and make the sign of the cross on their body as a symbol of making themselves spiritually clean before entering the house of the Lord.

Holy water is a symbol of cleansing, and is used at blessings, dedications, funerals, exorcisms, and "asperges."

Why is salt added to water to make it holy?

From the days of the ancient pagans, salt has been a symbol of purity. Historians reveal how the pagans put salt on the lips of infants in order to chase away evil spirits from their tiny bodies. Salt was carried as a symbol of incorruptibility over into the Hebrew and Christian traditions. It was used in the sacrificial offerings of the Jews to God (Leviticus 2:13); the covenant between God and Israel made at Mt. Sinai was called the "covenant of salt" (Numbers 18:19).

In the New Testament, Jesus said to his followers: "You are the salt of the earth" (Matthew 5:13).

Salt, therefore, carries with it the symbol of the eternal link between God and his people.

In effecting holy water, the Church combines water and salt because of their natural symbolic meanings. Water is known to cleanse and to put out fire; salt preserves from decay. Hence, holy water helps wash away the stains of sin, quenches the fire of passions, and preserves us from relapsing into sin.

Why is incense burned in some churches?

Incense is a granulated aromatic resin, obtained from certain trees in Eastern and tropical countries, especially those of the terebinth family. When it is sprinkled upon a glowing coal, it burns freely and produces an abundant white smoke of very fragrant odor.

The burning of incense has been a tradition in many religions—including Judaism and Christianity. In Old Testament times, incense was burned simply to mask unpleasant odors resulting from the sacrifice of animals, or those from a body lying in state before a funeral. At times, incense was burned as an independent offering of divine worship.

Christians were slow to include incense in their worship, since its burning was associated with pagan worship. During the persecutions of the Early Church, Christians were often compelled to demonstrate their loyalty to the emperor by burning incense before his image. Those who assented were deemed traitors by their fellow believers.

Once paganism had disappeared from the scene, the Church gradually adopted the practice of using incense (as early as the fifth century). By the tenth century, its use became common in conjunction with the blessing of altars and crosses used in a church. Pope Innocent III (elected in 1179) even saw some exorcistic value to incense.

Today, most Roman Catholic, Eastern Orthodox, Episcopal, and some Lutheran congregations burn incense from a container called a "censer" as a regular part of their worship. By its burning, incense symbolizes the zeal that should animate the faithful; by its sweet fragrance, the odor of Christian virtue; and by its rising smoke, the ascent of prayer before the throne of the Almighty as well as an offering acceptable to God.

What is more, the incense creates an aroma totally different from what a person would encounter elsewhere.

The unique sounds of church music, the pageantry of the service, and the smell of incense all contribute to making the service of worship different from any other experience in the Christian's life.

Why are the letters "XC" used in church?

The first and last letter of the Greek word *Christos* (meaning "Christ") resemble the English letters "X" and "C." Hence, this symbol represents the "Christ," which is to say the "Anointed One."

Why are the letters "IC" often seen in church?

The letters "I" and "C" are the capital letters in the Greek word *Iesous*, meaning "Jesus"

Why are the letters "INRI" inscribed on crosses and altar hangings?

The "INRI" symbol is a collection of the first letters of the Latin words: *Iesus Nazarenus Rex Iudaeorum,* translated: "Jesus of Nazareth, king of the Jews." These are the words that Pontius Pilate ordered written and to be placed over the head of Jesus as he hung on the cross on that first Good Friday (John 19:19). While Pilate may have interpreted the expression as one of mockery, Christians proudly display it as a sign of victory.

Why is the symbol "☧" part of altar hangings?

This strange looking symbol is a combination of the first two letters of the Greek word for "Christ"—*Christos* (pronounced Chris-tós). The first two letters—the "Chi" and the "Rho" are shaped like the English "X" and "P." They often become parts of altar hangings, stoles, and banners that serve as aids to worship for Christians in practically every denomination.

Why are the three letters "IHS" often misinterpreted by Christians?

People sometimes mistake the three letters "IHS" to represent the first letters of the popular phrase: "In His Service." The letters, however, were never designed to represent this or any other expression in English. Instead they stand for the first three letters of the Greek name for Jesus that resembles the English capital letters "IHS."

This monogram is sometimes thought to be the initial letters of "*Jesus Hominum Salvator,*" a Latin phrase meaning "Jesus, Savior of Human Beings."

Why is the shepherd's staff a symbol for Jesus?

Jesus said to his desciples: "I am the good shepherd. The good shepherd lays down his life for the sheep" (John 10:11). As a reminder of this eternal promise of Christ, the shepherd's staff is a common symbol in today's Christian houses of worship.

Why was the fish the first symbol of the Christian Church?

The first symbol of the Christian church was not a cross; this was a sign of death. Instead, it was a fish—something which had a much more positive significance.

During the early days of the Church, when Christians were severely persecuted, it was dangerous for the faithful to speak with one another in public about Jesus for fear that an enemy might overhear their conversation. So, they used a secret symbol for purposes of identifying who among them were Christians—the symbol of a fish.

The symbol was chosen because of the Greek word for fish—*ichthus*—the letters of which represent the first letters in the words of the Greek phrase which means: "*Jesus Christ, Son of God, Savior.*"

The fish was a rather natural symbol to be used because of its close connection with Christianity. Not only were Jesus' first disciples fishermen, but Jesus told St. Peter and St. Andrew to be "fishers of men" (Mark 1:17).

In ancient times, the symbol was etched in the sand in front of a house at which a worship would be conducted that day. Today, many Christians wear the symbol of the fish on the lapels of coats or on collars as an expression of identification as followers of Christ.

Why is the dove a reminder of the Holy Spirit?

Throughout the Bible, the dove is a symbol of the Spirit

of God. During the Great Flood, the dove was a sign that God had completed his destruction by water (Genesis 8:8ff). Each of the four Gospels records the Spirit of God descending *like a dove* from heaven at the baptism of Jesus (Matthew 3:16, Mark 1:10, Luke 3:22, and John 1:32).

In most European churches and in some American congregations, little children release doves from the front doors of their parishes as a symbol of this Spirit of God that covers the earth.

Why is the sand dollar a popular Christian symbol?

One of the most widely known and popular of all shells that tourists find on the Florida beaches is the sand dollar. Some contend that upon close examination, it tells the story of Christ's suffering and glory.

Legend has it that the five holes in the sand dollar shell represent the five wounds of Jesus resulting from his crucifixion on Good Friday. The Easter lily on the front of the sand dollar and the five-pointed star at its center represent the Star of Bethlehem. On the back is the shape of a Christmas poinsettia, symbolic of Christ's birthday. Inside the shell are five fragments representing the doves of peace and goodwill.

The sand dollar cross has become a favorite gift within the Christian community and can be worn as jewelry.

Why has violet or blue replaced the black stole worn by a priest or pastor at a funeral?

Until recently, a pastor or a priest who conducted a funeral of a Christian wore a black stole around his neck and shoulders, symbolic of a mood of mourning. Many clergymen, however, feel that black is not in harmony with the fundamental Christian teaching that through death the believer in Christ enters eternal life. They claim that such a display of mourning is in direct contradiction to the "good news" of the Holy Gospel. Therefore, one of the directives stemming from the Second Vatican Council issued in 1972 was to replace the black stole with violet or blue, symbolic of the victory of Jesus over death.

Black is still available for use as a liturgical color, but it is now generally reserved for Good Friday and for days of humiliation that might be brought on by such calamities as famine, assassination, or declaration of war.

Why are some church buildings consecrated?

When a house of worship is consecrated, the building can never be used for secular purposes. This is different from a typical blessing or dedication. When something is consecrated, it is set apart, exclusively, for the service of God.

Church buildings are not the only things consecrated. The bread and wine used during the sacrament of Holy Communion are consecrated; altars and other ecclesiastical aids to worship are consecrated; cemeteries for the departed faithful are consecrated; even people—such as bishops—are consecrated.

The act of consecrating something exclusively for God's use is, in the eyes of the Church, irrevocable. In most denominations, only a bishop can officiate at a consecration.

Why are some churches dedicated, not consecrated?

While some churches are consecrated—i.e., set apart for continual sacred use, never to be employed for secular purposes—other churches may be "dedicated." Dedication sets apart for sacred purposes a church that may be a temporary structure of a building for which the eternal fate cannot be guaranteed.

The earliest record we have of a dedication of a church building dates back to the year 314, when the cathedral of Tyre was set apart for worship.

The ritual of dedication normally includes six steps:

1. blessing the outside of the church;
2. blessing the middle of the church;
3. blessing the altar;
4. consecrating the altar;
5. procession of relics;
6. blessing of the altar vessels and ornaments.

The service of dedication is followed, generally, by an order for public worship.

Why are church benches called "pews"?

Our designation for the long seats that appear in so many churches comes from the French *puie*, meaning a "raised place." The term originated in the Latin word *podium*, which was a front balcony in an amphitheater reserved for royalty and prominent families. In colonial America, this tradition was continued, and certain sections were boxed off for families of stature so that they would be able to worship in public without being seen by others. These were the "pews." Later, when closed-in areas were eliminated in recognition of the fact that all people were equal before God, the term "pews" came to be applied to all the benches in a church.

Why are so many church doors painted red?

The tradition of painting church doors red—the color of the sacrificial blood of Jesus—came out of colonial America. It serves as a reminder to all who enter that, through the suffering and death of Christ, Christians have been granted forgiveness.

Why do most churches have peaked ceilings?

A rather long-standing tradition within the Christian Church is to construct houses of worship with ceilings that followed the peaked angles of a normal roof. The tradition is a carry-over from the first centers of worship shared by the faithful of the Early Church.

At its beginning, Christianity was an outlawed religion. In order to conduct worship in secret, for fear of punishment, many of the believers met under large boats that were overturned along the seashore. Today's modern architecture sometimes attempts to capture this scene by "recreating" the look of an inverted ship's hull. This led one architect to conclude: "If you turned most churches upside down, they would float."

The main part of the church sanctuary is often called the "nave"—the Latin word for "ship"—as a result.

Later, the Church carried the symbolism of the nave a bit further with the analogy that the Church is the ship which takes the faithful on their voyage to the port of salvation.

Why is the "narthex" a part of most churches?

The "narthex" is the name given to the hallway between the outside door of the church building and the sanctuary. The narthex was used in the Early Church as a place where the catechumens—those who were taking instruction in the Christian faith—would stand while the service of worship was conducted for the baptized. The sanctuary was only meant for baptized believers. Although potential converts no longer stand there during public worship, the narthex remains a part of most church buildings.

Why is the area of worship in a church called a "sanctuary"?

The main area of the Church in which the faithful gather for worship on Sunday mornings is called a "sanctuary"—a word that comes from the Latin *sanctuarium*, meaning "a consecrated area." The sanctuary was a place reserved in the Early Church for the baptized believers; those who were not baptized were required to remain outside the consecrated area during the liturgy.

Why do some churches have a "crucifix" hanging in front?

Some denominations emphasize the suffering and death of Jesus with a visual reminder called a "crucifix"—a cross with the body of Christ hanging by the nails in his hands and feet. These Christians believe that this one act was the supreme sacrifice made for all people.

Traditionally, the Roman Catholic Church has displayed the crucifix in its sanctuaries. The "open cross" is more common among Protestant circles.

Why do some churches display an "open cross" in front of the sanctuary?

The "open cross"—without the body of Jesus—symbolizes that the Lord has conquered death, is no longer hanging on the cross, and has risen to sit at the right hand of his Father in heaven. This is an emphasis that has been promoted traditionally by Protestant churches, although Roman Catholics show signs of adopting the symbol of the "open cross" as opposed to the "crucifix" that was so common in their houses of worship for centuries.

Why are "icons" a part of some churches?

An "icon" (the Greek word for "image") is a form of art peculiar to Christian churches—particularly those of the Eastern Orthodox tradition. "Icons" are rather crude paintings or sculptures with little emphasis on depth of field. They picture either biblical characters or saints of the Church.

Icons were visual aids, akin to primitive art, that served as reminders to the faithful of the people and events that shaped their faith. They appeared on the walls of caves, catacombs, and other places in which Christians worshiped secretly during the Early Church.

Today, the Eastern Orthodox Church allows only the icon style to portray holy men and women of God, for two reasons. First, it's in keeping with the tradition of the Early Church. Second, it's in harmony with the command of God: "You shall not make yourself a graven image, or any likeness of anything that is in heaven above, or that is in the earth beneath . . . ." (Exodus 20:4).

Why are certain houses of worship called "cathedrals"?

"Cathedral" is a word that comes from the Latin *cathedra*—the name for the official throne of a bishop. A "cathedral," then, is the designation given the building in which the occupant of the *cathedra*—the bishop—conducts Mass.

Throughout the history of the Roman Catholic Church, when the Supreme Pontiff (the Pope) renders an official pronouncement on matters of faith and morals, he does so *ex cathedra*—"from the throne."

Why are some church buildings called "kirks"?

Some church buildings are known by the Scottish designation "kirks"—a corruption of the Greek word *kyros*—meaning "power." One of the more popular churches in Bloomfield Hills, Michigan, for example, is still called "Kirk in the Hills."

Why do some churches have the word "evangelical" as a part of their official names?

It is common for a local church to carry a name such as "St. Mark Evangelical Methodist Church." Although the word "evangelical" is not really necessary, it serves as a reminder of an important emphasis of the Christian faith.

"Evangelical" comes from the Greek *euangelion*, meaning "glad tidings." By its inclusion in the official name of its church, the congregation reminds everyone that it proclaims the "good news" (Gospel) of Jesus as revealed by the four "Evangelists"—Matthew, Mark, Luke, and John.

Chapter 9

Pastors, Priests, and Popes

INTRODUCTION

St. Paul wrote to the church in Ephesus:

> And his gifts were that some should be apostles, some prophets, some evangelists, some pastors and teachers, for the equipment of the saints, for the work of ministry, for building up the body of Christ . . . (Ephesians 4:11–12).

Those men and women convinced that their calling in life is one of full-time service to the Christian Church quite often respond to that call by completing a prescribed course of schooling (usually college and seminary) for the holy ministry or priesthood. They take courses in Hebrew and Greek (the languages of the Old and New Testaments), homiletics (the art of preaching), exegesis (the study and interpretation of the Bible), Church history, as well as courses in psychology, sociology, theology, and philosophy.

When a man or woman decides on a career in full-time work for the Church, he or she has a variety of routes from which to choose. That choice may involve a parish, church administration, teaching, a foreign mission field, or life in a monastery.

Those who select a career in full-time church work have been called: "pastor," "father," "reverend," "priest," "parson," "bishop," "cardinal," or "pope." By whatever name he or she is called, each has felt a calling to serve the people of God.

It is to these dedicated men and women that this chapter is dedicated.

Why are clergymen ordained?

Clergymen are ordained in keeping with the practice of the Early Church as reflected in the New Testament. The act of appointing clergymen is shown to be an act of the whole Church, acting through its existing ministers. It conveys the gifts of the Spirit in the measure needed by each ordained (Acts 6:6; 13:1-3; 20:28; I Timothy 4:14; 5:22).

Ordination for clergymen is required as a sacrament by some denominations, and the earliest known rite is found in the *Apostolic Tradition* of Hippolytus (about 215).

The ordination of any priest or minister is a very solemn, impressive rite. The special ceremony, usually presided over by a bishop, marks the beginning of the active ministry of someone who has spent many years preparing for this day.

Ordination is a method whereby a particular Christian denomination says that a candidate for the ministry or priesthood has its blessing. He or she is thereby consecrated and set apart for full-time work in the Church.

Why are hands placed upon the head of a person at ordination?

From biblical times, designated representatives of the Church have ordained candidates for the holy ministry by placing hands on the head of the person. This act served as a sign that the newly ordained was sanctioned by the Church at large to minister to the spiritual needs of the community.

In the account of seven men who wanted to become

ministers of the Gospel shortly after Jesus ascended to heaven, we read: "These they set before the apostles, and they prayed and laid their hands upon them" (Acts 6:6). The practice is continued to this day at most ordinations.

Why do bishops normally officiate at ordinations?

The presence of a bishop at ordination insures that the consecration of a particular candidate for the ministry or priesthood has the blessing of the Church at large.

For those who insist on an unbroken line called "apostolic succession" for a valid ordination, some bishops are able to trace their authority back through history to one of the twelve apostles of Jesus.

Why do some Christians insist on "apostolic succession" for a valid ordination?

Most Christians believe that Jesus gave special authority to his apostles, beginning with St. Peter, to regulate the affairs of the Church. That authority, they feel, was meant to be passed from the apostles to the generations that followed. This teaching stems from the words of Jesus to Peter: "I will give you the keys of the kingdom of heaven, and whatever you bind on earth shall be bound in heaven, and whatever you loose on earth shall be loosed in heaven" (Matthew 16:18-19).

Some Christians—Roman Catholics and Episcopalians in particular—insist that this authority is passed at ordination through the physical laying on of hands. Therefore, the one who officiates at an ordination must be able to trace his authority through an unbroken line of laying on of hands to one of the apostles of Jesus. He then belongs to the core of those who possess "apostolic succession."

Why do some Christians not require apostolic succession for a valid ordination?

Some denominations, especially those of the more fundamental Protestant groups, feel that the only necessary criterion for a valid ministry is an inward call on the part of an individual to preach the good news of Christ. To these Christians, any imposition of an historic record of apostolic succession by those who lay on hands as a requirement for ordination is a demand that is in conflict with the witness by some of the biblical prophets such as Isaiah whose ministry was marked only by a personal response to God's call with the pledge: "Here I am! Send me" (Isaiah 6:8). These people also point to the fact that the Bible issues no direct command that apostolic succession is necessary for a valid ordination of candidates for the ministry.

Why is it a mistake for a clergyman to refer to himself as "Reverend"?

The term "reverend" has been associated with clergymen since the seventeenth century in England. The designation comes from the Latin *reverendus,* meaning "worthy of respect" or "honorable." It was a label given by the townspeople to the local minister as a gesture of respect for the spiritual leader of their parish.

If the term is to be used at all, the proper salutation is *"The* Reverend Mr. (or Dr. or Fr.) _____." In line with the original meaning of the term, it would be presumptuous of any clergyman to refer to himself as "Reverend." By doing so, he is saying: "I am the honorable _____."

Those who understand the meaning behind the term "reverend" commonly prefer the titles: "pastor" or "father."

Why are some clergymen called "priests"?

Clergymen of the Roman Catholic, Eastern Orthodox, and Episcopal churches are called "priests" in the tradition of the Old Testament. The role of the priest in biblical days was to officiate at a sacrifice of an animal as a symbol of the atonement for sin. Christians, primarily of the liturgical churches, feel that the clergyman who officiates at the consecration of the bread and wine at Holy Communion, offers again the body and blood of Jesus who died on the cross for sins. Hence, the clergyman assumes a role similar to that of the priest of the Old Testament.

Why is the term "pastor" the most popular title of a clergyman?

Most clergymen prefer the term "pastor" as a designation of their office. "Pastor" is a Latin word meaning "shepherd." A minister is the "shepherd" of his flock (i.e., of his parish). He is responsible to fill their spiritual needs and to preach the Holy Gospel.

Jesus, of course, was the supreme example, and often referred to himself as the "Good Shepherd" who was willing to lay down his life for his sheep (John 10:11).

Why were clergymen in early America called "parsons"?

In Colonial America, those who settled the land had little time for education. While children were taught the basics in English, math, and writing, institutions of higher learning were few and far between. Consequently, whenever anyone needed information, the townspeople looked to the one person in the area who possessed the formal education necessary to assist them. That man, in most locales, was the town minister, often referred to as the town "person." The word "person," when spoken by those with a heavy New England accent, became "parson," and the popular designation in this section of America remains to this day.

Why are certain preachers called "evangelists"?

The term "evangelist" comes from the Greek word *euangelion,* meaning "welcome message." The evangelist is deemed the bearer of good news.

The writers of the four Gospels—Matthew, Mark, Luke, and John—are often called "The Four Evangelists." The term was also applied to the circuit riders who traveled on horseback to their assigned churches in the western frontier of the United States during the 1890s. Today, traveling preachers of the Gospel such as Billy Graham are still called "evangelists."

Why are some Roman Catholic clergymen called "monsignor"?

The term "monsignor" comes from *monseigneur* (pronounced "mon-seén-ure"), a French word meaning "my lord." It is an honorary title bestowed by the Roman Catholic Church upon a priest who has given years of service to his people. While the title carries with it no increased authority, it is one of the most cherished and revered within Church circles, since it is an honor given a priest by his peers.

Technically speaking, this title denotes a rank beneath that of a bishop. The lowest grade is a "Very Reverend Monsignor." Next comes a "Right Reverend Monsignor" (who has the right to wear some of the insignia of a bishop). Every bishop is a "Most Reverend Monsignor." In some countries (France, for example), the bishop is always called "Monsignor" (Monseigneur).

Why are certain clergymen called "father"?

Roman Catholic, Episcopalian, and Eastern Orthodox Christians refer to their clergymen as "father," because they regard their spiritual leaders as spiritual parents as a result of their baptisms.

According to Christian teaching, baptism bestows a new birth of supernatural grace. The one who administers this source of new birth is the priest who, in a sense, becomes like a "father" to the one who is baptized. Further, the priest, by his office, is considered by his parishioners as their spiritual father in all matters of the faith.

Why are there so many levels of authority within the Roman Catholic Church?

In any organization, a system of authority is necessary in order to "get things done." The Church is no exception. While all denominations incorporate some chain of command, the Roman Catholic Church designates authority through the titles bestowed upon its clergy.

Heading the Catholic hierarchy is the "Pope" who has supreme power over his church.

A "cardinal" is one who serves as an adviser and assistant to the Pope. He is a member of the so-called College of Cardinals that acts as a senate of the Pope. Cardinals elect new popes who, almost always, come from their ranks.

An "archbishop" has authority over the rather large territory called an "archdiocese" which is divided into dioceses presided over by "bishops."

A "pastor" serves as chief administrator of a parish (or congregation).

Why do some clergymen discourage the use of any distinguishing titles?

In the minds of some clergymen, particularly those of the more fundamental Protestant groups, any title which distinguishes them from the people they serve would create a false barrier. They point to Jesus and Paul as their models and remind us that these servants of God never insisted upon being called "Reverend," "Father," or any other name commonly associated with clergymen today.

Why does a bishop wear a "miter"?

One of the distinguishable symbols of the office of a bishop is the liturgical headdress known as the "miter." The miter is worn during processions and when the bishop is seated at solemn functions. It is removed during prayers.

This special head covering that is shaped somewhat like a shield was not used until the eleventh century. Its shape is symbolic of the role of the bishop as a defender of the faith. It has two points that stand for the Old and New Testaments which the bishop has the duty of interpreting to his people.

Some miters are rather simple, made of white linen. Others are much more elaborate, covered with embroidered satin and bedecked with rare jewels.

The miter is worn today by bishops of the Roman Catholic, Eastern Orthodox, and Episcopal churches.

Why do bishops wear special rings?

In the Early Church, Christians were discouraged from wearing rings. Such ornamentation was deemed by the Church hierarchy as "ostentatious." The only members of the faith who were permitted to wear rings were Church officials (such as cardinals, abbots, and bishops) as symbols of their authority. Each ring carried with it a religious symbol which reminded them of the spiritual "marriage" they had contracted with the Church.

Today, a bishop in the Roman Catholic, Eastern Orthodox, or Episcopal Church wears his ring of authority on the third finger of the right hand to differentiate between his ring and the ones worn by the laity (placed, for the most part, on the third finger of the left hand).

Wearing the official ring on the right hand also symbolizes that Christ always receives the place of honor (the right side) of the bishop.

Why are Roman Catholic priests not allowed to marry?

Three reasons are given for prohibiting Roman Catholic priests from marrying. The first concerns dedication. A priest who is free from the responsibility of supporting a wife and family theoretically is better prepared to direct his energies and concerns for the welfare of his church.

The second reason concerns flexibility. If the Catholic hierarchy feels that a certain priest should be transferred from one parish to another, an unmarried man is free to change immediately, without being encumbered by a family. One Roman Catholic priest explained it pointedly: "All I have to do," he said, "is pack my coffee pot and razor; I'm ready to go anywhere."

And, there is symbolism. By giving up the fundamental and deepest of all human relationships—marriage—the priest expresses his total attachment to God.

The first pronouncement that celibacy be required for priests was issued in 305 during the Council of Elvira in Spain. Convinced that the demands of the Church required the total dedication of its pastors, the Council ruled that all men engaged in performing priestly functions refrain from enjoying the company of women—wives included—else forsake their priesthood.

The Council drew upon the advice of St. Paul who wrote: "The unmarried man is anxious about the affairs of the Lord, how to please the Lord; but the married man is anxious about worldly affairs, how to please his wife, and his interests are divided" (I Corinthians 7:32–34).

In 325 the Council of Nicaea declared that those who were unmarried at ordination could not marry afterward and noted that this was a long-standing tradition. But those who were married before ordination could continue their married life. This rule still holds for the Eastern Orthodox Church.

The Western Catholic Church put more and more emphasis on celibacy for priests. Finally, at the Second Lateran Council in 1139, it was made obligatory for all priests of the Latin Rite. This rule was reiterated by the Council of Trent in 1563.

Still, today, were a Roman Catholic priest to announce that he wished to marry, he would have to be removed from the clergy roster of the Church.

Why is a bishop of the Eastern Orthodox Church not permitted to marry?

While the Eastern Orthodox Church has married men on its clergy roster, no bishop of this denomination may be married. The reason for this requirement stems from the condition of the Church centuries ago, when a bishop was responsible for a diocese that covered hundreds of miles. Since modes of transportation were limited, it would not be unusual for a bishop to be away from his home town for months at a time while visiting his parishes. This, in the eyes of ecclesiastical hierarchy, would place an unfair burden on the married bishop and his family. Hence, the requirement for unmarried bishops remains to this day.

According to many modern priests in today's Eastern Orthodox denomination, this requirement may one day be stricken from the books, since the reason for its inclusion no longer exists.

Why is there a strong movement today to abolish the requirement for celibacy for Roman Catholic priests?

Many modern Roman Catholic lay people feel that the demands for celibacy of their priests no longer apply to today's world. In addition, this requirement has excluded some otherwise strong candidates from entering the priesthood. Official Catholic spokesmen, however, present every indication that their church is far from giving serious consideration toward a married priesthood.

As recently as 1979, Pope John Paul II wrote a letter to all the priests of the Roman Catholic Church entitled: *Celibacy and Priestly Life,* in which he extolled priestly celibacy as a treasure and a gift from God, a gift of the Spirit. He termed it an eschatological sign which also has great social importance in our present life.

Why do some clergymen become monks?

A monk is a clergyman who chooses to live a life of near solitude in a monastery with others who have made a similar decision. The term "monk" comes from the Latin *monachus,* meaning "one who lives alone."

A monk normally takes the vows of poverty, chastity, and obedience. He dedicates himself to serving the Christian Church through prayer, study, and works of a social nature (teaching in schools or assisting in hospitals).

Many of the oldest records of history (both sacred and secular) are products of monks who were among the few learned people of their eras.

Why is the head of a monastery called an "abbot"?

When Jesus prayed to Almighty God in heaven, he referred to him as "Abba," which comes from the Hebrew *Ab*, meaning "Father" (see Mark 14:36). St. Paul picked up on this theme and urged his fellow Christians to use the same term when speaking to God (Romans 8:15 and Galatians 4:6).

For this reason, the head of a monastery is commonly addressed as "Abbot," which sets him aside as the spiritual "father" of the monks who dwell therein.

Today, an abbot must be at least 30 years old, have had a minimum of 10 years experience since taking his solemn vows, and be elected by the monks of his monastery for the position. His appointment is for life.

The abbot traditionally wears a ring on his right hand similar to that worn by a bishop or cardinal, symbolizing his authority.

Why are three knots tied at the ends of the rope worn around a monk's waist?

The customary garb of a monk is a long robe, around which is wound a rope. At the ends of the rope are three knots which remind the monk of the three vows—those of poverty, chastity, and obedience—which he took at his ordination.

The attire is symbolic of the simple life of the monk and reminiscent of the clothing worn by the leaders of the first monasteries founded in the third and fourth centuries.

Why did monks traditionally shave their heads?

One of the more noticeable traditions of the monastic community until recent years was the shaven crown atop the head of monks. This patch of baldness, called a "tonsure," served as a sign that the man was an ordained clergyman of the Roman Catholic Church. For centuries, the tonsure symbolized a man's willingness to "bare his head before Almighty God." It was his way of stating that there would be nothing separating his thoughts from his Heavenly Father.

The tonsure was not given to monks, alone. All ordained priests of the Roman Catholic Church received a tonsure of some nature, even if it meant the symbolic removal of a few locks of hair. A ceremony called "tonsure" was regarded as the first step toward the priesthood.

Tonsures, then, took various forms. The most widely accepted practice was to have a shaved crown (symbolic of the crown of thorns borne by Jesus at his crucifixion), plus five "notches" of hair (representing the five wounds in Jesus' hands, feet, and side suffered while hanging on the cross) removed.

Why are tonsures seldom, if ever, worn today?

Until 1972, the tonsure was a common mark shared by Roman Catholic priests and monks. With the Second Vatican Council, however, came many guidelines from Pope Paul VI which were aimed at bringing the Roman Catholic Church in line with modern times. One of these changes involved the elimination of the familiar tonsure.

Today, as part of the sacrament of ordination, some orders of the Roman Catholic Church still include a symbolic removal of a lock of hair as a remembrance of the tradition of the tonsure that lasted for centuries.

Why are certain full-time Church workers called "nuns"?

We call a Roman Catholic woman who dedicates her life

to serving the religious community a "nun," which is a corruption of the Coptic word *nane,* meaning "good" or "beautiful." Most nuns serve their Church by teaching school, working in missions, or performing work in a variety of social fields. Others live in relatively secluded quarters, dedicating themselves to lives of study, prayer, and penance.

In order to become a nun, a woman must possess a strong desire for this type of life, undertake several years of study, and be judged suitable in character by Church hierarchy. After taking temporary vows of poverty, chastity, and obedience over the first few years, perpetual vows are taken, committing her to a life of service. Even after these vows are taken, however, a nun may choose to leave her full-time work in the Church, and resume her life as a lay person.

Why is a nun's garb called a "habit"?

The word "habit" comes from the Latin *habitus,* meaning "appearance" or "dress." The habit of a Roman Catholic nun traditionally consisted of heavily starched collars and exotic hats that covered not only her head, but, in most instances, the upper half of her forehead. The black outfit literally covered the nun from head to toe.

Today, largely as a result of the emphasis of the Second Vatican Council to modernize the Church, nuns are encouraged to wear modified habits—with a hat similar to a nursing cap and dresses with skirts that reach to slightly below the knee—in order to bring the apparel more in line with the clothing worn by women of the community in which they serve.

Why are some nuns called "Poor Clares"?

A 17-year-old girl of the thirteenth century named

Clare, the daughter of a nobleman of Scifi, was so moved by the message of St. Francis of Assisi (d. 1226) when he preached at the parish in her hometown, that she dedicated her life to full-time service in the Church. Forsaking the life of luxury that would have been hers had she remained with her family, she accepted the challenge given her by the saint to serve the poor.

After taking her vows as a nun, Clare convinced her younger sisters to join her in forming an order dedicated to humility, simplicity, poverty, and prayer—the same pledges taken by the male followers of St. Francis. She and her sisters adopted the name "The Poor Clares."

St. Clare was canonized by Pope Alexander IV in 1255. Her feast day is August 11.

Why are some people called "vicars"?

The term "vicar" comes from the same root as the word "vicarious." It carries the meaning "substitute" or "representative." The term may apply to a seminarian who is serving a term of internship, since he represents the pastor of the congregation; it may refer to a clergyman who is in charge of a dependent chapel; or it may denote the Pope, who is called the "Vicar of Christ" by Roman Catholics.

Why is the Pope called the "Vicar of Christ"?

The Roman Catholic Church believes that Christ gave special power to St. Peter, making him the ruler of the entire Church, when Jesus said to him:

> I tell you, you are Peter, and on this rock I will build my church, and the powers of death shall not prevail against it. I will give you the keys of the kingdom of heaven, and whatever you bind on earth shall be bound in heaven, and what-

ever you loose on earth shall be loosed in heaven (Matthew 16:18–20).

With this promise, according to Catholic teaching, Peter received the "keys to the kingdom," and became the representative (or "vicar") of Jesus here on earth.

The power given to St. Peter, according to Catholic teaching, was passed from him to each of his successors who assumed the role as Bishop of Rome and as head of the Church. Thereby, they too were the "Vicars of Christ."

As a result of this title, the Pope issues official statements of Church teaching with the same authority as if Jesus himself were speaking.

Why is the Pope called the "Supreme Pontiff"?

The word "pontiff" stems from the Latin word *pontifex*, meaning "bridge builder" or "way mender." It is commonly associated with anyone bearing the title of "bishop," since a bishop's role is often one of settling disputes that arise within his diocese. More important, the bishop, as it were, builds a bridge between God and his people. The Pope is, first and foremost, the "Bishop of Rome." As such, he is the "Supreme Bishop" (or "Pontiff") of the Roman Catholic Church.

Ceremonies presided over by the Pope or by any other bishop, then, are properly called "pontifical ceremonies."

Why do onlookers in Vatican Square cheer when they see white smoke coming from the chimney of the Sistine Chapel?

When a Pope dies or resigns from office, the Roman Catholic Church is without its leader. It is imperative that this office be filled as soon as humanly possible. Word is sent to the cardinals around the world to meet at Rome in a solemn conclave no earlier than 15 and not later than 18 days after the vacancy is pronounced. Here they remain in seclusion in a specially prepared part of the Vatican palace.

After Mass is celebrated, they retreat to the Sistine Chapel to cast votes for the new Pope. A secret ballot is taken on paper printed for this purpose. A two-thirds, plus one, majority is required for election. Two ballots are taken each morning and evening until a decision is reached. If no decision results on a given day, the ballots are burned along with some wet straw in the fireplace, producing a heavy black smoke. Hundreds of the faithful gathered outside sigh in frustration and wait for what they hope will be better news the next day.

When a candidate does receive the two-thirds majority plus one, the ballots are burned, this time without the damp straw. White smoke ascends from the chimney, and the gathered crowd cheers the election of a new Pope.

Why does the Pope wear a special ring engraved with a picture?

The Pope traditionally wears the "ring of the fisherman." The ring shows a picture of St. Peter fishing from a boat. This is symbolic of the time when Jesus said to Simon Peter, the outspoken apostle and fisherman believed by Roman Catholics to be the first Pope: "Upon this rock I will build my church" (Matthew 16:18).

The ring worn by the Pope is used to mark an imprint on the wax which seals all official papal letters and pronouncements.

Why is the official ring of the Pope destroyed at the time of his death?

The ring of the Pope is used to authenticate official documents and pronouncements. Because of the belief held by Roman Catholics that the Pope is "infallible" in matters of faith and morals, any decree coming from the papal throne must be authentic. In order to insure the integrity of papal correspondence, the Pope's ring is immediately removed from his right hand at the time of his death and destroyed by the Chamberlain (the personal representative of the late Pope). The destruction of the ring guards against the possibility of someone else using the ring to mark unauthorized documents which could cause havoc within the Roman Catholic Church.

Why is the Vatican called the "Holy See"?

The word "see" is a corruption of the Latin word *sedes*, meaning "seat." In this instance, it refers to the official headquarters (or "seat") of the bishop. Since the Roman Catholic Church regards the Bishop of Rome as the highest level of authority, his place of residence is called the "Holy Seat" or "Holy See."

Why does the Pope wear special shoes?

The Pope, like every other bishop, wears shoes which reflect the color of the liturgical season. During Lent, for instance, he wears purple shoes; during the Easter season, he wears white; after Pentecost, green.

It was once believed that the earliest Popes wore the actual shoes of St. Peter, symbolizing a continuation of the apostolic line. Modern scholars, however, discount this mythical story about the "shoes of the Fisherman."

Why are some papal announcements called "bulls"?

Before Martin Luther was excommunicated by Pope

Leo X in June 1520, official charges were brought against him in the form of a papal "bull" entitled *Exsurge Domine* ("Arise, O Lord"). In this document, Luther was given 60 days to recant his writings.

The term "bull" that is given to such communications from the Pope comes from the Latin *bulla,* referring to a round, leaden seal attached to official documents that come from the Holy See. It was in this manner that the receiver of the document knew, with certainty, that the communication was genuine.

Why do Popes issue encyclicals?

In addition to a bull, the Pope can issue briefs and apostolic letters. The most important among the latter are encyclical letters, popularly known as "encyclicals." These are widely published and generally refer to a subject of interest to Christians throughout the world. Sometimes, as in the case of Pope John XXIII's *Pacem in Terris* ("Peace on Earth"), they are addressed to all people because of the subject matter.

Some other famous encyclicals have been "On the Condition of Labor" *(Rerum Novarum)* of Leo XIII in 1891; "On Biblical Studies" *(Divino Afflante Spiritu)* of Pius XII in 1943; "On the Sacred Liturgy" *(Mediator Dei)* of Pius XII in 1947; and "On the Development of Peoples" *(Populorum Progressio)* of Paul VI in 1967.

Why is the Pope considered "infallible" to Roman Catholics?

Although Popes have sinned and made errors in judgment concerning astronomy, geology, and the physical sciences, Roman Catholics believe that every "Vicar of Christ," from the days of St. Peter until modern times, has been infallible in his official statements on faith and morals. Delegates to the Second Vatican Council explained in 1964 this concept of infallibility when they declared:

It (is) a dogma of divine revelation that when the Roman Pontiff speaks *ex cathedra*—that is, when he, using his office as shepherd and teacher of all Christians, in virtue of his apostolic authority, defines a doctrine of faith or morals to be held by the whole Church—he, by the divine assistance promised him in blessed Peter, possesses that infallibility with which the divine Redeemer was pleased to invest his Church in that definition of doctrine on faith and morals, and that, therefore, such definitions of the Roman Pontiff are irreformable in their own nature and not because of the consent of the Church.

The Pope is not infallible as a private person, as a learned person, or as a priest and bishop. He is not infallible in his philosophy of life or government. He is infallible only in his capacity as supreme Shepherd and Teacher of the Roman Catholic Church—and then only when he proclaims that a given doctrine of faith or morals must be held by the members of his denomination.

Thus this quality of infallibility affects only a minute amount of papal pronouncements issued through the centuries.

Why do non-Catholics refuse to accept the Pope as "infallible"?

Most of the Christian community accepts the Pope as an important leader within the Church. Non-Catholics, however, do not regard him as "infallible" in matters of faith and morals. These non-Catholics believe that all human beings are subject to error. They also point to past pronouncements by Popes of bygone eras that are now subject to "reinterpretation."

Why were there once three Popes who claimed supreme authority?

One of the most confusing times in the history of the Christian Church was when not one, but three men claimed the title as "Supreme Pontiff."

In 1378, Urban VI was elected Pope, and assumed his duties in Rome. Some French cardinals, however, maintained that Urban had not been properly elected. Consequently, they conducted their own election, naming another "Pope" who called himself "Clement VII."

In an attempt to settle the problems resulting from having two Popes, a third group of cardinals declared that both Popes were to be considered unauthorized, and then elected "Alexander V." The results? Three men claimed title to the papacy, and each refused to relinquish the position.

A General Council was called, and the problem was resolved in 1417—39 years after Urban VI (who had since died) was elected. Urban's successor resigned his office; the successors of Clement and Alexander were declared unauthorized and unduly elected. This paved the way for the election of Pope Martin V who, according to Roman Catholic teaching, continued the tradition of apostolic succession begun by St. Peter in Rome.

Why do some clergymen wear clerical collars?

The clerical collar is a symbol of the office of the holy ministry. This collar, which appears to be worn "backwards," stems not from a spiritual source, but from a more practical experience.

Public speakers in the ancient Roman Forum wore a

scarf around their throats and necks to protect them from the cold. The thin, white material wound around the neck was also a convenient way of protecting the neckline of the shirt from perspiration stains.

In keeping with the conservative tradition of retaining the old mode of dress by the Romans, clergymen of the sixth century adopted the inverted collar as a "badge" of their occupation.

In England, by the way, not only Christian clergy, but also rabbis (whom the British call "Jewish ministers") continue the tradition of wearing clerical collars.

Why do some clergymen refrain from wearing a clerical collar?

For every ordained priest or minister who seeks to be identified as a Christian clergyman by wearing a clerical collar, there is at least one other who prefers to "blend in with the crowd" by wearing more conventional attire.

Those who refrain from wearing the clerical collar do not necessarily wish to hide their identities, but desire to relate in a special way to those whom they serve. Some go so far as to feel that the distinguishing clerical collar creates a psychological barrier between a clergyman and his church members.

Traditionally, clergymen of the Roman Catholic, Eastern Orthodox, Lutheran, and Episcopal churches prefer to wear clerical collars, while ministers of the other Protestant denominations generally prefer a more "standard" mode of attire.

Why do some clergymen wear a cassock and surplice while conducting public worship?

Some clergymen, particularly those of the liturgical traditions—i.e., Roman Catholic, Lutheran, Eastern Orthodox, and Episcopal—often wear a cassock and surplice while conducting public worship. A cassock is a black robe-like vestment that reaches to the ankle; the surplice is a shorter white garment worn on top of the cassock.

The black cassock is symbolic of sin; the white surplice represents the forgiveness of sin. Together, they remind us that Christians are still sinful, but through the sacrifice of Jesus, they are looked upon by God as though they had not sinned.

The cassock and surplice are results of a conservative tradition of the clergy who refused to conform to a "modern" form of dress adopted by the Romans of the sixth century.

The leaders of the Early Church prohibited the clergy from separating themselves in appearance from the other members of the fellowship. They promoted, instead, a philosophy that clergymen should give the appearance of being "one with the people" through the wearing of cassocks—the standard dress of Roman men. Pope Celestinus, in 428, reprimanded any bishop who encouraged clergymen to wear anything different from the people they served.

When the more modern forms of dress—trousers, cloaks, etc.—were adopted as part of the common dress by sixth-century Romans, the conservative clergy rebelled, and fought to retain the long-standing tradition of wearing the cassock. Pope Gregory the Great (d. 604) sympathized with their attitude, and, in spite of the reprimand issued by Pope Celestinus a century earlier, ordered that all clergy continue to wear the older Roman garb of a black cassock and, during public worship, a white surplice for the sake of symbolism.

Why does a clergyman wear a stole around his neck and shoulders during public worship?

Clergymen, especially those of the liturgical churches, often wear stoles made of silk or other material around their necks, draped over their shoulders and chests. Usually, these stoles—made in the colors of the liturgical year—are ornamented with crosses or other symbols.

The stole is symbolic of a towel worn around the neck and shoulders by those in the Bible who served others by washing the dust-covered feet of weary travelers who arrived at a home following a trip over dirt roads. The stole, then, represents the pastor's responsibility to serve the Lord and the Church. It becomes a part of his official garb when conducting public worship, offering private Communion, hearing confession, and performing other official acts.

Traditionally, the stole is placed around the neck of a priest or minister for the first time at his ordination. Therefore, it is to be worn only by ordained clergy.

Why do future clergymen attend seminaries?

Candidates for the ministry or priesthood in most Christian denominations must complete a prescribed course of study at an institution known as a "seminary."

The word "seminary" comes from the Latin *seminarium,* pertaining to "seed." Generally a student enrolls in a seminary after he has completed four years of undergraduate work at a college or university.

A seminary is normally a denomination-sponsored school dedicated to instructing students in the official teachings of this specific Christian community. In the seminary, the student takes courses not only in the dogma of that denomination, but also in Church history, biblical studies, philosophy, and the original languages of the Bible—Hebrew and Greek. In addition, he may study homiletics (the art of preaching) and exegesis (the interpretation of sacred writings).

Graduates of seminaries generally are awarded a Master's degree in theology.

Why do some future clergymen refuse to attend a seminary?

In the opinion of some future clergymen of the more fundamental Protestant denominations, a seminary education breeds liberal thinking. After all, they feel, what is so complicated about the simple Gospel that needs to be explained or rationalized by higher education? Instead of spending three or four years in seminary, these future clergymen would rather use this time to proclaim publicly the story of Jesus.

Although this view has been held traditionally by some fundamental denominations, today's modern trend is definitely toward required formal education at a seminary.

Why do students of theology sharpen their skills in "exegesis"?

"Exegesis" is the name given to the technical analysis of a passage from Holy Scripture. Through the study of the verse in its original language—Hebrew for the Old Testament and Greek for the New Testament—the biblical scholar can more clearly discover the meaning behind the verse.

Although the Bible has been studied for thousands of years, scholars still uncover deeper meanings through modern methods of study enhanced by archeological discoveries.

As an example, were a student to study St. Paul's famous chapter (13) about "love" in I Corinthians, he would have a better concept of what Paul meant were he to read the original Greek text. The word for "love" used by Paul is the Greek word *agape*, which refers to an extremely self-giving love. *Agape* is the sort of love, for instance, that expects nothing in return. It says, in effect, "I will love you in spite of the fact that you may not love me in return." Once the student understands this concept of "non-conditional love," he will understand what Paul meant when he wrote: "So faith, hope, love abide, these three; but the greatest of these is love" (I Corinthians 13:13).

Why do seminarians serve an internship?

A growing practice in recent years is the requirement that all students preparing for full-time service in the Church take a year's internship at a designated parish under the guidance of an appointed pastor. During this year (often the third of four years of seminary training), the young intern (or "vicar") serves people in real-life situations. He has the opportunity to preach, make hospital calls, visit shut-ins, recruit new members, teach Sunday school, and work with the organizations of the congregation.

The purpose of the year's internship is to offer practical experience in addition to the theory learned in a classroom.

Why do future clergymen speak of an "inner call"?

When a candidate for the ministry feels that God has summoned him for full-time work in the Church, he speaks of this as an "inner call." This conviction is similar to that of St. Paul who testified that he was "called" to be an evangelist by the grace of God (Galatians 1:15). In his letter to the church in Ephesus, he asked the early Christians to "lead a life worthy of the calling to which you have been called" (Ephesians 4:1). In the same epistle, he wrote that some were called as prophets, some as evangelists, some as pastors, and some as teachers (Ephesians 4:11).

Some students for the ministry of the fundamental Protestant denominations feel that the only thing necessary for a valid ministry is this "inner call."

Why do some seminarians await an "outer call"?

In addition to the "inner call" to serve the Church which the future minister feels he receives from God, many seminarians await an "outer call" from a bishop or a parish. This "outer call" is one from a parish or a representative of the denomination which tells him that he is deemed worthy of serving a congregation of the faithful. In the Roman Catholic, Eastern Orthodox, and Anglican churches, priests are called by the bishops and appointed to serve various parishes throughout the dioceses. Most Protestant clergymen are recruited by the members of a specific congregation through a "letter of call," inviting them to serve as pastors.

Before a candidate for the ministry can be ordained in many circles, he must have received both the "inner" and the "outer" calls.

Why do some denominations discourage women from entering the ministry?

St. Paul, perhaps more than anyone else, is responsible for the prohibition against women performing certain duties in the Church, including, for many denominations, assuming the role of a pastor within a congregation.

Paul often spoke of a woman as playing a submissive role to her husband:

> Wives, be subject to your husbands, as to the Lord. For the husband is the head of the wife as Christ is the head of the church, his body, and is himself its Savior. As the church is subject to Christ, so let wives also be subject to their husbands (Ephesians 5:22–24).

According to this principle, a woman who attempts to fulfill a pastoral role would, by her very nature, delegate all final authority to her husband. She, then, would not be a pastor in the true sense of the word.

Even if she were not married, the most telling blow to a woman's potential for the ministry is recorded in Paul's first letter to the Corinthians:

> The women should keep silence in the churches. For they are not permitted to speak, but should be subordinate, as even the law says. If there is anything they desire to know, let them ask their husbands at home. For it is shameful for a woman to speak in church (I Corinthians 14:34–35).

On top of this, Paul offers some strong advice to Timothy: "I permit no woman to teach or to have authority over men" (I Timothy 2:12).

Today, Roman Catholic, Eastern Orthodox, and some Lutheran churches prohibit women from entering the ministry.

Why are many denominations changing their concept of women in the ministry?

One of the differences in attitude resulting from the "women's liberation" movement in the '70s and '80s is the change in position of many denominations regarding women in the ministry. Although European churches have ordained women for decades, most American Protestant congregations are just now beginning to adopt this practice.

The gnawing question remains: "What about St. Paul's stand against women speaking in church?" Those who endorse the right of women to join the clergy ranks would say that Paul's admonition was necessary for a specific time and society in which women were considered second-class citizens with few rights of their own. Modern times, they claim, demand a fresh approach to the concept of the ministry.

Chapter 10

Saints and Sinners

INTRODUCTION

The sixteenth-century Reformer, Martin Luther, once commented that a Christian is both "saint" and "sinner" at the same time. What he said was not new; he reflected the confession of St. Paul: "I can will what is right, but I cannot do it. For I do not do the good I want, but the evil I do not want is what I do" (Romans 7:18–19).

The following pages tell about the lives of those men and women who committed themselves to serving their Lord through their gifts and talents, often in the face of incredible odds.

This is not to imply that all of them gained universal acceptance within the Christian Church. Some of these zealots are praised by the vast majority in both Roman Catholic and Protestant circles as "saints"—holy men and women of God. Others, because of their life-styles, are dubbed by many as "sinners"—scandals to the faith. Some have been officially sanctioned by the Church through "canonization" or "beatification"; a few have had a special day marked on the Church calendar in their memory. Others, in spite of their expressed intents, will never receive official recognition.

Are these people "saints" or "sinners"? Who is to judge? History has often exaggerated the good works of saints far beyond any verified accomplishments. On the other side of the coin, the alleged evil deeds of the "not so saintly" have also been blown out of proportion.

Whether we praise or condemn their efforts, we must admit that each of the following personalities has, in some way, molded the Church into its present form.

The stories and witnesses shared through the lives of these individuals are but a few that could be told. Even in our modern times, new personalities are emerging who may have a profound impact upon the Church. Time will tell.

The men and women chosen for this chapter represent the fact that the Church has seen a wide variety of approaches to proclaiming the Gospel of Christ. Even today, the zealous actions of some vibrant witnesses cause those in the more "traditional" circles to shake their heads in astonishment at what is done in the name of the Gospel.

Lest we become too judgmental, let us recall that the Church originally condemned many of the people it now regards as heroes.

Why are certain people called "saints"?

The word "saint" comes from the Latin, *sanctus*, which means "one who is holy." In the real sense of the word, *all* Christians are "saints" in that they have eternal life as promised through Jesus Christ. Paul addressed the "saints" who were living in Rome, Corinth, Ephesus, and other cities that fell under his guidance. Meanwhile, the Church has seen fit to designate over 750 people as "saints" in the common sense of the word: those who are venerated because they are both close to God (because of their holiness) and accessible to humans (whose nature they share).

The practice of venerating saints claims biblical foundation, e.g., Genesis 18:16-21; Matthew 19:28; Hebrews 12:1; Revelation 6:9ff. Roman Catholic, Lutheran, Eastern Orthodox, and Anglican Christians emphasize the lives and contributions of the saints, while the majority of other Protestants generally "play down" the importance of the saints.

Throughout the history of the Church, hundreds of· saints have been recognized by the faithful. Because no standard was established for the veneration of saints, and because superstitions arose that caused their alleged deeds to be blown out of proportion, the Council of Trent (1545-1563) treated the subject in moderation, stating that the faithful should address themselves to certain saints whose lives, deeds, and performance of miracles had been authenticated, in order to seek assistance in winning favors from God. Since then, saints have been officially named only by the Pope after a long legal process.

Why are certain people "beatified"?

"Beatification" is a papal decree which permits members of the Church to venerate a person after his or her death. This veneration is not binding upon the whole Church, but is limited to a particular locale. At the same time, beatification is the preliminary step necessary before a departed soul may be "consecrated" as a saint, though the act of beatification does not guarantee elevation to sainthood.

Papal pronouncements of beatification are given after study and consultation. Nonetheless, the decision is not regarded as "infallible." The pronouncement gives only *permission* to venerate, not a *command*.

When the soul of a person is beatified, the name of the person receiving such an honor may be prefixed by the term "blessed."

The first record of beatification is in the fourth century when martyrs were memorialized in this special manner.

Why are certain departed souls "canonized"?

When the Pope declares that a departed soul who has

been previously "beatified" has left purgatory and now resides in heaven, that person is "canonized"—i.e., designated as a saint. Normally, in order for anyone to be considered for canonization, substantiated miracles in the name of that person must be made known.

The first such canonization took place in the year 993 when the Church (through Pope John XV) declared Ulrich (d. 973) a saint.

Canonization confers seven privileges:

1. The name of the person is listed in the catalog of saints.

2. The name may be invoked in public prayers of the Church.

3. Churches may be dedicated to God in honor of the saint.

4. Masses may be publicly offered to God in the name of the saint.

5. A day is set aside on the Church calendar for the saint's memory.

6. Pictures of the saint may be surrounded by a heavenly glow of light.

7. Relics of the saint may be publicly honored.

Why have some saints been "suppressed"?

Saints have not only been canonized, they have been "suppressed"—i.e., removed from the official list of those recognized by the Church as enjoying the seven privileges mentioned in the previous answer.

Throughout the history of the Christian Church, the lives of some devout leaders have been viewed as examples for all to follow. Often, however, the reported work of these individuals has been exaggerated as time passed. On the basis of these flamboyant tales alone, some have been venerated to sainthood. Subsequent research, however, has cast doubts on their accomplishments. On occasion, evidence revealed that it is highly improbable that some of these people actually lived at all.

In light of the additional information resulting from bona fide research, a Pope can suppress a saint just as he has the authority to canonize a saint. Pope Paul VI in 1968, for instance, abolished 40 feast days for saints from the Church calendar. Although not all of these saints were "revoked," their lives and works were no longer considered as sufficiently documented or meaningful.

Of the saints in recent years who have been "suppressed," the best known are St. Philomena (removed from the list of saints in 1960) and St. Christopher (removed from the calendar observance in 1969).

Why does the Church honor saints with special days?

Once a person has been canonized, the name of that saint is affixed to a particular day on the calendar. Each year on that date, Christians are urged to remember the life and works of this person of God and to render worship to God in honor of the saint. Certain Christians (such as Roman Catholics) will offer special prayers to God through this saint on that day.

Saints' days are honored particularly by Roman Catholic, Eastern Orthodox, Episcopal, and Lutheran Christians. These churches believe that every form of holiness in the Church and its members proceeds from Christ and flows back to Christ. This is true of all the saints beginning with Mary—the mother of Jesus, the apostles, and the martyrs. All have, in one way or another, exemplified for the faithful one aspect of the infinite holiness of Christ.

By imitating the saints, Christians imitate Christ, who is the King and Crown of all the saints.

Although Christians have traditionally honored saints

on particular days, the majority of Protestant denominations disregard these calendar designations.

Why are some saints' days called "black letter days" and others "red letter days"?

In the Book of Common Prayer, the basis for the worship of the Anglican (Episcopal) Church, there is a listing of the various days on which the saints are remembered. Those who were deemed the "lesser saints," because their lives are not substantiated by the Bible, were mentioned on the Church calendar with black numbers. The more important saints were honored by having their dates listed in red.

To this day, when something important occurs, not necessarily a religious event, people refer to it as a "red letter day."

Why do paintings of saints often include "halos"?

A "halo" is a circle of light painted around the head of a saint by an artist. It is a symbol not of Christian origin, however, dating to centuries before Christ. Natives of various cultures often wore feathered headbands depicting their association with the sun god. Other people used additional ornaments to represent circles of light which indicated divine intervention.

In this tradition, artists who painted Christian-oriented portraits distinguished holy people from others with a circle of light surrounding their heads. Not only did this serve as a designation for holy figures, but it also provided excellent backgrounds for facial pictures so important to the artist.

Why is St. Anne revered by many Christians?

According to the oral tradition of the Church (i.e stories that have been transmitted from generation to generation by the *spoken* word rather than by *written* records), St. Anne was the mother of the Virgin Mary. The Bible makes no mention of St. Anne; in fact, there is no reference whatsoever to any mother of Mary. Nonetheless, by the second century, St. Anne was recognized by Christians as being the mother of the Virgin Mary.

Emperor Justin I, who died in 565, erected a church in her honor at Constantinople. In 1382, Pope Urban VI established a feast day on July 26 in her memory, fixed to coincide with the marriage of Richard II and Anne of Bohemia.

In the sixteenth century, the dubious e· stence of St. Anne was one of the hotly debated issues arr ing Reformers of the Church. Today, Anne is honored by most liturgically-minded Christians; the majority of Protestants, however, do not hold Anne in high esteem.

Why are some early Christians known as "Fathers of the Church"?

The "Fathers of the Church" is a title accorded to theologians and ecclesiastical writers of the first eight centuries who were outstanding both for their purity of doctrine in the face of adversaries of the faith and for their personal holiness. It was they who transmitted the faith received from the apostles, protected the faith of Christians, and enabled the Church to grow in the world.

They are usually divided into two main groups. The *Apostolic Fathers* are those of the second and third generation of Christians who heard the apostles and their immediate successors: among them were: Clement of Rome, Ignatius of Antioch, Polycarp of Smyrna, Justin the Martyr,

Irenaeus of Lyons, Clement of Alexandria, and Cyprian of Carthage.

The *Dogmatic Fathers* are those who beginning with the conversion of the Emperor Constantine labored to set forth the Christian doctrine and to defend it against heretical sects. They are subdivided into the *Greek Fathers* and the *Latin Fathers*. The greatest of the Greek Fathers were John Chrysostom, Basil the Great, Gregory Nazianzen, and Athanasius. The greatest of the Latin Fathers were Ambrose, Augustine, Jerome, and Gregory the Great.

The last Fathers were Isidore of Seville (died 636) in the West and John Damascene (died 750) in the East. The golden age of the Fathers is regarded as extending through the first four General Councils of the Church—from Nicaea (325) to Chalcedon (451). The number of the Fathers is usually given as about five hundred.

Why is the "Cross of St. Andrew" in the form of an "X"?

St. Andrew, the patron saint of Scotland, was an apostle of Jesus and the brother of Simon Peter. He appears throughout the New Testament sporadically, remaining for the most part in the background.

Tradition tells us that in about the year 70, Andrew was martyred for the faith in Scythia on a cross shaped like an "X." To this day, this has been called the "Cross of St. Andrew."

The feast day for Andrew is November 30, a day for joyous celebration in Scotland.

Why was Polycarp's death an inspiration to the Early Church?

From its beginning, Christianity was a persecuted faith.

Although Jesus' teaching was revered by his disciples, the Roman Empire remained unconvinced and unsympathetic. Of chief concern to the government was the unwillingness of the growing band of Christians to offer sacrifices to the Roman gods. In the minds of the civil leaders, this refusal symbolized disloyalty. This conflict between Christianity and Rome grew in intensity over the next few centuries.

Among the leaders of the Early Church was Polycarp (65–151), the Bishop of Smyrna, in Greece. His remarkable preaching of the Gospel, his sincere love for all of God's people, and his exemplary life-style endeared him to the hearts of both Christian and non-Christian.

In the middle of the second century, a great festival was held in Smyrna, attended by Statius Quadratus, a proconsul of Caesar. The proconsul, in an attempt to teach a lesson to all, demanded that the beloved Polycarp, now in his mid-eighties, be brought to the arena. There Polycarp was ordered three times to swear by the fortunes of Caesar and to deny Christ. With each order, Polycarp refused.

"For eighty and six years I have served him [Christ], and he has done me no injustice," said the Bishop firmly. "How, then, can I blaspheme my king and Savior? Hear me declare with boldness, 'I am a Christian.'"

The answer infuriated the proconsul, who ordered him taken, bound, and burned alive at the stake.

As the fires were lit, and the flames licked his body, Polycarp was heard to pray: "I thank thee, Heavenly Father, that thou hast thought me worthy of this day and hour, that I should have a part in the number of thy martyrs in the cup of Christ."

Over the centuries that followed, Polycarp's unwavering faithfulness in his hour of death inspired countless other Christians who were "put to the test" for their faith by torture and death.

The feast day for St. Polycarp is February 23, the date, according to tradition, of his martyrdom.

Why were the writings of St. Augustine so inspirational to the Early Church?

One of the most influential of all leaders in the Early Church was Aurelius Augustine (354–430), revered by many as the leader among the Church Fathers. But it wasn't the inspirational speaking of this African-born saint that left such an impact upon the Church; it was, instead, the appeal of his writings to the average citizen.

In his *Confessions*, St. Augustine disclosed the inner struggles he had with himself as he tried to do right in the eyes of God, but fell victim to the temptations and the ways of the world. His personal battles notwithstanding, Augustine studied for the priesthood and, five years after his ordination, was appointed Bishop of Hippo in his native Africa. While serving as a bishop, he dedicated himself to writing.

His most influential work, entitled *City of God*, promoted the theme that in spite of what was about to happen to those who professed to be Christians, God was going to have the last word. According to Augustine, in the long run of history, righteousness will prevail, and the earthly city in which human beings live today will be transformed by the heavenly city of God in which the faithful will reside for eternity.

This assurance gave confidence to Christians that while it may appear that the enemies of the Church are victorious, these triumphs are but temporary. In fact, it was this confidence that Augustine, himself, needed when, at age 76, he lay weak and dying as the Vandals stormed the city of Hippo and seized it.

St. Augustine's feast day is the 28th of August.

Why is the bright red cross of St. George a part of the English flag?

St. George, who was highly venerated by the crusaders,

was made patron saint of England in 1350. The record of his alleged accomplishments, however, is suspect.

According to pure legend, George was 17 years old when he became a soldier for Emperor Diocletian. Here, he gained a splendid reputation while serving as a knight. On one of his tours, he reportedly came to a town in Lybia called "Silence." There he met a young maiden, the daughter of the king, who was to be sacrificed to a fire-breathing dragon. George, alone, challenged the dragon to battle and killed it. The king was overjoyed and gave George a large reward which the brave soldier, in turn, donated to the poor.

Through some ruthless trickery, Emperor Diocletian was led to believe that George was a conspirator against the government. This suspicion was amplified when George refused to offer a sacrifice to the Roman gods, and bore witness, instead, to his loyalty toward Christ. Under direct order by the Emperor, George was tortured and beheaded on April 23 (his feast day) in 303.

In spite of the fact that much of the legend of St. George is apocryphal, it inspired many soldiers who went to battle. His badge is often worn to this day by men and women who serve in the British army, and the bright red cross—called the "cross of St. George"—appears on the flags of England and its territories.

Why do some Christians still place statues of St. Christopher on their automobile dashboards?

Some Christians still consider St. Christopher as the "patron saint of motorists" in spite of the dubious history associated with his name.

Legend tells us that St. Christopher was a martyred Christian of the first century. Most historians have no difficulty accepting this as true. Nevertheless, countless far-fetched accounts fill his biography. Christopher was supposed to have carried the Christ Child upon his shoulder while fording a river; hence he was called "Christ-bearer" (in Greek: *Christophoros*) from which comes his familiar name in English.

Another story says that a drop of his blood healed a wound that a king suffered while attempting to execute Christopher, giving rise to the belief that anyone who saw the image of Christopher would be free from harm that day. For this reason, Christopher was regarded as a protector during travel.

Although some Christians continue to wear St. Christopher medals around their necks and place his medal or a statue of his likeness on the dashboard of their cars, his alleged accomplishments are viewed with skepticism. His feast day was officially removed from the Church calendar in 1969—but he was not removed from the rolls of the saints.

Why is St. Francis of Assisi often pictured as preaching to the animals?

Francis Bernadone (1181-1226) was born in Assisi, Umbria, Italy to well-to-do parents. He was an intelligent young man, and his father had plans for him in business. However, after trying his hand as a merchant and a soldier, Francis chose, instead, to give his life to serving the poor. Although he was never ordained as a priest, he was determined to serve the Church which, at that time, had become morally corrupt with uneducated clergy and monasteries that had lost sight of their original purposes for existing.

In his missionary ventures in Italy and Spain, Francis founded three monastic orders—the Friars Minor, the Poor Clares (for women), and the Brothers and Sisters of Penance. All were dedicated to humility, simplicity, poverty, and prayer—known as the "four foundation-stones of the Franciscan Way." "Above all the graces and all the gifts which the

Holy Spirit gives to his friends," wrote Francis, "is the gift to conquer oneself."

Part of "conquering oneself," according to Francis, was the willingness of people to recognize their part within God's creation. In his *Canticle of the Sun,* he called the animals his "brothers and sisters" and wrote of "brother sun" and "sister moon."

Stories were told that as he went into the woods in order to preach to them, wild birds lit on his shoulders, and other animals ate out of his hand. All the while, Francis behaved as if he were one with all of creation. Today, therefore, it is not unusual to see pictures of Francis surrounded by animals.

In 1224, as he was deeply engrossed in prayer, Francis was startled when strange marks suddenly appeared on his hands, feet, and side, as though he had been wounded as was Jesus on Good Friday. This was one of the first documented cases of someone receiving the "stigmata" of Christ.

Because of Francis' tremendous contribution to the Church, he was canonized as a saint just two years after his death. His feast day is October 4.

Why do French children receive gifts on November 11?

November 11 marks the feast of St. Martin, the patron saint of France. On this day, often called "Martinmas," the faithful in France celebrate the end of the harvest. Children awake in the morning to find gifts of apples and nuts. Residents of French towns parade through the streets singing special songs of the season in honor of St. Martin of Tours.

Martin was born in the fourth century. While a catechumen (one receiving instructions before joining the Christian Church), he volunteered as a soldier in the Roman army. During his term of service at Amiens, in northern France, he saw a begger by the roadside freezing in the cold weather. Out of pity, Martin gave him half his cloak. At that exact moment, a vision of Christ appeared. Martin, out of fear and awe, pledged to become baptized and to devote his life's work to the service of the Lord.

After he left the army, Martin became a monk and served his Church faithfully. In 372 he was consecrated Bishop of Tours, France. He dedicated the remainder of his life to the establishment of monasteries in France. As a result, monasticism grew rapidly in the country, one of the prevailing reasons for the increased popularity of the Christian faith among the French.

Why do Christians honor St. Valentine?

While St. Valentine's Day (February 14) is not an official observance within the Church, the legend of the saint has been adopted by most Christians as one worth remembering.

St. Valentine was a Christian priest in Rome, according to tradition, who taught the dogma of the Church during the third century, when Christianity was still considered by Rome as an "outlaw religion." One of the teachings stressed by Valentine was the importance of marriage for those men and women who desired to live together. Marriage, however, had been forbidden by Claudius II, who believed that family ties made soldiers less willing to fight. As a result of St. Valentine's persistent teaching, he was jailed, tried, and convicted of promoting dogma contrary to government law—a capital offense. He was executed on February 14 for his direct violation of an edict by Emperor Claudius.

On the eve of his execution, Valentine sent a note to the jailer's daughter who had befriended him. In it he thanked her for her care and kindness, and signed it: "Your Valentine." Thus was born our modern practice of exchanging similar notes to our special "valentines" on February 14.

Why is the "Actor's Chapel" in New York City named in honor of St. Malachy?

Located on West 49th Street in New York City is St. Malachy's Chapel, erected in 1902 for actors and other performers, thanks, in part, to the benevolent contributions of famed showman George M. Cohan. The actors chose the name for their chapel for two reasons. First, St. Malachy was a saint familiar to the Irish actors who dominated the theater in the early 1900s. Second, the saint's nomadic life-style was similar to those of the struggling actors whose bookings led them to cities throughout these United States.

St. Malachy (1094-1148) was a priest in the early twelfth century. Instead of accepting an appointment to serve a parish, he elected to be a missionary in Ireland. His method of operation was to travel constantly the roads of Ireland on foot, preaching the Gospel from parish to parish. He had no personal possessions or income. He inspired his country-men to raise Bangor from the ruins caused by the invasion of the Norsemen, and founded the abbey of Iveragh. In 1125, he was appointed a bishop, and later became the papal legate to Ireland.

The story is told that in his last moments on earth, Malachy touched the paralyzed hand of a young boy and cured it instantly.

Malachy was canonized by Pope Clement III in 1190. His feast day is celebrated on November 4, especially by actors.

Why was Jonathan Edwards able to frighten so many people in early America?

One of the names most inseparably linked with the colorful period in American History known as "The Great Awakening" is that of the fiery preacher, Jonathan Edwards (1703-1758).

In his theological studies as a student for the ministry,

Edwards gradually became convinced of the absolute sovereignty of God and people's utter dependence upon the Lord for survival. This belief not only influenced his thinking but dominated his preaching as well.

Because he became the center of controversy over various theological issues, Edwards was dismissed as the pastor of his Congregational Church in Northampton, Massachusetts, but not before the impact of his sermons was felt throughout all of Colonial America. His subsequent journeys as a free-lance missionary further promoted his teaching that not only are people dependent upon God's mercy for salvation, but they are unable, on their own, even to choose to follow God. In his most famous sermon: "Sinners in the Hands of an Angry God," Edwards proclaimed that God holds sinners over the fires of hell as he would a spider from its web, all the while debating with himself whether to save them or not.

As a result of his style of preaching, "The Great Awakening" flourished, and some people went out of their way to demonstrate that they were among the "chosen of God." Some of Edwards' followers fell into trances and awakened to report visitations from God. Others awoke barking like dogs and exhibiting other "signs of the spirit." Those who were not able to demonstrate their faith through such outward signs were often labeled by preachers such as Edwards as "hell-bound."

Edwards convinced many of the Colonists that he was "engaging to fight against the world, the flesh, and the devil to the end of life." He regarded anyone who dared challenge his message as an agent of Satan and urged the friends and family of such a scoundrel to avoid associating with him. Those who believed his claims regarded Edwards as a "modern saint"; those who suffered persecution as a result of his attacks sometimes considered him akin to the Antichrist.

In the last years of his active ministry, Edwards tempered his flamboyant preaching and became engrossed in an attempt to combine Christian theology with the teachings of the great philosophers of old. His unique approach developed into what is often called "New England theology"— a combination of the Bible and teachings by selected scholars. Two months after he became president of the College of New Jersey (later, Princeton University) in 1758, he died of smallpox.

Why was Henry Ward Beecher called "the greatest preacher since St. Paul"?

The brother of the author of *Uncle Tom's Cabin* (Harriet Beecher Stowe) also achieved fame as a superior orator and popular leader of his church. Those who heard him speak in church often called him "the greatest preacher since St. Paul."

Henry Ward Beecher (1813–1887) was the pastor of Plymouth Congregational Church in Brooklyn, New York, at a time when tensions in America were high. Controversies over states' rights and slavery were but two of the issues dividing the nation. While most clergymen tempered their remarks about such delicate issues for fear of creating dissension within their congregations, Rev. Beecher boldly and dramatically emphasized his stands.

In one of his famous antislavery sermons, Beecher brought a slave child into the pulpit as an object lesson and offered her for sale to the highest bidder among the Sunday morning worshipers. This unforgettable scene has been cast in bronze and stands today in the garden of the Plymouth Church.

After the Civil War, Rev. Beecher was outspoken in his support of a moderate policy of reconstruction for the South, Grover Cleveland's 1884 candidacy, women's suffrage, evolutionary theory, and scientific biblical criticism.

Henry Ward Beecher used his pulpit as a platform, and he became one of the most effective clergymen in calling

American Christians to respond to the social concerns of the day.

Why was Dwight L. Moody called "a businessman for Christ"?

He wasn't a preacher, because he was never ordained; and he wasn't a businessman, because he never owned a business. Yet, Dwight L. Moody (1837–1899) has been considered by many to be the foremost Christian businessman-preacher in American History.

While selling shoes in Boston, Massachusetts, Moody, a high school dropout, formed a Sunday school class at a nearby Congregational Church. His energetic teaching and powerful promotion techniques caused his class to swell in attendance beyond all expectation. Unfortunately, the well-bred members of the Congregational Church were not happy with the social standing of the new worshipers whom Moody attracted, and he was forced to leave.

Moody left this atmosphere for Chicago where he sold shoes at another store and formed a Sunday school class at an inner-city church. His effervescent appeal enabled him to gather plenty of followers. Together they formed the undenominational Illinois Street Church for the purpose of preaching the word of God and serving the needs of the community.

Moody's popularity grew. Often he was invited to speak at various conventions. At one of these meetings in 1870 in Indianapolis, Moody heard Ira D. Sankey sing Gospel hymns. "I want you to come with me to Chicago," said Moody. Sankey did. Afterward, the two conducted a series of revivals that were spiritually and financially successful.

Moody and Sankey used the proven tools of business—pamphlets, billboards, and banners—to publicize their crusades in the United States and Europe. In New York City alone, better than 11,000 gathered each evening over a four-month stand to hear Moody's sermons about the need for a personal conversion to Christ. A special appeal always went out to businessmen to share their profits with the Lord. Those who did testified that their earnings rapidly increased the day they began to fulfill their pledges.

Moody converted his earnings into profit-making ventures from which were formed the Bible Institute in Chicago (now called the "Moody Bible Institute"), a girls' school in East Northfield, and a boys' school in Mt. Hermon.

During his last years, Moody lived in seclusion, with one exception. He came out of retirement to preach under the huge canvas of a circus tent at the Chicago World's Fair in 1896. One last time, he proclaimed the Gospel to a new generation of businessmen, many of whom pledged a percentage of their earnings to the work of the Lord.

Why was Aimee Semple McPherson able to gain instant popularity throughout the United States?

In the heart of Los Angeles, The International Church of the Foursquare Gospel stands as a monument to its founder, Aimee Semple McPherson (1890-1944). "Sister Aimee," as she preferred to be called, became as much a part of the American scene in the early 1920s as Prohibition and the New York Yankees.

In her mid-twenties, Aimee Semple McPherson had already been through two marriages that left her penniless, impatient, bored, and with one child. Perhaps as an avenue of escape, Aimee packed her belongings and hit the trail as a self-proclaimed evangelist.

She struggled with limited success until 1921 when, during a rally in southern California, an elderly woman unexpectedly rose from her wheelchair, walked toward Aimee, and praised God for the "miracle of healing power." Others followed that night, and at other rallies that week, tossing aside crutches, leaving wheelchairs, and praising "Sister Aimee" for her ability to heal.

"I'm not the healer; God is," insisted Aimee. Despite her disclaimers, the public flocked to hear her preach. Her reputation spread rapidly, aided by her willingness to broadcast her services over a new invention—radio. Unlike the familiar "fire and brimstone" approach of most evangelists, Aimee wooed her radio flock as she would a lover. Her sweet, sugary, hushed tones were an appealing contrast to her contemporaries.

Each Sunday from her spanking new headquarters in Los Angeles—a $1,500,000 structure called the "International Church of the Foursquare Gospel"—Aimee delivered sermons sometimes accompanied by simulated lightning and thunder.

When she preached, her church, which seated over 5,000, was filled to capacity by those bent on hearing the famous evangelist who wore the long white robes of purity. Afterward, some of the devotees inspected the "miracle room" lined with crutches and wheelchairs of those who were cured by the prayers of Sister Aimee.

One daring stunt, however, tumbled her from the throne of popularity to the depths of disgrace. In May 1926, Aimee retreated to a California beach for a brief swim and private devotions. When she failed to return home, rumor spread that she had drowned. The faithful panicked. One hopeful rescuer died from exhaustion in his frantic attempt to find the body.

A ransom note appeared 15 days later, stating that Sister Aimee had been kidnaped and would be released for the sum of $500,000. When the ransom was paid, the evangelist appeared in a Mexican border town, stating that she escaped from her captors. The authorities, however, were suspicious, since she seemed none the worse for wear; instead, she looked as radiant as ever, without as much as a scratch marring her velvety skin. Further investigation revealed that both Aimee and her married boyfriend were seen together at several hotels weeks before the incident.

While others might have withdrawn from the spotlight and gone into seclusion, Aimee Semple McPherson bucked the odds as she had done before, and set out once again on the evangelism trail.

On a September morning in 1944, after addressing a particularly zealous crowd the night before, Aimee Semple McPherson was found unconscious in a hotel room. She died within hours. Cause of death: suicide through an overdose of sleeping pills.

Why was Billy Sunday called "God's cheerleader"?

William Ashley ("Billy") Sunday (1862–1935) was a "cheerleader for Christ" whose zealous style of preaching gained him as many enemies as converts. Some considered him a ham actor; others called him a "fighter for the right."

Billy Sunday was a better than average major-league baseball player who lived a fast life both on the base paths and in the city streets. His conversion to the Christian faith happened in Chicago. While sitting on a curb alongside his inebriated pals, he heard a small band across the street play a familiar Gospel hymn. "I told my friends I was through," he said, "and that I was going to Jesus Christ."

Over the next five years, during baseball's off-season, Billy Sunday traveled the circuit, preaching in makeshift tents set up in obscure farming towns. As time passed, the fireballing evangelist became increasingly popular. His audience heard him speak in simple terms, without much regard for proper grammar, about the dangers of whiskey, card playing, wild women, and the lusts of the devil. His sermons were punctuated with outlandish gestures and peppered with gymnastics and slapstick antics. Crowds cheered as he pounded the pulpit, broke chairs, and shattered benches. His favorite routine was pretending to be a sinner sliding into home plate, only to have God call him "Out!"

At the close of each rally, he challenged the devil to join him on stage for a fight. When the devil failed to appear, Sunday raised his arms over his head, symbolizing victory.

At the height of his career in 1917, Sunday was an established millionaire, something made possible through freewill offerings from his faithful followers.

Times changed, but Billy Sunday didn't. The impact of World War I and Prohibition made his message obsolete. Without a popular cause, he quickly vanished from prominence, and returned to preaching in tent revivals in the same small farm towns where his ministry began.

Why was a Roman Catholic priest once considered the second most powerful man in the United States?

Father Charles E. Coughlin (1891–1979) was an unheralded local parish priest who helped the members of his flock with their problems, performed marriages, baptized babies, and buried the dead. All this changed in 1926 with the broadcast of his Sunday morning sermon over a new medium called "radio." This started him on a road to popularity that caused many observers to regard him as the most powerful man in America, outside of the President of the United States.

Father Coughlin's radio series grew in popularity. Gradually, stations were added to his private "network." Before long, radio stations in every major city throughout the country were airing the priest's weekly sermons. By the middle 1930s, the tough-sounding Irish priest was receiving nearly 100 letters a day from listeners. That was a greater response than that enjoyed by any Hollywood celebrity of the day.

Father Coughlin's sharp rise to fame did not result from his unique insights into Holy Scripture. Instead, his "gospel" consisted of diatribes against the problems of the day. With over 30 million Americans struggling with the woes of the Great Depression, Father Coughlin became their champion. He singled out politicians such as Presidents Hoover and Roosevelt (whom he called "the great liar and betrayer"). His views were also promoted through his popular magazine, *Social Justice*.

Father Coughlin's influence came to a sudden halt after a series of mistakes in judgment. He backed the unsuccessful presidential candidacy of Congressman William Lemke, attempted to link the leaders of the Communist Party with the Jews, and editorialized that the Jews were "getting what they deserved" at the hands of Adolph Hitler in Germany.

His audience dwindled, and his Church superiors ordered him to cease his broadcasts and magazine publication.

Father Coughlin continued to preach at his parish—called "The Shrine of the Little Flower"—in Royal Oak, Michigan, until his retirement in 1966.

Until his death in 1979, Father Coughlin was on occasion invited to deliver a sermon from the pulpit that he had made so famous 30 years earlier. According to members of the parish, whenever Father Coughlin returned to the pulpit, attendance at church services shot up perceptibly.

Why was a New York minister called "The Black Messiah"?

George Baker (1864–1965), the son of a sharecropper from Georgia, was better known to Americans as "Father Divine." This small, rotund former Baptist preacher mesmerized his followers into believing that he was, indeed, "God on earth," or, as some called him, "The Black Messiah."

Father Divine preached a gospel of hope, promising that anyone who joined his crusade would "live forever." During the Great Depression, he attracted the downtrodden with his teachings, and provided five-cent meals to those who visited his communal dwelling in New York City.

His flock increased steadily. Many believers abruptly left everything and followed him. Some adopted different names, such as "True Love," "Chosen One," and "Inner Glowing." The money flowed in. One millionaire left him an estate valued over nine million dollars.

Continually surrounding himself with lovely ladies whom he called "secretaries," who catered to his every need and wore sweaters with a "V" (for "virgin"), driving a Duesenberg, and sporting $500 silk suits, Father Divine left a trail of irate husbands who sued the self-proclaimed prophet for wrecking their marriages.

Perhaps his greatest source of controversy came in 1926 when he married a 22-year-old white girl, Edna Rose Kitchings, who adopted the title: "Mother Divine."

When he died in 1965, Father Divine left property valued at over 10 million dollars. In lieu of a solemn funeral service, "Mother Divine" hosted a gigantic feast.

"Father would have wanted it that way," she said.

Why was Harry Emerson Fosdick forced to resign from his parish?

One of the most controversial figures in twentieth-century Church history was the persuasive preacher Harry Emerson Fosdick (1878–1969). His sermons became the focal point in America for the debate between the fundamentalists (those who believed in a literal interpretation of the

Bible) and the liberals (those who accepted a more philosophical approach to Holy Scripture).

During the time when fundamentalist-liberal controversies were at their peak in the mid-1920s, Fosdick served as minister at the First Presbyterian Church in New York City. There, his sermon entitled: "Shall the Fundamentalists Win?" sparked arguments not only among members of his congregation but also within larger circles of the Christian community. His remarks and those of his enemies were widely circulated through the press.

The higly publicized sermon, at first, seemed innocent enough; its theme called for tolerance on both sides, stating that Christianity could embrace both fundamentalists and liberals. This angered the less tolerant fundamentalists of the Church and of his congregation who forced him to resign.

Immediately thereafter, John D. Rockefeller, Jr., invited him to become pastor of what is now Riverside Church, in New York City. It was from this pulpit that Harry Emerson Fosdick had his greatest influence. His weekly radio broadcasts and his books of sermons demonstrated to his followers how the Christian Gospel could meet the pragmatic needs of people of that day. "Unless a sermon can provide a solution to a genuine problem," said Fosdick, "it is useless to the man sitting in the pew. The Bible can solve our day-to-day problems if we let it."

To the end, Fosdick was unsympathetic toward the fundamentalists who claimed that their literal interpretation of the Bible provided eternal answers to any theological question. "If anything on earth is tentative," he said, "subject to the push and pull of changing science and philosophy and to shifting population moods of optimism and despair, it is systems of theology."

The fundamentalists would never agree. When Fosdick died in 1969, one popular fundamentalist preacher proclaimed: "God has ridded his Church of its last enemy."

Why was Dietrich Bonhoeffer called "a prisoner for Christ"?

The persecution of the Christian Church did not end with the fall of the Roman Empire. Dietrich Bonhoeffer, a German Lutheran pastor, was hanged by the Nazis at the Flossenburg prison on April 9, 1945, by special order of the Gestapo because he dared to preach the Gospel and was accused of participating in an assassination attempt on the life of Adolph Hitler. He was only 39 years old.

Dietrich Bonhoeffer had studied theology in Germany and the United States prior to entering the holy minstry in the early 1930s. When Hitler came to power in 1933, Bonhoeffer joined the anti-Nazi pastors who struggled to maintain separation of the Church and Nazi philosophy.

Soon, his outspoken support of the anti-Nazi movement caused concern not only among government leaders but also among many friends who labeled him "unpatriotic." The Nazi government ordered him to stop preaching. Bonhoeffer, however, defied his country's leaders and continued to speak out. The Union Theological Seminary in New York City offered Bonhoeffer a faculty appointment—something that would have insured his safety. The pastor refused, saying: "If I do not minister to my people when they are in danger, I have no right to minister to them after the danger is past." In 1943, as he was smuggling Jews to Switzerland, Bonhoeffer was arrested.

While in prision, he wrote some of his most powerful works, including *The Cost of Discipleship, Letters and Papers from Prison,* and *Way to Freedom.*

His execution failed to still his message. On the contrary, his ideas sparked and shaped diverse movements including ecumenism, Christian resistance to war, opposition to political dictatorships, and a new insight into Christian martyrdom.

Why is Bob Harrington called "the Chaplain of Bourbon Street"?

Bourbon Street in New Orleans, Louisiana, is a popular attraction for tourists who want to experience the best in adult entertainment. Stripper bars, massage parlors, and brothels are hawked by carnival-like pitchmen. Into this setting steps a contrast in the form of the Reverend Robert L. "Bob" Harrington (b. 1927), an ordained Baptist minister who, at least once each week, visits his "congregation"—the pimps, prostitutes, derelicts, runaways, and drunks—who work on Bourbon Street. To them, he's their "chaplain."

For those who challenge his ministry to "this kind of people," Harrington calls attention to the words of Jesus, who was also accused of associating with the wrong crowd: "Those who are well have no need of a physician" (Luke 5:31).

On a nationally televised talk show, Harrington was asked: "How can you be so naive as to think you can rid the area of prostitution?" "I can't," was Harrington's candid reply. "I only work with the prostitute, the drug user, the alcoholic, or anyone else who needs the message of Jesus."

Harrington's unique brand of ministry, coupled with an amazing ability to communicate his philosophy, has made him a welcome guest on talk shows and on the banquet circuit. His fees enable him to live "comfortably." "Just because you're a Christian doesn't mean you have to be poor," he says.

Bob Harrington's life has been marked with criticism, controversy, editorial rebuke, and a bitter divorce. "They're all just a part of the territory," he says.

Why was Pope John XXIII accused of being "too ecumenical"?

Angelo Giuseppe Roncalli (1881-1963), the eldest of 12

children, left his family farm in Bergamo, Italy, to study for the priesthood. At 23, he was ordained and served as an army chaplain. Over the next 40 plus years, he rose through the ecclesiastical ranks, assuming increasingly important duties until he was elevated to cardinal in 1953.

After the death of Pope Pius XII in 1958, the College of Cardinals was hopelessly deadlocked in its selection of a successor. A "compromise candidate" was offered for consideration. Within hours, a stunned former Cardinal Roncalli stepped out onto the balcony above St. Peter's Square, smiled to the throng below, waved, and gave his first blessing as Pope John XXIII.

Although many considered him a "compromise Pope," John XXIII was uncompromising in his mission. It was clear to him that the Roman Catholic Church for too long had isolated itself from the rest of Christianity. It was his feeling, too, that many of the differences between Catholics and Protestants were no longer of significance, but were often more a question of semantics than of theology. As a result, he called for the Second Vatican Council on January 25, 1959, and invited Protestant leaders to be official observers.

Not everyone endorsed Pope John's efforts. Some of the more conservative Roman Catholics accused him of "selling out" to the Protestants. Most, however, applauded the results of his work.

Today, Christians are freer in their conversations with one another, and different denominations show deeper respect for what others have to offer.

The life of John XXIII ended much too swiftly for most of Christendom when he died in 1963. Francis Cardinal Spellman captured this feeling when, upon seeing non-Catholics openly weep at the news of John's death, he wrote: "He was their Pope, too."

Bibliography

Albright, Raymond W. *A History of the Protestant Episcopal Church.* New York: The Macmillan Company, 1964.

Baker, Archibald G., ed. *A Short History of Christianity.* Chicago: University of Chicago Press, 1940.

Bevan, R.J.W., ed. *The Churches and Christian Unity.* New York: Oxford University Press, 1963.

Bishop, Jim. *The Day Christ Died.* New York: Harper and Brothers, 1957.

The Book of Common Prayer. Greenwich, Conn.: The Seabury Press, 1977.

Bowie, Walter Russell. *Men of Fire.* New York: Harper and Brothers, 1961.

Buttrick, George A. *Prayer.* Nashville: Abingdon Press, 1942.

Cross, F.L., ed. *The Oxford Dictionary of the Christian Church.* New York: Oxford University Press, 1974.

Davis, John D., ed. *The Westminster Dictionary of the Bible.* Philadelphia: Westminster Press, 1944.

Douglas, J.D., ed. *Dictionary of the Christian Church.* Grand Rapids, Michigan: Zondervan Corporation, 1978.

Ferm, Vergilius. *Pictorial History of Protestantism.* New York: Philosophical Library, Inc., 1957.

Fox, Matthew. *Religion U.S.A.* Dubuque, Iowa: Listening Press, 1971.
Harrington, John B. *Issues in Christian Thought.* New York: McGraw-Hill Book Company, 1968.
Howe, Reuel L. *The Miracle of Dialogue.* Greenwich, Conn.: Seabury Press, 1963.
The Interpreter's Bible. 12 volumes. New York: Abingdon Press, 1952.
The Jewish Encyclopedia. 12 volumes. New York: Funk and Wagnalls, 1912.
Kolatch, Alfred J. *The Jewish Book of Why.* New York: Jonathan David Publishers, 1981.
———. *The Family Seder.* New York: Jonathan David Publishers, 1967.
Lamm, Maurice. *The Jewish Way in Death and Mourning.* New York: Jonathan David Publishers, 1972.
Lewis, C.S. *Miracles.* New York: The Macmillan Company, 1960.
Maier, Paul. *The First Christmas.* New York: Harper and Row, 1971.
Maus, Cynthia Pearl. *Christ and the Fine Arts.* New York: Harper and Brothers, 1938.
McCollister, John C. *So Help Me God.* Minneapolis: Landmark Books, 1982.
———, ed. *A Child Is Born.* Minneapolis: Augsburg Publishing House, 1972.
Mead, Frank S. *Handbook of Denominations.* Nashville: Abingdon Press, 1970.
Morris, James. *The Preachers.* New York: St. Martin's Press, 1973.
The New Catholic Encyclopedia. 15 volumes. New York: McGraw-Hill, 1967.
Puckle, Bertram S. *Funeral Customs.* London: T. Werner Laurie, Ltd., 1926.
Reed, Luther D. *The Lutheran Liturgy.* Philadelphia: Muhlenberg Press, 1947.

Richardson, Alan, ed. *A Theological Word Book of the Bible.* New York: The Macmillan Company, 1957.

Stuber, Stanley I. *Primer on Roman Catholicism for Protestants.* New York: Association Press, 1953.

Selby, Donald J. *Introduction to the New Testament.* New York: The Macmillan Company, 1971.

Theiss, Herman. *Life With God.* St. Louis: Morse Press, 1969.

Tillich, Paul. *Systematic Theology.* Chicago: University of Chicago Press, 1967.

Ward, Hiley. *Documents of Dialogue.* Englewood Cliffs, New Jersey: Prentice-Hall, 1966.

West, James King. *Introduction to the Old Testament.* New York: The Macmillan Company, 1971.

Wilhelm, Anthony J. *Christ Among Us.* New York: Paulist Press, 1975.

Index

fulfilled prophecies about Messiah, 4, 33
God incarnate, 8, 17
Good Shepherd, 9, 263, 275
Good News of, 274
held no title, 278
his followers believed in his resurrection, 37
IC, 261
IHS, 262
Immanuel, 5
imposed silence about his miracles, 18
INRI, 262
instituted Lord's Supper, 224
instituted sacraments, 91
interpretation of his life, 2
Jewish carpenter, 1
King, 2, 7, 23, 29, 243
King and Crown of Saints, 303
King of the Jews, 14, 16
King of kings, 2, 252
killed by crucifixion, 32
knowledge of, 4
knowledge of must be put into practice, 4
known through oral tradition, 4
Lamb of God, 9
Last Supper of. See Holy Communion.
Latin form of Joshua, 7
Light of the World, 212, 213, 220, 252, 258
lived in Palestine, 3
Lord of lords, 2
love for all human beings, 33
in marriage, 190, 196
meaning of name, 7
mentioned by Jewish historian, 3
mentioned by Roman historians, 3
mentioned by Syrian Stoic, 3
merits used in indulgences, 167
message of, 325
Messiah, 1, 4-7, 67
miracles of, 17-19
miracles rejected by some, 19
mystery of star at birth, 13
name, 7, 219, 237, 261
name given by angel, 237
name means God with us, 219
nearly executed as a child, 16
new Adam, 10
not recognized by Jews as Messiah, 67
offering of body and blood, 275
parables of, 20
Passion Narratives of, 2-3
and Pharisees, 21-22
placed in manger, 12
possessed two natures, 8
post-resurrection appearances, 37
prayed before arrest and trial, 27

prayed often during life, 153
predicted his death, 24, 25, 28
predicted his resurrection, 38
presence in blessed homes, 237
presence in Holy Communion, 105-108
promise to thief on Calvary, 90
public life of, 3
put to death on eve of Passover, 231
questions about, 2-39
real name, 7
real presence, 106, 107-108, 156
received gifts from Wise Men, 212
record found in Bible, 2
records of, 1
referred to destruction of Jerusalem, 32
rejected through mortal sin, 165
resurrection of, 211
resurrection greatest miracle, 20, 37-38
resurrection known as the Pasch, 221
returned to Father on Ascension Day, 238
rode into Jerusalem on Palm Sunday, 24
rose on first Sunday of Passover, 232
and the Sabbath, 22
sacrificial death, 227
and Sadducees, 22-24
scourged and crowned, 29
Second Coming, 46, 203, 254-55
and the Shroud of Turin, 34
as Son of God, 52
Spirit descended on him at baptism, 264
spiritual king, 29
stabbed with a spear, 32
star at birth, 210
stigmata, 172, 311
symbolized by shepherd's staff, 263
taken to Egypt as an infant, 16
taught Lord's Prayer, 60
taught in parables, 20
tempted by Satan, 221
third party at a Christian marriage, 183
tomb not visited until two days after death, 36
trial and execution, 27-28
used unleavened bread at Last Supper, 26
used wine at Last Supper, 26
Via Dolorosa, 229
Vicar of, 285-86
visions of, 157
visited by Wise Men, 202
was a Jew, 67
was without sin, 10
will destroy the Antichrist, 84
and the women of Jerusalem, 31
worshiped by shepherds at birth, 15, 204
youth of his mother, 11